love - from

Grandma

Ringo's Gift

Ringo's Gift

To Charlotte,
When the horse
whispers back

Sarah Rees Howell

Sarah Rees Howell

To order additional copies of this book, contact:
Xlibris Corporation
1-888-795-4274
www.Xlibris.com
Orders@Xlibris.com
43235

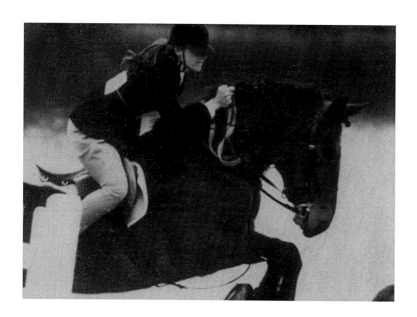

"This book is dedicated to my children, Tayo and Richie; to all woman
who have unfair limitations imposed on them by others, and to the
animals that help such women overcome those limitations."

Contents

Elm Tree Farm

I was brought home from the hospital where I was born to Elm Tree Farm, my family's home in Chagrin Falls, Ohio. Mary Meyers, Nanny I called her, was one of the first and surely best things I remember about Elm Tree Farm. My memories are not so much of the words she spoke, but of my sense of her entire being. She made me feel safe, loved, and wanted. I sought her out the way a blind puppy pursues the scent of its mother. I would have been completely lost without her. I knew my brother and sister were there but they were unapproachable, as though on the other side of a glass wall. My feelings told me, "Yes, they are your family, but you can't go where they are." It wasn't allowed. I was a member of my family without being a part of it.

I knew I was born with something that made me different long before I could understand what it was and might mean for my life. Was that my first lesson, not to be included in our family? I didn't try to seek comfort from them. Or perhaps I tried but denied that I was trying because I was always disappointed. In any case, I never found any warmth. But Nanny was open. I instinctively knew that Nanny accepted me. Her large body enveloped me and carried me along in her world of unconditional love. My feelings told me I was safe there, accepted for the child I was. The squeak of the rocking chair provided a constant rhythm for my dulled nervous system, and her sweet Jergens Lotion filled my entire being as she rocked me to sleep at night. I would sit on her lap, with my nose pressed into her neck, and she would wrap her huge arms around me so that not one part of my unfeeling left side was exposed. In bed, the cold sheets made my left side tense up and jump; but in Nanny's arms, I melted into sleep.

My mother later told me that she and Nanny took turns rocking me at night, but my body doesn't remember my mother holding me. Rather, my feeling from as far back as I can remember was that my family had built this invisible divider between them and me. I wasn't allowed to cross over into their world. If I'd been allowed in, I think I'd have memories of my mother's arms around me, protecting and comforting me. Instead, I remember only that I sought out Nanny, and she was always there.

If my family had opened to me, they wouldn't have been able to pretend things were normal, that we were a healthy family. My mother liked the game of normality, which she played with considerable skill. But Nanny didn't care. She wasn't trying to prove herself to anybody, at least not in our family. So I focused on Nanny and the animals because Nanny and the animals were allowed to pass out through that glass wall to me. They weren't required to play my mother's game. My limited sense of family with my elder sister, Dindy, and our elder brother, Murray, was based on our shared connection with the animals. The animals provided sort of a demilitarized zone for us. Part of it was that they made us laugh, the cats, when they rolled on the floor or leapt around in the leaves, and Dindy's pony, just for being a playful pony named Peanuts.

Because I found Peanuts such good company, I wasn't afraid to try horseback riding. It proved to be one of the few physical activities I actually enjoyed. I liked being up high, plus I rode bareback most of the time so that I could feel Peanuts' warm, fuzzy coat against my legs. The sensation took my mind off my left side, which in turn caused it to relax. Nanny would bridle Peanuts and help me up, and off I'd go. The first time I rode, I found the rocking motion natural and soothing. I held Peanuts' mane and watched his shoulders go back and forth. Every time his leg moved forward, there would be a rocking feeling that threw me slightly forward and then back again. It gave me the giggles, but it also relaxed my side. That was important because while I was riding, I felt completely healthy, and afterward I invariably slept better. So from the very beginning, I couldn't get enough of it. I would have ridden all day if I'd been allowed to.

I liked the rustling sound of Peanuts' feet shuffling through the leaves. I also liked his smell, as well as the smells of wood, hay, and manure in the barn. His mane was stiff, bristly, and long enough to grab onto if I needed, which I did when I started trotting. But cantering was the most fun. It gave me a feeling of complete freedom from my physical limitations. When I was riding, my left leg relaxed so that it could grip as well as the right. During such times, I felt outside myself, free from any physical problems. When I was on foot, walking, the tense and twitching muscles of my left side ruled my every move; but when I was aboard Peanuts, they did what *I* asked *them* to do. When I was riding, I was relieved of the frustration of having to deal with my body without understanding what was wrong with it.

Not being able to tie my shoes was a major source of frustration. It was the cause of regular temper tantrums, especially when I started kindergarten. In school, where everyone tied his shoes at the same time, it became clear how slow I was. I remember looking around the room at how the other kids were doing. Some were slower than the others, but at least they could do it. All of them would be putting on their jackets and doing up their zippers, and I'd still be sitting on the floor, tying. And then I'd get stared at when we were all in our shoes and one of my laces immediately became untied, and the teacher had to come over and tie it for me. I remember my teacher asking me, "Why can't you tie your shoe?" Her question made me flush with shame.

My problem with shoes was what made me feel different. It wouldn't have occurred to me, except for the other kids. Their teasing made me think, *Why am I like this? Why doesn't my hand work?* I had ventured out into the world without Nanny, and I couldn't go to her and dive into the comfort she offered. It was proving very difficult. I wonder what my life would have been like without Nanny. Would there have been any bonding with anyone for that little girl? How many more insecurities would I have developed if I'd been all alone outside the glass wall?

My mother couldn't see the value of exposing Murray and Dindy to the handicapped child. She couldn't accept me because she couldn't accept the truth about life. It was easier for her to mold Dindy and Murray because they had no apparent defects. So my relationships with my brother and sister were controlled so my mother could keep them apart from me and mold them and protect herself from the truth. Murray and Dindy were kept off in the distance, in the mist, as if watching me through binoculars. But they couldn't focus the binoculars, so they couldn't get a clear picture of me. And that was the way it remained until we all grew up.

My mother was a complicated person. Facing the truth about me, and thus about her family, was more than she could handle. She relied on what she knew, which were her social skills. She was pretty and charming, and she knew how to put up a good front, how to make things look normal. It was this part of her that always succeeded in finding me the right clothes or getting me into what she considered the right school. That's how she got me into Dindy's school, Low-Haywood, when we moved east to Stamford, Connecticut.

Looking back, I think I experienced a bond, a quality of love with Nanny that my brother and sister never had. Because of my handicap, Nanny took me under her wing. In a way, I was saved by my disability, whereas Murray and Dindy were condemned by their good health. Whereas Nanny accepted me completely and told me the truth, Murray and Dindy had to beg for conditional acceptance at best from our mother. Plus they had to try to get the truth from someone who couldn't look at life straight on, and was therefore fundamentally dishonest. Yet I was the one who had the "disability."

My first home, Elm Tree Farm, Chagrin Falls, Ohio, 1950. I remember every room. As a child, they all seemed huge and the driveway, endless.

Siesta Key, Florida, 1951. By the time I was 3 or 4, my frustration with my left hand had caused me to begin having temper tantrums. Not understanding, Mom's friends urged her to curb my outbursts, but she indulged me. Sometimes she'd take me off alone and allow me to work through it. I loved the sensation of the warm sand on my skin.

Elm Tree Farm, 1953, Murray, 7, Dindy, 10, and me, 4. I can tell from my expression that I felt part of the family, included, when we sat for this portrait. The feeling wouldn't last.

Elm Tree Farm, 1953. Nanny would take me out to the barn, help me bridle Peanuts, then climb up on. I liked riding bareback because Peanut's fur was soft and warm, a comfort to my left leg.

Colorado, 1954. When I was 5, we took a family trip out west to a dude ranch. I loved riding and being outside. The fresh air and exercise made it easier for me to get to sleep at night.

Peanuts, Tabby, Angel, and Joe-Joe

My father went along with Mother and her decisions. He was kind, but he was also quiet. He didn't make waves. Luckily, I had Nanny, so I didn't have to make demands on him or look to him for comfort. I have no strong memory of my father at Elm Tree Farm. My sense is that whereas Mother was dogged about staying on the other side of the glass from me, and Murray and Dindy followed her example, Dad occasionally came over to my side. But he didn't come often, and he didn't stay long because Mom always yanked him back. It was as if he was torn in half and unable to sew himself back together. I think Mother preferred keeping him in pieces. It exposed every part of him to her so she could pick and choose which part she wanted to draw out next. That way, she could keep things the way she thought they should be. His kind of love for his children, accepting them for who they were, was too risky for her. It challenged her insecurities. She couldn't help herself. It was the only way she knew how to be. So she and Murray and Dindy treated me like an outsider, and Dad usually acquiesced. And I turned to Nanny and the animals and was separate from my family.

We moved from Cleveland to Stamford when I was six. My father, who worked for *Fortune* magazine, was promoted to advertising director and transferred to New York. It was a difficult transition for me. I was shy and didn't make friends easily. But the hardest part was that Nanny stayed in Cleveland. I don't know why or if she was even asked to come with us. I have no memory of the move, but Mother said I had a fit over leaving Nanny. I'm sure I felt I was being cut off from my only source of love and might therefore not survive. I've tried to go back and recall saying good-bye to Nanny, but there's nothing there. I know and feel everything about her, except parting from her. I've often wondered if the memory would come back if I were hypnotized. I'd like to be able to remember it because I'd like to know how I felt and what I did that day. I feel that more truth about those early years would come out if I could retrieve that single memory. But it's too deep. I guess it was so painful that I buried it.

All I remember is the sense that I was uprooted from my home, jammed into new ground, and expected to keep on growing. But at least Peanuts and the other animals had come with us. We had some cats and a black Lab mix named Jiggers, and Dindy had her Welch terrier named Sandy. Sandy was very attached to Dindy and had no interest in me. But the animal I remember most was Peanuts. He had become my friend even more than Dindy's, and I was glad to have him. Unfortunately, I wouldn't have him for long.

Poor old Peanuts died shortly after our arrival. They said he was eighteen. At the end, in Ohio, I have a feeling I may have transferred my attention from Nanny to Peanuts because he was coming with us to Connecticut. Maybe that's why I don't remember saying good-bye to Nanny and why I was so upset by his death.

When we found Peanuts dead in his stall, he was blown up like a balloon and his back leg was pointing straight up in the air. Mother accused Daddy of feeding him too many green apples. She said the apples had given him colic, and the colic had then killed him. The way I understood it at the time, Peanuts had filled up with the gas that had been inside all the green apples he'd eaten. For years afterward, I thought red apples contained less gas than green.

My parents decided to call the glue factory. I thought that was strange. Why would a glue factory want a dead horse? Mom explained that they make glue out of horses' hooves. But I didn't want him to be taken away. I wanted to bury him at home. I guess they thought he was too big. It was a lot of facts and logic, and I had to make an extra effort to understand.

When Mother told me that a big truck was going to come and they were going to put Peanuts in it and take him away, I insisted on staying out to watch. Mom urged me to come in, but I sat in the field beside the barn, arms around my knees, crying and rocking in an effort to comfort myself. I pulled my legs up into my body as tight as they'd go and recreated Nanny, conjured her up to comfort me. I did it a lot at first because, once I got her there, I invariably felt comforted by her presence. On that occasion, I got to feeling that it was all right for the truck to come. And then, sure enough, there it was, pulling into the pasture, its high plywood sides wobbling back and forth as it came over the rough ground. The driver made straight for the barn, veered away at the last minute, stopped, and backed up to the door.

I got up and walked around to the back of the truck. When the ramp slammed down onto the ground, the noise made me jump. I guess I wasn't expecting such disrespect for the dead. The truck was old and dirty, with lots of debris scattered around the bed. When the dust cleared, I saw two buckskin horses already in the truck, lying on their sides. A huge chain was wrapped around the hind legs of one of them. Horrified, I wiped my tears with my sleeve and forgot I was sad.

There were two men. They didn't say much. I suppose it was all very normal, business as usual. One of them removed the chain from the dead buckskin and went in to Peanuts. I walked away from the barn. I didn't want to see what was going to happen next, but I couldn't stop looking. The man wrapped the chain around Peanuts's neck, just behind his head so it caught in the corner of his mouth. Then he hooked the other end of the chain onto a crank bar at the front of the bed, swung down into the cab, threw the engine into gear, and yanked Peanuts out of the barn.

Someone came and stood beside me. I don't remember who it was. I asked if it hurt Peanuts to be pulled like that. I didn't want him feeling any pain. Whoever was there assured me that he wasn't feeling a thing.

The chain pulled him onto the truck, and he ended up between the two buckskins. His back leg was still sticking up in the air. The men didn't waste any time. Together, they slammed the ramp back up then climbed up into the cab and started back across the field. I followed the truck out to the road. The only part of Peanuts I could see was the hoof and white sock of that stuck-up leg. I told myself it was good that he was with the other horses, that they'd comfort him during their journey. Maybe they'd talk about the things they'd do in horse heaven. I hoped Peanuts would tell them about me and all the fun we'd had together. I stood watching Peanuts' foot, waving good-bye to me as the truck went down the road. It. I kept looking until the truck went around the corner. When it disappeared and I realized that Peanuts was gone forever, I broke down all over again.

Peanuts's death left a huge void in my life. Dindy had her horse, Lady, but I no longer had a horse to ride. Lady had her problems and was too mean for a seven-year-old, so I spent the time I would have been with Peanuts with our two cats. I was especially close to Tabby. He was black with a white tip on his tail. He jumped up on my bed every morning to wake me then followed me around. He helped me get over the loss of Peanuts.

I occasionally rode at a stable my mother had found. It was fun though it couldn't take the place of Peanuts. I did make a new friend though, a neighbor named Susan Flatow who was also taking lessons.

Tabby was great to come home to. He carved out his own little space in my heart. But he met a tragic end when our neighbor's boxer caught him and shook him to death. I watched it out the living room window. Tabby was in our yard when the dog came out of nowhere and grabbed him. Maybe I screeched, or perhaps Murray was watching too because he let out a holler and ran for his BB gun. I sat there, paralyzed, as the boxer shook the life out of poor Tabby. I heard Murray's and the housekeeper's voices, but it was as if I wasn't in the same room. And everything slowed way down. It was as if the instant I'd seen the dog grab Tabby, I'd drawn back into some sort of shadow, another dimension in which everything happened in slow motion. Murray gave the dog a couple of BBs in the butt, but it was too late. When the dog ran off, Tabby was a lifeless heap. I was again devastated.

I don't remember if Tabby was buried or what the next few days were like. Our housekeeper, a woman named Jay, felt awful about what had happened. I think she blamed herself for letting Tabby out. In the weeks that followed, Jay saw how I missed Tabby, especially in the morning. The sun still shone through my bedroom window, but it wasn't the same without Tabby jumping up on the bed to wake me.

Feeling guilty I suppose, Jay went out and bought me another cat. It wasn't just any cat, but a genuine grey Persian. She was so beautiful I named her Angel. She didn't have the spunky personality Tabby had, but she had her own sweet way. I had fun taking her to cat shows.

Jay insisted on calling the cat Princess, which meant the poor creature had two names, which didn't seem like a good way to develop her personality. Jay was okay, I guess. I know she really liked me, but she babied me too much. She didn't give me the same kind of love that Nanny had given me. It was as if Jay felt sorry for me. That was it: she couldn't accept me because she felt sorry for me. It bugged me. I was grateful for Angel but Jay's attitude made me indifferent to her.

I missed Peanuts, but I continued to ride. Angel got digestive problems. At first, it just meant that I couldn't play with her, but they became steadily worse to the point where we finally had to put her to sleep. I don't think she was much over a year old. I was sad, but it was nothing like losing Tabby. I think I was learning to deal with the death of my pets. I reasoned that Angel was better off because she wouldn't have to suffer anymore. And of course, it was a painless death, at least that's what I was told. So I got on with my life. By then, I had two friends: Susan, who lived on one side of us and with whom I rode, and Beattie, who lived on the other side of us from Susan. The three of us rode our bikes together, and Susan had a pool at her house.

My life was completely separate from my sister's and brother's. Except when he was teasing me, Murray never spoke to me. He teased Dindy too, but I felt it was just fun with her. But it wasn't fun for me. I hated it. It was cruel and scary. My father saw it, and it drove him crazy. Sometimes, he'd chase Murray with a rolled-up newspaper and hit him over the head to make him leave me alone. Once, out on the driveway, Murray came after me with a kitchen knife. He made an evil face and laughed, but I didn't think it was funny.

When he wasn't teasing me, Murray kept me at a distance. I don't recall him ever saying anything nice to me. The only time I ever thought he cared about me was when he tried to save Tabby, but that was probably more about his feelings for Tabby than for me. And he certainly wouldn't have a conversation with me. Down inside, I felt he hated me. I rationalized it by thinking that all big brothers hate their little sisters.

As for Dindy, she was too involved with Murray and her friends to even notice me. I felt she had no use for her little sister. I didn't like the way she looked at me. Her look said, "Get away from me!" And I did. I stayed away from her even though I desperately wanted her to be my friend. I thought she was beautiful, and I bragged about her to my friends. Sometimes I made up stories about Dindy and Murray, stories in which I felt more like their sister. In my stories, they entered my world with my animals, and we all had fun together. The stories were what I did to feel part of the family.

I continued to ride as long as we stayed at our first house in Stamford. I became a fairly competent rider at a young age, and as I improved, my parents saw how it was helping me physically.

I kept after my parents about replacing Peanuts, and they kept checking the paper. One day, there was an ad for a burro. I remember the black-and-white picture, a side view of this small creature with longish hair and huge ears. The owners were asking $95 for him. I remember feeling I had to have him. My eighth birthday was coming up, and I decided I'd bug my parents to death for the entire nine months if that's what it would take to make them get that burro for me.

I worked on them, but I couldn't tell how I was doing. Then Christmas came, and the matter was resolved. The living room in our house had a cathedral ceiling, and we always had a tall tree. It was a storybook scene. On Christmas morning when I came out onto the upstairs balcony and looked down the tree from the angel at its top to the presents around its bottom, I noticed a small Western saddle with a bridle next to it on the arm of the couch. The tree lights were blinking on the shiny leather, and when I got closer, I saw that the saddle had a capped pommel and loops and circles etched across the back of the seat. The leather was dark, suggesting warmth and comfort; and the etched lines were playful, promising fun and adventure. The bridle was small, but also elegant. It looked as if I wasn't going to have to spend the next seven months lobbying for my burrow.

My parents brought him home in the station wagon for my eighth birthday the following July. My friends, Susie and Beattie, were there. My new pet made a big hit with them. When we'd first moved to Stamford, I'd been known as the new kid who had horses; so I was keeping up my reputation with the arrival of Joe-Joe.

Joe-Joe, still just a few months old, was small and skittish. I thought he was incredible. I couldn't get over his ears. They were long and full of shaggy hair, and they stuck up so high he had trouble getting out of the car. His hair, a nice red color, hung off him in clumps. Like a baby, he was knock-kneed. As I watched him, I thought that his head must have difficulty holding his ears up. On the ground, he took short jerky little steps as if he was on stilts; and his tail twitched with each step. It seemed his legs and tail were connected, like a pull toy in which the turning wheels make other things happen.

I led him over and hitched his halter to the rope attached to the post my father had sunk in the ground for that purpose. My friends were there. It was a fun day.

I couldn't wait for Joe-Joe to grow big enough to ride. Meanwhile, he hee-hawed every morning. He sounded as if he was gasping for air. I thought he would have made a good fire alarm.

As he grew, it became increasingly difficult to keep him in the pasture. Dindy couldn't take Lady out without Joe-Joe wanting to follow her. He liked to wiggle out through the pasture fence. He was very social such that if our neighbors were outside, he'd escape and go visit them.

When the time came, riding was half hoot, half adventure. Joe-Joe turned into a very stubborn creature when you got up on him. You couldn't just jump on him and take off like you could with Peanuts. Joe-Joe simply wouldn't move unless someone was leading him. But Joe-Joe hadn't planned on Sooner. Sooner was a little part-beagle mongrel who belonged to Lowell, the man my father hired to keep the place up. When I wanted to ride, I'd tell Lowell; and Lowell would let Sooner out of his truck, and Sooner would race around and nip at Joey's back feet. Well, Joey was afraid of yippy dogs, so he'd buck and start running on his stiff little legs. And I'd clamp my mouth shut so my teeth wouldn't crack or bite my tongue, grab the pommel, and hang on for dear life. Riding Joey was like riding a can of paint while it's being mixed in one of those hardware store machines. I'd try to steer, but Joey usually went in a straight line.

Plus Joey was a master of the sudden stop. When he realized that Sooner was no longer on his heels, he'd just—*bang!*—stop. On a dime, no slowing down. But Sooner would be watching; and the minute Joey stopped, he'd come after us and nip at those little burrow heels, and I'd grit my teeth, and off we'd go again. We must have been a sight. I remember hearing my mother roar and, looking over, seeing her hug her stomach with laughter. But I was matter-of-fact about it. If it hadn't been for Sooner, or my friends leading me, I wouldn't have been able to ride.

Beattie's real name was also Susie, so I called my friends the two Susies. One summer, we got the idea of raising money for the Stamford Hospital by giving neighborhood kids rides on Joey. It worked out well. Joey was fun for the most part, though he could also be mean. One time, he bit down on all four of my fingers and wouldn't let go. Some days, when he didn't want to go, it made me really mad.

Even though I loved Joey, I was often unhappy. I knew I wasn't like the other kids, but I still didn't know why. My parents thought my frustration with Joey wasn't healthy, but I felt the good outweighed the bad. There were things I loved about him, things that made up for his stubbornness and mean streak. Sometimes in warm weather, for example, if I was up in the playroom watching TV and Joey was outside and some sound on the TV caught his ear—maybe a horse whinnying or cantering, he'd come see what was up. He'd come in through the screen door, opening it with his nose, up the stairs, down the landing, and right into the playroom. I'd hear his hooves on the landing and know he was coming. And he'd come in and stand next to where I was sitting and watch TV with me. He wasn't very gracious though. Sometimes he'd stand directly in front of the TV so I couldn't see, and I'd have to push him aside or sit on the floor. Either that or I'd sit up on the back of the couch and watch through his ears. He favored shows with galloping horses. I learned to put newspaper on the floor under his tail if it was a long show.

One day, my parents just up and gave Joey away. They didn't tell me they were going to. When I woke up, he was gone. They took me into the living room to talk about it. I remember that when I asked where he was, they walked away from me. Finally, they had me sit down, and Mother told me they'd given him away. I was both sad and mad. As I sat there, I got increasingly more upset to the point where I went out of control. Dad mumbled something to Mom about it being a mistake to give Joey away, but she insisted it was for the best, that Joey wasn't a healthy pet for me. I thought, *What does she know?* I looked at Dad as if to say, how could you let her do this? I knew Dad understood me and accepted me and my handicap better than Mom did. Why didn't he stand up for me? Why did he just sit there, mumbling? My frustration spread through me like fire spreads through dry hay, jumping from straw to straw. One minute, I was sad about losing Joe-Joe, the next I was furious at Mom for giving him away, and finally I was outraged at Dad for letting her do it.

I sat on the floor and screamed and threw my arms around and kicked my feet back and forth. Dad watched with a pained look on his face, but Mom just sat there, showing no feelings. When she spoke, she had the nerve to say that my hysteria, the way I was behaving, was the reason they'd given Joey away. That made me the maddest, for her to assume that she knew what was going on between Joey and me when, in fact, she knew nothing. When it was over and I thought about how she'd behaved, I thought my mother had to be the cruelest person on earth.

That day was the beginning of my habit of not letting people pass a certain point with me. When it comes to my relationship with animals, I put a shield around us, and there are very few people allowed behind that shield. I particularly keep out the people who assume they know me and draw conclusions based on their false assumptions. Those people may think they can get into a relationship with me, but they can't.

A few weeks later, my parents called me into the living room again. They had something else to tell me. Or rather, Mom had something to tell me. It was obvious that my father didn't want her to tell me. But she insisted. She sat me down on the couch and showed me a picture of Joey in his new home. As I was looking at the picture and missing Joey, she told me that he was dead. She said a horse in Joey's new pasture had run Joey into a fence. Joey had torn his chest open on the barbed wire, with the result that his new owners had put him to sleep. The picture had been taken before the accident.

I was confused. Poor Joey must have been very scared to run on the fence like that. Dad was protesting. Why was she telling me all this? But once she started in, of course, I wanted all the details. Staring at the photograph, I started crying. I asked if the horse in the background of the picture was the one who had chased Joey onto the fence. Mom said she didn't know. My father stood up and said there was no reason on earth that I needed to know what had happened, that I could just as well have gone on thinking Joe-Joe lived to a ripe old age. But what he said didn't matter. Mother had put this horrible vision in my head, and I was stunned and numb. Mom turned without saying a word and walked out of the room. I watched her go; then I sat, staring out the door after her, not really looking at anything. I didn't know whether my father was still in the room or not. I felt so alone. I had no idea where Dindy and Murray were. All I knew was that, as usual, they weren't around when I needed them. Neither my mother nor my father ever talked about Joey again, at least not around me.

It was as if my mother had singled me out for punishment. She'd thought she was doing the right thing when she gave Joey away, but when I'd gotten mad, I made it look like her decision had backfired on her. My first reaction was to fight. I talked back to her and screamed, and she lost control. To regain control, she then set out to hurt me, to make me draw back into myself. But that was the last time I let her ambush me like that. From that day on, I expected her to hurt me. I kept a part of me on guard, watching for the attacks.

Every detail of how Joey came into my life and then left has stayed with me all these years. It's such a sad memory, I'm surprised I didn't block it. I was a handicapped little girl who depended on her animals for fun and acceptance. When they were taken away, I was left with a brother and sister who could have cared less what I was feeling and parents who never encouraged them to care. What if Dindy and Murray had been taught to see the value of having me as their sister? Was Mother so powerful that they didn't dare strike out on their own and spend time with me? Was Mother's jealousy and need for control simply too much for them?

My mother thought Charles Lindbergh was a great man, but not just because he was handsome and flew across the Atlantic. I think, like him, she was prejudiced against certain people—blacks, Jews, and so on. Was she prejudiced against the disabled too? Did she discriminate against me because there was something wrong with me? She had a perfect husband, perfect houses, and two perfect kids. I was the only thing in the house she couldn't fix or hide. I think that's why she denied there was anything wrong with me. If there was nothing wrong, there was nothing to make a special effort for; therefore, she didn't have to make Murray and Dindy be friends with me. So I, who I really was, didn't exist on a day-to-day basis. I only existed when I was a problem, and that's how Murray and Dindy related to me. I was always treated like someone who had nothing to offer and nothing intelligent to say. When I think about all they could have learned from me if they'd had the courage to stop judging and listen, it makes me sad.

Joey slowly faded into the past when we moved from our first house in Stamford to the house on Tyler Drive. I was surprised that my mother would agree to live in that house. In the first place, it was new and we'd always lived in old houses; Mom was into antiques. Her friends also thought it was unusual, but she said she and Dad were tired of the maintenance of old houses. The new house wasn't that great looking, plus it was in a development. But the worst part for me was that I liked being close to my two Susies. The move meant I had to be taken to visit them by car, instead of riding my bike. At least I didn't have to switch schools.

I was going to the same private school for girls that Dindy attended. She'd been there a couple of years. I liked it because I had friends there and the teachers let me do what I wanted. They didn't make any demands on me like they did on the other kids. I think they were afraid to handle me any other way. Needless to say, I didn't learn much.

My two Susies came to the new house to visit. We had a great basement, all finished off, in which the three of us played. The most interesting thing about the new house was that it was at the edge of a ravine. The land dropped off behind it, straight down into dense woods. I thought that was so cool. There were two small patios—one outside the basement door, and the other up a flight of steps on the level of the kitchen, dining room, and family room. I was eleven or twelve when we moved into the house. I liked it, though it was strange not having a barn.

I met a lady at the end of our road who had a horse, and before long, she was letting me ride him. His name was Chris. He wasn't very well trained, but I had fun. The woman would let me do anything I wanted with him, so I decided to teach him a few things. There was a flat area in his pasture where I could work with him. We got along, Chris and I, such that the woman was amazed by how well he behaved with me. He became safe enough that the woman let me bring friends from school to help me with him and, in some cases, even ride him. He wasn't the greatest-looking horse. There were no markings on him, but he had a pretty color. I liked tying him outside in the sun and brushing him. His coat would shine like a penny that's just come through the wash cycle.

During the winter when I couldn't ride, I'd take a friend and visit Chris. If there was snow, we'd slide down the hill in his pasture. I was making more friends at school.

My last year in Dindy's school, my sixth-grade year, we had a young teacher we all really liked. There were fourteen of us in her class, and she called us "my fourteen angels." It was a fun year. Every one in the class liked everyone else. But the school still demanded little of me, and I got poor grades, especially in math. Nor was I given any extra help. At the end of the year, my mother was told to find another school for me. I was surprised by the news. It didn't seem right that they'd let me do whatever I wanted then fault me for my grades and ask me to leave. I guess everyone was doing better than I was, but no one told me. It made me feel misled and gypped. I was also mad because I didn't want to leave my friends.

Looking back, I think that when I was diagnosed with cerebral palsy and they then had that label to hang on me, my mother and the school let everything slide. They no longer made any demands on me. When I was a student having trouble, they tried to help me; but the minute I became the one with cerebral palsy, they wrote me off.

That was when my mother told me I wasn't "college material." I didn't know how to deal with that. What did it mean? My twelve-year-old mind didn't understand. Did it mean I was going to be a nobody? I knew I wasn't the best student in the class, but I thought I was getting by. Besides, how did Mom know? Neither she nor the school had made any effort to measure how smart I was or determine what kinds of things I might be good at. They had no idea of my potential because they'd never considered it!

In all fairness, Mom had other things on her mind. It was around this time that my father was diagnosed with colon cancer. Maybe that was why we moved into that tract house. At any rate, he had an operation and came home to recuperate. Mom took care of him. I visited him once in the hospital, but I have only a vague recollection of his illness. I remember that on the way home from our visit, I asked Mom if he was going to die. She said nobody knew. That's all I remember. After that, my father faded even further into the background in my life. When he went back to work, he came home every night, but he wasn't a significant figure in my life. For me, his illness just sort of came and went. I was unaware of its lasting effects on him. All I remember is that during his recovery my world came crashing down around me.

*Stamford, Connecticut, 1956. Susan Flatow, Joe-Joe and me.
When we got Joey, he was just a soft, fluffy baby with a jerky walk.
He was hysterically funny and the neighborhood kids all wanted
to come over and play with him. He got me a lot of attention and
new friends.*

*Camp Songadewin, Vermont, 1958. Susan Flatow, middle, and me,
to her right. Susan's mother talked my mother into sending me to this
camp. I hated it because I couldn't do anything right and no one knew
why, so the counselors blamed and shamed me. I also hated it because
Dindy and Murray got to take a boat trip to Martha's Vineyard
with Mom and Dad while I was there. They send me a postcard.*

Off to School

Mom started looking for another school for me. When spring came and the local public school had made it clear that they didn't want me, I had no idea where I might end up. I hoped the school I was in might change its mind. Being sent away to private school was never mentioned, so I had no reason to think it was a possibility. But it went from a possibility to a necessity, and then to a fact—all without my having the slightest idea.

I was sad about leaving my friends. Sometimes our teacher would talk about keeping the class together when the school year ended. We all knew there would never be another class like the fourteen angels.

Adolescence was coming on, and it made me more aware than ever of my differences. I felt dumb, and I knew I was becoming more of a burden for my mother. When I learned that I was being sent away to school, September seemed so far off that I didn't give it much thought.

One night, I overheard my father and mother talking in their bedroom. Dad kept insisting that there had to be another solution, that I shouldn't go away. It was as if he didn't believe my mother. Up until that night, I hadn't questioned my mother's motives in sending me away; but if my father thought there was another answer, maybe there was. Why was she giving up? In the end, I went along because I thought she knew more than Dad. What I couldn't understand was how much my life was going to change. I assumed life would go on as it always had. Little did I know that when I went away, the delicate thread that held me to my family would be severed once and for all.

That last summer, Mom decided to send me to camp, a dude ranch in Arizona, to get me used to being away from home. My father and I were to fly out to California to visit his mother who was in a nursing home, and then he was going to accompany me to the camp. On the way out, we laid over in Chicago to see my mother's sister who was dying of cancer.

I hadn't been away from home that much, but I liked the idea of going to a place that had horses. It was my mother's idea and once she got it into her head she seemed relieved. It was as if she'd finally found a school for me and then the ranch, and if she could just get me to them, everything would work out.

Part of her plan was for me to get braces before I left for the ranch. It made me feel as if I was being spiffed up, packaged so I could be shipped off from dude ranch to school.

In order for me to arrive at the camp on time, the braces had to go on immediately and all at once, instead of in steps. It was a process that normally took weeks, but Mom dropped me off at the orthodontist's office with the instructions that he was to do it all in one appointment. When Dr. Sorenson heard the instructions, he got mad and said absolutely not. As a result, I spent the entire hour-and-a-half appointment in his waiting room, bored.

When Mom pulled into the driveway, I went out to meet her. Seeing that I didn't have braces on, she asked what had happened. I explained that the doctor had refused to put them all on in one appointment. When I told her that, she pushed past me, marched into his office, and demanded that he do what she'd ordered. She said I was going away soon, and she'd been through enough, and it wasn't fair to her or me for him to get in the way of what had to be done. Embarrassed and not knowing what to do, I just stood there. I didn't want the braces put on all at once, but I didn't understand why it was a big deal one way or the other. Dr. Sorenson tried to tell my mother how sore my mouth would be, but she kept interrupting him until he finally shook his head and gave in. When he got the braces on, I learned what he meant by sore. There wasn't a spot in my mouth that wasn't in agonizing pain.

But I got to the ranch on time, and I liked the horses, and I wasn't homesick. I didn't make any friends. The kids were different, not very nice; and I was lonely, but I was all right as long as I could ride. The bad stuff just kind of stayed in the background.

Everyone had to take turns waiting on tables. It was hard for me because I couldn't carry the trays without spilling things. At school, I was used to getting help from my friends, but no one offered to help me at camp. Once again, I felt different, as if I stood out, and ashamed.

I spent the last two weeks in the infirmary getting over heatstroke. We'd gone on a long ride up into the mountains, and it had been 104 degrees and bone-dry. I'd been wearing a hat, but it wasn't enough; and I passed out, fell off my horse, and rolled down a hill. I remember waking up under a tree, flat on my back, with a counselor holding my legs up in the air. I was sick to my stomach and feeling completely alone. I wasn't homesick, but I sure was glum. When it finally came time to go, I was relieved to get out of there.

I'd gotten a French poodle the previous Christmas. We'd named him Fundy, and he and I had become very close; but when I'd gone away to camp, he'd bonded with my mother. She was matter-of-fact about it. The poor dog slept under my bed for the first week I was home, but then I guess he gave up. It seemed Mom had gotten him for me, become jealous of how close we'd became, and stolen his affection while I was away. She loved the fact that he'd go to her over me. I remember she said, "Well, you weren't here and I was." Yeah, well, whose fault was that? I didn't ask to go to the camp. I hated Mom for that.

It was becoming clear what was happening. I was no longer a little girl. I was a teen, and I was becoming pretty, and Mom was threatened; so she took pleasure in putting me in my place. Fundy followed her around for the rest of his life and paid no attention to me. The last time I saw him, I was living in Vermont and taking care of him. Fourteen and deaf, he wandered out onto the road and got run over. I saw the whole thing, but this time I didn't cry. Poor old Fundy had come to symbolize the way my mother cut me out and put me down. In a way, it was like watching her get run over. And when I buried Fundy, it was like burying the part of her that had hurt me so much by sending me away then stealing him from me.

Fundy became mixed up in my feelings when I went away to school. I was terribly homesick, and I hated my mother for giving me a dog and then sending me away. It was as if she'd planned the whole thing. I was becoming more aware of myself as a teen, and she was becoming jealous of that, jealous of my youth. I suddenly understood what her sarcastic remarks really meant. As a child, I was no threat to her; but as I got older, we came into competition, and I tested her insecurities. I was so alone and scared at my new school, House in the Pines, that I begged her to let me come home. I'd call home and just beg her. But there was always this cold voice on the other end of the line saying there was no other choice because no other school would take me. "You know why we're doing this, Sarah," she'd say. "You can handle it. Now, I'm going to say good-bye." And, *click*, she'd hung up; and I'd be standing there holding a dead phone in a dorm full of strangers.

I cried a lot. At first, I cried almost continuously. My whole body would shake. The beds were hard and uncomfortable, and I missed my room at home. Plus I had to share the bathroom. At night, I'd sit on my bed with my knees up against my chest, rocking back and forth, and the tears would stream down my cheeks, and I'd feel frozen in time. My roommate cried too, but I didn't talk to her. All I could think about was my parents leaving me. I kept seeing them driving away. My mother wasn't upset. Dad seemed concerned, but he was in his defeatist mode. Sometimes I hated my father for not standing up to Mom.

My first night at the school, I sat in the corner of my bed, rocking and crying. I felt like a puppy that's been dropped off at the pound. At one point, the headmistress, Ms. Johndroe, came in to try to comfort me; but it was all rehearsed. I could tell she'd said it thousands of times. There was no warmth in her voice. In fact, she frightened me. Her smell was strange, and she was disgustingly fat. I drew back from her and pressed myself against the wall. When she finally got off my bed and stood there looking down at me, she told me I was not to use the phone again for two weeks until I got over being homesick. I spent the next four years at that school without getting a warm hug from anyone.

But warm hugs weren't a part of my life anyway. As an adult, I realize how unnatural that was; but at the time, I just missed Nanny. Ms. Johndroe was certainly no replacement. Whereas Nanny was large and soft and had a warm glow, Ms. Johndroe's largeness was hard and angry. Whereas Nanny's speech was spontaneous, Ms. Johndroe's was all rehearsed.

I liked being in my own room at home, imagining Nanny. It was familiar, and she was familiar. But there was nothing familiar at the school. When Ms. Johndroe left and I looked around, all I saw was barren emptiness. It wasn't *my* dresser against the wall, *my* curtains, or *my* bed. The room had had countless girls pass through it. The walls were bare, a faded, dull pink. I had the sense that the room didn't care who I was.

There was one window, opened slightly. The breeze was making the curtains ripple; and occasionally, if they moved just right, I could see the moon. The movement of the curtains mesmerized me, and as I stared at them, I gradually grew numb. Lynn, my new roommate, was sniffling in the bunk above me. We hadn't spoken to each other. All I could let in was the movement of the curtains. I was in a bubble with my hurt and loneliness, seeking comfort from the flow of the curtains.

It was like a nightmare that wakes you up. I wanted to go to sleep because I thought that maybe, when I woke up, it would all be gone. But it was a nightmare I'd awakened to, not from. I knew it wasn't going to be better in the morning, and because I knew it, I couldn't get to sleep. As the night wore on, I became steadily more exhausted. Then fear set in, replacing the numbness, and I shook. The curtains ceased to comfort me. I relapsed into tears, hugged my knees still tighter, and pushed myself even harder against the wall. I imagined the wall opening and swallowing me up, but I knew it wasn't going to. My mind hopped around like it was tiptoeing across hot coals. Unable to keep up with my feelings, I fell into a panic and my breathing came in fits and starts, and sweat poured out of me. When rocking and pushing my back against the wall no longer worked, I turned and pushed my face against it.

Gradually, another feeling crept into me. It was hatred. I hated. But I wasn't sure whom or what I hated. Was it someone else, or did I hate myself? I didn't know. I couldn't tell. While trying to figure it out, I finally drifted into a light sleep.

The next thing I knew, sunlight was streaming into the room. I was still in the corner of the bed, back to the wall and hugging my knees. I was also worn out, emotionally as well as physically, to the point where it took me a while to figure out where I was. I stretched out one leg then the other. The sheets, rolled up around me, were sticky. Had I made a mess? I looked up. Lynn was sitting at the foot of my bed. When I saw her, I jumped and pulled my legs back up. She was staring at me through tired, red eyes. Her hair was short and light brown. When it seemed our eyes might remain locked forever, I willed myself to look down. She was wearing a T-shirt and underpants, nothing else, and I could see that she was incredibly thin. Her bones stood out on her knees and ankles. Everything about her was unfamiliar as was everything in the room. When I looked back up into her face, I saw the most beautiful blue eyes. It was then that she spoke. Her lips started moving before any sound came out. In slow motion, she said, "My name is Lynn."

Though I jumped a little at the sound, her voice snapped me out of my stupor. Drawing my legs back up to me, I searched for my voice. Did I still have it? I looked around the room. The curtains were still, and in the morning light, the walls were a darker pink. Realizing I was wet and chilled, I drew the covers around me. I cleared my throat then looked around again, seeking some source of comfort.

Lynn's head sagged, and she started sniffling again. I watched the tears slide down and drop off her cheeks, on one side then the other. When she started to get up, I realized I didn't want her to leave. It was as if I was watching my mother drive away all over again. *Oh god*, I felt like saying, *don't go. Don't go!* Before I knew it, I'd reached out and put my arms around Lynn, and we were sobbing into each other's shoulders.

"Sarah," I said.

"What?" she replied, trying to catch her breath.

"My name is Sarah."

The sound of my voice calmed me, but feeling awkward, I pulled back. We both did, but not completely. While we were shy, neither of us wanted to return to feeling separate and alone. Lynn stood up and climbed back up on her bunk. I got up and stood below her, not knowing what to do. We watched each other without making eye contact. My arms felt funny at my sides, and I crossed them and sat back down on my bunk. Immediately feeling alone again, I leaned forward and looked up. To my surprise, Lynn was looking back down at me. Feeling inhibited, I drew back where she couldn't see me.

I looked at the clock. We had an hour before Ms. Johndroe was going to come wake us. I was embarrassed, and god, how I wanted to go home. There I was, in a room no bigger than a walk-in closet, getting undressed and sleeping in front of a complete stranger. And the two of us would have to share the bathroom with two other girls. There was no place to hide and no escape.

I started thinking about my parents. Why was Mom so cold when she left? "This is the way it has to be," she'd said. I imagined her, Dad, Murray, and Dindy at home, waking up together. I wanted to be awakened by Mom and Fundy. As I imagined them all together, I was determined to get home; but at the same time, another thought was there. It occurred to me that my family felt I was a fifth wheel. But how could they? How could they go through their days with a family member missing? And then I realized that they were going to share all kinds of things that I was going to miss. They were the family now. But if that was the case, if I was no longer part of my family, who was I?

Lynn snapped me out of my thoughts and back to reality. I heard her voice, but not what she'd said. Anger from my daydream gave me the courage to stand up, look up at her, and demand, "What did you say?" Just then, Ms. Johndroe opened the door and came in.

When I turned to face her, Ms. Johndroe's bulk hit me like a truck. I smelled her breath, even felt it on my face, and was awestruck by the size of her bosom. She announced that we were to be in the dining room at the main house by eight o'clock. "Being late will *not* be tolerated." And then, as quickly as she'd appeared, she turned and was gone. She closed the door gently but firmly behind her.

I turned back to Lynn and gave a sigh as if to say, "Wow!" She burst out laughing and said, "You look like you've seen a ghost."

"She scared me," I said. Lynn laughed. "I guess it was pretty funny," I allowed. "I thought her bosom was going to eat me alive."

At last we were past the tears. We were stuck in a tiny room for God knows how long with a headmistress and housemother who looked like an amoeba and talked like Mussolini. The good news was that by being who she was, she'd broken the ice between Lynn and me.

Our next challenge was to figure out how to get our turns in the bathroom. We quickly discovered that it was the bathroom for the entire floor and there were four, not two, girls living with us. With towel and toothbrush, we passed in the hallway, sizing one another up. Not knowing whether to smile or look cool, I decided the situation called for both. I had a hard time with the smile.

I got more of a stare from the other girls than Lynn did. At first, I wondered why, but I found out when one of the girls demanded, "Why are you limping?" The question caught me by surprise. When I turned to face her, I was struck by how cold her blue eyes were. They seemed to be looking at something behind my head.

I lowered my eyes and bought some time by clearing my throat. It was the same question everyone had always asked: what was wrong with me? I'd been asked the question so many times I should have gotten used to it, but I hadn't. It was the way she was asking—cold and impatient; it made me feel put on the spot. The words *cerebral palsy* wouldn't come to my lips even when other girls gathered behind her waiting for my answer. All I could muster was, "I sprained my ankle." After saying it, I waited to see if it would satisfy her. She shrugged, mumbled something I couldn't quite hear, and walked off.

I shut the door and looked in the mirror. I was white as a sheet. Leaning over and staring into the white sink, I splashed cold water on my face. To open the door and go out into the hall again would be a brand new experience for me. It frightened me more than being without my family. It was the way the girl had asked why I was limping. It was mean, unaccepting, even rejecting. That's why I'd said it was a sprained ankle. I wanted her to believe it would go away, that I was like everyone else, because I couldn't stand any more rejection. I'd fit in with the fourteen angels. As long as I'd had them, everything else was okay. But I no longer had them. And now I no longer had my family either. That's why I'd lied, because I felt all alone. I *had* to fit in with these new girls.

It was my cerebral palsy again. It was always just a matter of time before it came up, crashing to the forefront like Ms. Johndroe's bosom. How was I going to survive?

An impatient bang on the door made me jump. I wiped my face and hastily gathered up my things. I dropped my toothbrush while fumbling with the lock. Gathering it up, I took a deep breath, opened the door and, trying not to limp, set off down the hall.

Lynn seemed to sense my anguish. She didn't ask how I'd sprained my ankle. She knew there was something else. After all, we'd spent the night together. We'd looked into each other's eyes long enough for her to notice how my left eye wandered. When I realized that she'd noticed without saying anything, I decided Lynn would be the first one I'd tell about my disability.

And that's how it was that first morning. Neither Lynn nor I talked as we walked out of the dorm and up to breakfast. We were both away from family and friends for the first time, and we knew we wouldn't be going home anytime soon. We understood without talking about it: it was just the two of us, and we were going to have to stick together.

The main house was huge, yellow with white trim and surrounded by the tallest pine trees, hence the school name. It was there at the main house that we gathered for classes, ate, and got our mail. Our mailboxes were our link to everything familiar to us. On the top floor, the house was also the ninth-grade dormitory. If I survived the next two years, that's where I'd live. My reward would be dealing with a long, curving flight of stairs.

The path led up to a terrace from which we could look in through large windows to the dining room. It was still empty, so at least we weren't late. The large square tables had white linen tablecloths neatly pressed. Our places were set, and each had a high-back spindle chair in front of it. While Lynn and I were staring in at this scene, a woman—I guessed a teacher—appeared at the door, cleared her throat, and told us to come in. As we passed her, I looked up into her face for some hint of warmth, but she looked away.

We entered a dark corridor. On the left were row upon row of brass mailboxes, running on up the hall, each with a tiny keyhole. After the phone, my mailbox would be my primary connection to my family. Every day, I'd find and unlock my box, reach into the unknown, and grab whatever had come from home. It was as if my hand actually went into my family while the rest of me stayed on the outside. Standing there in the dark hall waiting to go in to lunch, I had the sense that my ties to my family were unraveling, tearing was perhaps more like it; and they'd never be restitched.

My eyes were filling with tears again. When I failed to see a step and stumbled, someone caught my arm, pulled me back, and hissed, "You can't block the dining room doors!" I'd become separated from Lynn and had no idea what was going on.

A few minutes later, the teachers came down the staircase two by two and marched past us into the dining room. When each had taken her place at the head of one of the tables, we students were allowed to file in. I spotted Lynn up ahead, waiting for me; and when I caught up, we chose a table and stood behind our chairs.

Ms. Johndroe stood up and made announcements. Among other things, she said that from then on, our seats would be assigned and that the assignments would change every two weeks. She said the first assignments were on the bulletin board upstairs and that we should check them before returning to our dorms. It would be the last time Lynn and I sat together for a while.

We sat down, and everyone put their napkin in their lap. Everyone but me; I just sat in my fog, staring straight ahead. Behind me somewhere, I heard dishes banging in the kitchen. I couldn't stop thinking about my family. I saw them in my mind, all except Nanny. Where *was* Nanny? It made me so sad I didn't think I'd be able to eat.

Lynn gave me a nudge, and I snapped out of my stupor. The teacher at the head of our table was giving me the evil eye because I hadn't put my napkin in my lap. Her name card said she was Ms. Pence, but she looked more like Ms. Frog, with eyelids that rose and fell like venetian blinds and nostrils the size of golf balls. I snatched up my napkin, spread it across my lap, and looked back for her approval. There was none, but I couldn't stop looking at her. She was amazing. Was she real? With that down-turned, snarly mouth and short white hair slicked back, and skin like dried leather? Her body was short and round, and she had a hump on her back that made her lean in over the table. Like most of the other teachers, she was in her sixties and wore no rings on her left hand. I later found out that her nickname was the Toad.

At least I was back to reality. The thoughts of my family were gone. I'd been dumped at the school, and they were going on with their lives. Nanny was gone, too. It was time for me to start thinking about how I was going to get through it all.

The two girls to the right of Ms. Pence got up and stood behind their chairs. They would carry the trays and wait that day. The next day, we'd all move around two seats, and the next two girls would wait. I assumed that since I couldn't carry the trays, they'd skip me. But I couldn't be sure, and not knowing made me nervous.

Ms. Pence looked around the table, parted her thick lips, and said, "At my table, you may have one helping only. There will be no exceptions. If you forget and ask for seconds, you will get an extra turn waiting. Do I make myself clear?" We all nodded. The two girls who were to serve were still standing behind their chairs, waiting to get the nod to go get breakfast. Ms. Pence dismissed them with a flick of her wrist. They were clearly old students.

The servers from all the tables went over and got into a line that led to a hole in the wall. The kitchen was on the other side of the hole, and the girls leaned in to pick up the trays of food. There was a swinging door next to the hole, and every once in a while, a woman in white with a net on her hair came out to see how things were going. As the clatter of dishes grew louder, people were forced to raise their voices. The dining room was huge, with a plaster ceiling and dark hardwood paneling that reflected the noise. The windows we'd stared through were at the end of the room looking out over the campus. It was much lighter under the windows, and I later learned that the girls hoped they'd be assigned to those tables. Ms. Pence's table was in the middle of the room. It was a far cry from our dining room at home.

One of the waiters placed a tureen of oatmeal in front of Ms. Pence. She removed the top, handed it to the girl to take away, and signaled for us to begin passing our bowls. Wielding her spoon with frightening dexterity, she took each portion from the same place at the edge, turning the tureen as she progressed. Finally, when she'd served everyone precisely the same amount and nothing remained but the center, she took it for herself. It was a mesmerizing performance. God only knows how many times she'd done it. Having served us all, she helped herself to the sugar and cream then started them around the table. We helped ourselves, put our hands in our laps, looked up at her, and waited. When everyone's eyes were on hers, she raised her spoon and nodded for us to begin.

It was the best oatmeal I'd ever had, and it calmed me to the point where I began to accept my lot. Daily meals with my family were a thing of the past. House in the Pines was my life now. Perhaps I'd survive it after all.

Before I knew it, that first breakfast was over, and we were all headed up the stairs to see the seating assignments for the next two weeks. Afraid we'd be separated, Lynn and I clung to each other as we were swept along toward the bulletin board. When we got close, we became packed in like sardines. At the board, fingers ran down the list of tables. Some girls—clearly not "newbies"—cheered and went giggling off with friends when they learned where and with whom they'd be.

When it came our turn to search, Lynn found her name first and looked at me with disgust. "What?" I asked.

"I'm with Ms. Pence," she said with resignation. I found my name at Ms. Wood's table, across the dining hall from Ms. Pence's.

I grabbed Lynn by the hand and pulled her aside. "Look at it this way. You won't have her again for a while." My encouragement didn't seem to help.

We walked back to our dorm. It was Sunday, and we had the rest of the day to settle in and unpack. In our cubbyhole of a room, we couldn't help but bump into each other as we put our clothes away. After excusing ourselves for a while, we stopped and stood facing each other. Both of us had bundles of clothes in our arms. Lynn smiled and said, "We just don't have space for everything. This room is ridiculous." She leaned back against the windowsill and took a deep breath.

"We could put some of the stuff under the bed," I suggested. And that's what we did, and it worked out just fine. When we had everything put away, we climbed up on the top bunk, proud of ourselves, and shook hands.

As we were giggling about the absurdity of it all, our door flew open, and a dark-haired girl burst in. She introduced herself as Joan Loring from Maine. "I'm just looking around," she said. "Want to come and check out the living room?" Lynn and I looked at each other, climbed down, and followed Joan out the door.

The dorm was busy, with girls hurrying to put their things away. Once they'd done so, the newbies checked the place out as we were. The girl who had asked me about my limp was coming up the stairs as we went down. She stared at me again and brushed against me as we passed each other. Even though my back was to her, I could tell she'd stopped to stare at me. Sure enough, when I turned, she was standing at the top of the stairs, watching me. Embarrassed at having been caught looking, I turned back. But it was already too late; I missed the bottom step and stumbled out into the living room.

Lynn grabbed me. "What's the matter?"

"I don't know why that girl stares at me."

"Who?" asked Joan, overhearing us. I pointed up the stairs just as the girl was being called away by a friend. "Oh, that's Meg Ferguson," Joan explained. "She lives in Rhode Island. Her parents have a Morgan Horse Farm. They're loaded." I was impressed, but I didn't understand why Meg Ferguson was so mean.

The living room was a long, bright room with lots of windows and a Dutch door that exited out onto a small patio. It had a couch and several chairs and looked like what it had been, a room in someone's home.

On our way back to the stairs, we came to a door in the hallway. "Do we dare?" asked Joan. It was Ms. Johndroe's door.

"I don't see why not," said Lynn. "It's the only way to the kitchen, and we're allowed to go into the kitchen, aren't we?"

We opened the door with caution, as if a ghost might pop out at us. Inside, there were two girls, looking terrified. "Oh my god!" one of the girls hissed. "We thought you were Ms. Johndroe!" We all laughed. "Oh my god," the girl said again at the thought of it.

We introduced ourselves. The girl who'd spoken, a blond, was Betsy; the other girl—who had brown hair, large blue eyes, and a big smile—was Ellie, from Darien, Connecticut. I told her I was from Stamford, but we didn't pursue it. Neither of us wanted to talk about home.

We went through Ms. Johndroe's bedroom to the kitchen. There was a wall phone in the kitchen. Lynn and I would have to pass through Ms. Johndroe's bedroom to get to it. We agreed that we didn't want to have to do that in order to talk to our families, and we especially didn't want to have to pass back through *after* talking to them.

There was a small bedroom behind the kitchen. The girls who lived there would have to pass through Ms. Johndroe's bedroom every morning. We felt sorry for them. As we were checking out the kitchen and back bedroom, we decided Ms. Johndroe's bedroom was the only room big enough for her massive bed. It was a four-poster, covered with huge pillows. Betsy said it looked like the giant's castle in *Jack and the Beanstalk.*

We were staring at the bed when we heard the front door open and Ms. Johndroe's voice in the front hall. Afraid we might meet her if we tried to get back out into the hall, but not wanting to get caught in the kitchen either, we were stymied. We could hear her footsteps coming toward us on the hardwood floor and then she entered her bedroom. She looked at us then at her bed, sized the situation up, and said, "Girls, it's time you started up for lunch."

I waited for one of the other girls to take the lead in passing Ms. Johndroe, but no one did. Finally, Ms. Johndroe came over, put her arm around my shoulders, and asked how I was managing the walk up to the dining hall. I didn't know whether the other girls thought it was weird or not, but I wasn't going to hang around to find out. I said fine, turned out from under her arm, and made for the door.

I didn't look back, that's for sure. Outside, Lynn called, "Hey, wait up," and ran to catch up. Betsy and Ellie were coming along behind, whispering to each other. I hoped they weren't talking about me.

"Why did Ms. Johndroe ask you that?" Lynn asked. I tried to avoid her. I wanted Lynn to know about my cerebral palsy, but I was really uncomfortable about Meg. She was acting so strangely around me as if she was looking for some fault or failing. She knew there was something different about me, and she seemed determined to find out what it was.

"So you limp and your eye's a little funny. What's the big deal?" Lynn blurted out.

"What did you say?" I barked. Betsy and Ellie walked by, talking, talking, talking.

"You limp. I already know there's something," Lynn replied.

"I have cerebral palsy," I said, looking down at the ground. "I didn't want to tell you because I was afraid Meg would find out. I never had a problem telling my friends at my old school. We all got along. But I can tell it's not going to be that way here."

"You have *what*?" Lynn's eyes were wide.

"Cerebral palsy. It's a birth defect. I suffered brain damage which effected the nerves and muscles on my left side. I'm blind in my left eye."

Lynn stared at me with her mouth open. Remembering lunch, we continued on. As we walked, Lynn made me explain my disability to her. She said she thought I was amazing because of all the things I could do despite it. And then we were at the main house entering the dining hall, and she was walking away from me to her table. After a few steps, she turned back, gave me a half wave, and said, "I'll wait for you upstairs, okay?"

Lunch was fairly uneventful. Ms. Elizabeth Wood was a young, freckle-faced, pretty woman who was assistant coach for the field hockey and lacrosse teams. She was quite a switch from Ms. Pence. For one thing, she didn't care how much we ate. I decided it was going to be a relief to be at her table for two weeks. I was still nervous about explaining that I couldn't serve as a waiter, but it seemed I was at a table where I'd be safe for a while.

As she'd promised, Lynn found me upstairs after lunch. We decided to go see the stables before returning to the dorm. The campus was beautiful. We passed an outdoor amphitheater surrounded by giant pine trees, then followed the sign to the stable. The barn was a large T-shaped building, with a grand entrance at the bottom of the T. Passing in through the huge green doors, we came to a buckskin, cross tied between two posts. He was switching his tail back and forth to keep the flies off. As we got closer, he shook, startling Lynn. "It's all right, he's just after the flies," I explained. "Wow, will you look at this place. Pret-ty ritzy."

I stepped past the horse and signaled Lynn to follow. As my eyes adjusted to the darkness, I saw an entrance to an indoor riding ring. The ring was large, with stands on either side, windows above the stands, and a high ceiling from which hung huge canopied lights. Underfoot, there was soft, deep sawdust.

From behind us a deep voice asked, "Can I help you, girls?" I turned and saw a shadowed figure but was unable to make out whether it was a man or woman.

"I wanted to see the stable," I answered. "I'm going to be riding here."

"I see," the figure replied. It laughed. As I drew closer, I saw that it was wearing high boots and breeches and had short bristly hair. And then I saw the birthmark, covering half its face, and the breasts, and knew it was female. "We're not open. I'm here to get things ready for tomorrow. You can look around, just don't stick your fingers through the bars of the stalls." She reached out her hand. "I am Ms. Keener," she said. "I run the stable."

When I hesitated, she grabbed my hand and ground the joints of my fingers together in her powerful grip. I tried to smile. After crunching Lynn's hand as well, Ms. Keener abruptly turned and reentered the stall from which she'd come. When she slammed the heavy gate behind her, the noise echoed around the barn.

I looked at Lynn. We were glad Ms. Keener had gone back to work so we could continue exploring. From where we were standing, we could look down two long isles of stalls. There seemed to be horses in all of them. It gave me a sense of hope. "I could live in this place," I whispered.

We walked down one isle and then the other. Some of the horses were munching hay while others were standing on three legs, taking an afternoon snooze. The common area outside of the stalls was white with green trim that matched the outside of the building. On our way back to the entrance, we ducked in to see the tack room. Ms. Keener was there, cleaning a bridle which was hanging on a hook suspended from the ceiling. Saddles lined the walls, and there was a sweet smell of leather saddle soap and neet's-foot oil.

Ms. Keener didn't look up, and we left without speaking to her. Her distance made me feel strange, but at the same time, I was happy to find such complete facilities. Lynn said she was "freaked" by Ms. Keener, whom she called "a poor excuse for a human being." We took a different path back to the main campus, passing an outdoor ring and white-fenced paddocks.

When the sun set on my first day at House in the Pines, we were back in our room. Lying on my bed, my thoughts returned to home and my old bedroom. Lynn, who was also thinking of home, said we should get out of our room to ward off the sadness. I was afraid of encountering Meg, but my fear wasn't as bad as my homesickness. She stayed in her room, I guess, because we didn't see her. When we finally settled in, we fell asleep immediately.

We were to begin classes the next day. It was hard for me to see Lynn disappear into the crowd at breakfast, but at least I had Ms. Wood's cute face to look forward to. Lynn wouldn't be waiting for me upstairs after breakfast because we were supposed to pick up our schedules and go immediately to the classroom building next door. After eating, I was anxious to leave, but I had to wait until everyone at our table was finished. I watched the slower girls eat their oatmeal.

When Lynn went by on her way out of the dining hall, I pushed back my chair and tapped my foot while staring after her. She stopped at the door, turned back, and made sign language at me. Not understanding, I formed my mouth into an exaggerated but silent what.

"Do you want something, Sarah?" asked Ms. Wood.

"Ah, no, Ms. Wood," I answered, embarrassed.

"In that case," she said, smiling, "you may all be excused."

Finally! I caught up with Lynn on the path to the classroom building. We had our notebooks, which we'd put together the night before. Our first period was free. As we filed into the study hall, I noticed how much alike we all looked. Although we didn't have to wear uniforms, our skirts were the same length, and we all wore kneesocks and loafers. Most of us were wearing plaid skirts and cardigans. It was the style. Plus we weren't allowed to have our bangs over a certain length.

I was dressed the same as everyone else. I had my A-frame skirt, sweater, kneesocks, and the "in" hairdo called the Marienbad—short behind the ears and parted on one side. I fit in. In fact, with my small waist, I was starting to look pretty good. Except for my shoes. I couldn't wear those slim little penny loafers. My left foot had a habit of rolling onto the ankle, and I couldn't keep slip-on shoes on. I had to wear tie shoes, with lots of support.

But I was too homesick and concerned about eating and staying away from people who noticed my limp to worry about my shoes. Lynn didn't care about my limp, but if anyone else did and I got challenged about it, there was no escape. Well, our dorm room was safe, but I couldn't hide in the dining room or classroom building. Walking into the study hall, my feet felt huge, and my footsteps sounded louder than everyone else's. At the front of the room, there was a teacher sitting at a desk. She watched me as I came down the aisle. When we made eye contact, she looked down at my feet and touched the tip of her index finger to her lips. I tried to put my left foot down more softly, but I had drop-foot, which caused it to slap down on the floor.

I got a dirty look from the tight-bunned, wispy-haired teacher. The nameplate on her desk said she was Ms. Downey. I tried to avoid more eye contact, but I had to walk to the front of the room to get to another aisle; and when I passed Ms. Downey, she reached out and grabbed my arm, forcing me to look at her. But then, immediately, she let go. When I got by her, Lynn, behind me, whispered, "What is the *matter* with her!"

I couldn't respond. My face flushed with embarrassment. Ms. Downey's treatment had made the girls near us stare at my feet. Tears came into my eyes. I looked down so no one would see them, took the first empty desk, and tried to hide my feet under it. God! I *really* wanted to go home. I had cerebral palsy plus I was becoming a teen. I *was* a teen, and everyone at the school was making me feel uncomfortable and different. My friends at home had liked me, but here I seemed to be getting an awful lot of cold stares.

It wasn't all bad. A few of the girls, well mannered enough not to stare, made eye contact and smiled. One even winked as she walked by. I turned and watched as she found a seat. She was tall and big busted, and her straight hair neatly framed her face and accentuated her dark eyes and delicate nose. I kept looking at her. I wanted to smile, but I didn't dare. She finally felt me watching her and returned my glance. Then I smiled. I desperately wanted some reassurance, some show of warmth, and I didn't care where it came from. She smiled again, very quickly, then turned away to talk to a friend. She looked older than I and, judging from her relaxed manner, was a returning student.

Ms. Downey interrupted the light whispering going on around the hall by banging a book on her desk. Everyone became still, sat up straight, and looked to the front of the room. Ms. Downey was now standing before us in midcalf-length skirt and black tie shoes with thick heels. The heels supported equally thick ankles and shapeless legs that ran up like pipes to her huge, fat bottom. Her head, neck, shoulders, and chest were far too small for the massiveness below. As I looked at her, it occurred to me that the teachers at the school looked more like animals than people. Ms. Pence had looked like a toad, and now Ms. Downey looked like a penguin. It made me giggle, which was a relief because I was dreading the coming classes.

Lynn and I made it through the morning. We got lost a couple of times, but everything was sensibly laid out, and it didn't take us long to get back on track. We had history with Ms. Hall, and then speech with Mr. Castle.

I remember the English teacher best of all from that first year. Ms. Pierce was a short, slim, older lady who drove an ancient DeSoto. That part was funny, but she knew how to teach. I really loved her classes. My problem was that I had no study skills when I arrived at the school. No one had ever made me work, and I had no idea what I could do. I actually thought *not* paying attention was the way to go, what you were supposed to do. I had been such a bad student that House in the Pines put me on probation before we even started classes. But Ms. Pierce, old-fashioned and strict, was crystal clear about what she taught and expected from us.

She immediately saw that I could read aloud fairly well, so she held my attention by surprising me with requests to do so. She also noticed my writing. My printing looked like typing. It was so good, I was the only student in our class allowed to print her papers. I was proud of that. Ms. Pierce's attention and demands were a godsend. They helped me learn how to study, which helped me in other classes as well.

Being on probation, I had mandatory study hall every night after dinner. They had the blue book in study hall. The blue book was where they put your name if you were late or made inappropriate noise. It rested on the front of the desk at the front of the room, where we all saw it continually. And it made me work hard, not just on my schoolwork, but also to keep my left foot still. I made an extra effort to keep it quiet when I had to get up from my desk to look up a word in the big dictionary at the back of the room. We all paid attention in study hall because if you got your name in the blue book, you could lose your weekend privileges, which meant you couldn't go home.

Sometimes, especially in the beginning, I would put my chin down on my hands, stare into my book, and daydream. I would think of my old classmates, the angels, and wonder where they were. I missed my friends, going over to their houses after school or having them over to my house. I missed the tomato soup that was always waiting when I got off the bus, or the tea and cinnamon toast Mom sometimes made us. I felt completely alone at the school, and I was always afraid of one thing or another. Besides, it didn't seem right that you should sleep at school, especially on weekends when there weren't any classes.

When the first morning of classes was over and Lynn and I were walking to the main house for lunch, the tall upperclassman who'd smiled at me in first-period study hall caught up to us. She was with another girl. She introduced herself as Prim Bullock, and the other girl as Bunny, her cousin. Bunny was blond and very athletic. When I told them Lynn and I had visited the stable, they said they rode too. "Yeah," said Bunny as she skipped along, "We've been trying to figure out if there's something going on between Ms. Johndroe and Ms. Keener." I could see why she was called Bunny.

"What?" asked Lynn.

"Shhh," said Prim, putting her hand over Bunny's mouth. Bunny pretended to bite Prim's finger, and we all laughed.

As the fall wore on, the days began to run on together, and Saturdays and Sundays became only slightly different from weekdays. Lynn and I became better friends. We were like sisters, the way I imagined sisters were supposed to be. Whether we were running around, giggling, or talking about serious stuff, we were completely relaxed with each other. I brushed her hair at night. It was brown, and she was letting it grow out.

My friendship with Lynn made me think about my sister, Dindy. Why couldn't we have the kind of relationship Lynn and I had? Without realizing it, I had regressed into making up stories about Murray and Dindy. I imagined playing with them and having Murray come visit me at school. It was real to me at first, like a movie in my mind. I even knew what we'd say to each other when he came. I did it with my father too. I imagined him and what he'd feel and say, and I played it out in my mind, and then I repeated it all to my dorm mates. We were getting to know each other, and it was our first time away from home, so we tried to describe our families to one another. I don't know about the other girls, but I created the family I wished I had. I did it not only to look good but also to feel better by pretending I had a loving family. That way, I didn't have to think about that glass wall between them and me.

It was a way to survive, imagining a warm, affectionate family waiting for me at home. I believed my creation because it enabled me to get through the Meg Fergusons at school. It also got me through missing my dog, Fundy, and the anger I felt toward my mother for sending me away. And when Ms. Keener finally put me on a horse, and it was a slow horse and wouldn't let me prove myself, my fantasy got me through that too. In fact, my imagined family got me through that entire first year. When it finally came time to go home for the summer, I was not only taller and developing a nice figure, but also off academic probation.

I learned to study that first year at school. Being on probation scared me into it. I also grew up a lot. I met girls from all over the country, learned to spot the friendly, accepting ones and avoid the snotty ones. My instincts about such things had always been good because of my family and my cerebral palsy, but they got even better. The hard part was living without cats and dogs. There were the horses at the school, but I wasn't allowed to ride up to my ability, so that experience was frustrating rather than relaxing. Oh, those horses! They were so old and slow, it was work just to keep them moving. I was a good rider, but I couldn't show it on those nags.

But the worst part about the horses was that I couldn't get my mind off my tense muscles. That's what riding has always done for me. It's not like other sports. I've been riding for so many years—since I was five—that the muscles on my left side have developed their own memory. They know what to do on a horse without my mind having to tell them. Plus they relax and stop being tense and jumpy, so they no longer distract me. When I'm riding a good horse, I'm free to think about anything I want, or not think at all. It's like meditation, when you slip down into your breathing or pulse. But with the school horses, it was so hard to keep them going that I couldn't get into any rhythm.

I remember one horse in particular. Her name was Dolly, and she was a buckskin in her twenties. The first time I got assigned to Dolly, my initial thought was, well, there are lots of horses, I won't get this one again. But sure enough, I did. I got her a second time that very same week. My friend Prim put her hand on my shoulder and smiled when she saw how disappointed I was. She was good at smiling when things went wrong, that Prim. So I got on old Dolly and headed for the indoor ring. Well, this horse liked to stand in the middle of the ring while the other horses walked around her. If you wanted to trot, you had to take your horse to the outside of the ring and trot along the wall so you'd be out of the way of the walking horses. I was so frustrated that day, I determined to get Dolly out on the wall and make her trot. And I could tell it had seldom been done with Dolly. She was a packhorse, stubborn beyond belief, plus she pretended she didn't understand. Either that or she actually didn't understand because she'd spent her whole life refusing to learn. I had to yank her head around and kick her constantly just to get her attention. By the time I got her to the outside, she was wet with sweat. When I saw how heated she'd become, I gave up, loosed my reins, and let her veer back into the center of the ring.

Some of the girls clapped. One rode over to me, at which point Dolly put her ears back. "Dolly, quit it!" I yelled.

"That's the first time anyone has been able to get Dolly out on the wall," the girl said. I could see she was impressed.

I was sweating by then too. "Well, what do you know?" was all I could think to say.

Ms. Keener came out to see what the clapping was all about, and immediately noticed the sweat on Dolly's neck. When I walked Dolly over to the crosstie and dismounted, she came over, pushed past me, and examined Dolly. Fear and embarrassment hit me at the same time. When Ms. Keener wouldn't look at me, I started to walk off, hoping I could get away without an incident.

No luck. "Sarah!" Ms. Keener demanded. I turned back to face her. "This is an old horse. She's too hot. If you do this again, you will no longer be allowed to ride in my barn. Do you understand?"

I was shocked by her tone of voice. My lips quivered as I searched for words. Ms. Keener left Dolly and marched up to me so that we were face to face. Terrified, I started crying. In a voice so shrill I could feel it all over, Ms. Keener screeched, "I expect some kind of response from you, Sarah."

I managed, "Yes, Ms. Keener." It seemed to suffice, for she turned and walked away.

A little while later on my way back to the dorm, my tears turned to anger. "This is all their fault," I muttered to myself. "If they'd put me on a decent horse, this wouldn't have happened."

"Muttering to ourselves, are we?" chided Meg as she and some other girls passed. I wiped my face and pretended nothing was wrong. I'd noticed that Meg was one of the few girls who hadn't clapped for me. She must have loved the scene with Ms. Keener. Meg and her fancy Morgan horse, I thought. Who needs her? I bet *she* couldn't have gotten Dolly out to the fence! I made a face at her back as she and her snooty friends went on ahead. They were so boring. There was Dudley, whose father was a famous gambler, and Tara, from California, who had never seen snow before. Sometimes Joan Loring was a part of their group too. Clara Rosengarten was another one. She looked just like a great tortoise, except that she had no neck. Her shoulders started at her ears.

Lynn met me at the dorm door. "What happened? Everyone's saying Ms. Keener got angry at you." Her face was full of concern.

"I didn't do anything. You know Dolly, right? Well, I got her to the outside today. She even trotted a little. But she was *not* that heated up." And just then, when I said that, I realized that it wasn't about Dolly. In fact, it had nothing to do with Dolly. The school was afraid I was going to hurt myself because of my cerebral palsy.

I was staring past Lynn. "Hello. Are you there?" she asked. I pushed around her and plopped onto the common room couch. She came and sat next to me.

"That's it," I said.

"What's it?" she asked, leaning closer.

"Don't you see? This is a test."

"What do you mean a test?" Poor Lynn was completely confused.

"I proved that I can ride today—by getting that horse out on the wall and making it trot. Now, if they give me Dolly again, it means they're afraid I'm going to get hurt. Because of my cerebral palsy. Oh god, what am I going to do?" I had to tell my parents. I couldn't let it happen. My ability to ride had never been mentioned, much less questioned. They'd just assumed I couldn't. It was a whole new thing for me to deal with.

"Do you really think that's true?" Lynn asked. "That they'd keep you off certain horses because of your handicap?"

"I'm sure of it."

"But you're amazing. You can do everything."

"Yeah? Well, if I'm so amazing, why am I on the reject field hockey team? You know what? I'm never going to get off that either!" I started upstairs to change for dinner.

And that's the way the year ended, with my realization about the school's attitude toward me. They saw me as being different, and some of the not-so-nice girls had picked up on it, and it was going to get worse my second year. Little did I know that I was going to face something that summer that would make my second year far worse than I had imagined.

Images from the 1964 House in the Pines Yearbook

The main building, with offices, dining hall, and third floor rooms.

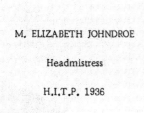

M. ELIZABETH JOHNDROE

Headmistress

H.I.T.P. 1936

Miss Johndroe, as she looked 27 years before I met her.

MRS. BARRY
Nurse
H.I.T.P. 1955

MRS. DITCHETT
Housemother
H.I.T.P. 1958

MISS DOWNEY
Mathematics
In Charge of Study Hall
H.I.T.P. 1928-30, 1936

MRS. HORTON
Mathematics
Librarian
H.I.T.P. 1962

MISS JESINSKA
Latin, German
H.I.T.P. 1951

MISS KEENER
Riding
H.I.T.P. 1951

MRS. JOHN PIERCE
Nurse

MRS. VIRGINIA PIERCE
English

MISS WOOD
Physical Education
H.I.T.P. 1959

Some of the teachers and staff responsible for my confinement and instruction.

RIDING GLUB

We in the Riding Club have learned much since the beginning of the year about sportsmanship, riding, and about the horses themselves. We have produced and enjoyed costume rides, breakfast rides, and horse shows. We have exhibited our Drill Team for school occasions and horse shows.

On behalf of the whole club, I wish to express our gratitude to Miss Keener for her expert instruction.

Prim Bullock
PRESIDENT

PRIM BULLOCK
President

TOP ROW: Cornwall, Clark, Bullock, Lawson, Chase, Thiessen, Ferguson. MIDDLE ROW: Bandler, Becerra, N. Thomas, Robinson, Barleon, J. Thomas, Borntraeger. FRONT ROW: Tananbaum, Dario, Baugh, Spurling, Gage, Cook. ABSENT: Case, Duer, Fenn, Gordon, Hayden, Howell, Land, Miller, Sim, Walker, Russell.

Under the Knife

I arrived home at the end of my first year having adjusted to being away at school. I'd made friends, and I'd learned to imagine a warm, loving family at home when the friends weren't enough. I went home as a teenager who desperately wanted to be like her peers, but had been made to feel she wasn't. Thanks to Ms. Pierce, I'd learned to study. And I could share a bathroom without having it bother me. But the worst thing was, I came home as a girl who was no longer respected for her riding ability.

All my parents could see was how I'd grown and gotten stronger. I didn't tell them how sad I was about being seen as different and not being respected. And of course, I didn't tell them how estranged I felt from them. I felt further outside than ever because they'd molded into a unit and settled into a routine, neither of which included me. My dog, Fundy, barely recognized me.

So many changes had occurred. It was a mixed bag. I was crushed that I couldn't wear heels like everyone else. But on the other hand, I'd made a new friend in Lynn; and I missed our nights together, gabbing after lights-out. I'd wanted to leave school, but I'd also wanted her to come home with me. In a way, I no longer had as much desire to fit into my family because my real family wasn't as nice as the family I'd created in my mind. So the upshot was that I pretty much did my own thing. There was no pressure to be Murray and Dindy's little sister. It didn't matter anymore.

I went to visit Lynn in Rhode Island. I was familiar with Lynn's family because she'd taken me home from school for weekends. Her family had a small, cozy house, a cat named Pluto who weighed twenty-one pounds and a brown, furry guinea pig named George. Lynn had taught George to climb up and down a ladder. It was amazing how he got his short legs from rung to rung. His favorite part was coming down. He came down like a sped-up movie. Lynn and I laughed hysterically when he did it. We decided he could tell he was delighting us. While he may have started out doing it for the exercise, he'd become a regular little entertainer.

Lynn and I talked about school and going back. Ms. Keener had given me Dolly again, so I knew I was right about the school babying me. Lynn was growing up too. We were getting interested in boys and we talked about them a lot.

While we planned for me to visit again, I didn't get back to Lynn's that summer because of my foot. It was rolling over worse than ever, causing my toes to tuck under. This was back in 1962, and no one in Stamford knew what to do with cerebral palsy victims to help them walk better. Mother made an appointment for me to go to the Hospital for Special Surgery in New York. I was to see Dr. Phillip Wilson, Jr., supposedly one of the best orthopedic surgeons in the country.

It was the beginning of the first of four operations I would have over my next four summer vacations. I'd had some good summers to remember though. There had been all those summers in Cleveland, with the bareback rides on Peanuts. I hadn't liked the camps I'd been sent to, but I had good memories of the trip Mom and Dad and Murray and I took to England in 1958. We'd gone across on the *Queen Elizabeth* and stayed with friends of Mom's and Dad's outside of London—Stevenson was their name. Mr. Stevenson, who worked in the London office of Time, Inc., my dad's company, had a daughter, Susie, who was my age. I remember my mother made a pact with the Stevensons that I'd go back and stay with them when I graduated. Mom had it in her mind that I'd live in England, but I didn't pay much attention to the idea at the time.

We also got to see Nicole again. Nicole was a Belgian girl who had been an American Field Service exchange student and stayed at our house in Stamford one year. She and Dindy had been seniors together at Low-Heywood. Nicole came over from Paris to visit us at the Stevensons. It was nice seeing how she'd grown.

The first house we'd lived in back in Ohio was in my thoughts that summer too. I was so uncertain about the future when I heard I might have to have an operation that the past came rushing up. I thought about Nanny a lot. All those days waiting to go for my appointment with Dr. Wilson, all I could think about was the good summers I'd had. I thought about Chagrin Falls and how the animals there had accepted me so completely. I wanted to go back. I wanted to be in Nanny's arms again, rocking, rocking, rocking. Sometimes in my daydreams, Nanny would be with me in England, sitting in the Stevensons' glider under the willow tree by the pond. In my daydreams, I was always safe when Nanny was with me. And I daydreamed a lot because daydreaming was what I did when I was frightened, and I had a lot to be anxious about that summer.

My life was also uncertain because I was fourteen. I'd said good-bye to the angels, and pretty soon I was going to bid farewell to my two Susies as well. That was because at the same time we were talking about me getting surgery, my parents were also talking about moving again. We'd lived in that, our second house in Stamford, for five years, but while I didn't know it because no one told me anything, we were about to move to Rhode Island.

My feelings about our house in Stamford were different when I came home from my first year away at school. When I'd lived there before going away, I'd liked the basement and ravine out back and having my friends over, but I wasn't going back to that life. I'd been a child then, but I'd grown a lot at House in the Pines. The house wasn't like home anymore. It was the house I'd been sent away from, the house in which my dog had forgotten me while I was gone, plus it was the house where my father had struggled with colon cancer. And it was the house I was about to be sent away from once more, this time to go into the hospital. So there was that change too.

It wasn't that I didn't want my foot fixed. I did, but at the same time, I felt that between school and adolescence, I was going through a lot. I'd gone away to school a girl, the little girl Nanny knew, but I'd been forced to grow up. So while I was resigned to getting help, I was also feeling overwhelmed by all the changes.

My mother drove me into the city in her Mercedes. It was a 1957 convertible with red leather seats, and she drove as fast as she thought she could get away with. We cruised along at about seventy though it seemed more like forty in that car. She liked to weave in and out of traffic on the East River Drive. Her hands would be opposite each other on the wheel. When she saw a gap, she'd grab the shift lever on the steering column with her right hand, shift down, and zip into the other lane. She clutched and changed gears smoothly, like a racecar driver, and no matter how fast she drove or how much she wove in and out of traffic, she never missed her turns or got lost—even on the first trip to Dr. Wilson.

As we got close to the hospital, a huge building overlooking the river, my mouth started getting dry. When we turned into the parking lot, Mom reached over, patted me on the thigh, and said, "Here we are, dear." I felt like saying, oh, Mom, that's so affectionate, so comforting, but I didn't utter a peep.

A doorman was waiting for us when we got out of the car. Mom greeted him politely, and he turned to me and said, "Norman is my name. What's yours?" He put some candy in my hand, kind of sneakily, then looked at our car and gave me a thumbs-up. I smiled. I'd never seen a doorman like that. From then on, whenever we returned, Norman always knew us by our blue Mercedes. He'd get a gleam in his eye as he slipped into the red leather seat to park it. I think he found the car a welcome distraction from the anxious mothers and endless stream of kids with twisted backs.

That was what the hospital was all about. People came from all over the country to see Dr. Wilson. There were special wards for scoliosis, polio, and other orthopedic problems. He did a lot of back surgery. Mom told me Dr. Wilson's father, who was also a well-known surgeon, had operated on President Kennedy. I think Mom gave me all that background to soften me up for the news that Dr. Wilson had never operated on a child with cerebral palsy before.

I didn't think about it much when she told me. I was still distracted about having been sent away and coming home to a different world. And then, on the way to the hospital, I didn't want to think about why we were going there. I was in such denial that when we entered the lobby, I started for the gift shop. I wanted something, anything, to take my mind off the appointment. Mom had to call me back and lead me to the elevator. Though we were alone in the elevator, neither of us said a word. The reality was beginning to set in.

A seriously overweight but jolly nurse showed us into the examination room, and before I knew it, Dr. Wilson was staring intently into my eyes. He was a big man, bald, with striking blue eyes and beautiful skin. Mom did her usual social graces thing, which meant she did most of the talking. Dr. Wilson was patient with her, but at one point, he turned to me and winked. It was as if he was signaling that we knew the score and reassuring me that I'd get my chance to talk. I was amazed at how I could read that wink. I must have had a surprised look on my face because he smiled and chuckled. Then he took my foot in his warm hands and, starting with the toes, felt every bone. He went very slowly and seemed to feel each detail of every single bone. Each of his fingers seemed to have its own job, and his mind seemed to memorize everything they sensed. No one talked. When he was through, he put his fist under the ball of my foot and asked me to push against it. I tried, but I couldn't put much power into it. He smiled, said, "Good," then with one hand on my toes and the other holding my heel, he twisted the foot back and forth. That part felt weird, and I pulled back a little. "That's all," he said, patting my foot one last time.

He got up and sat on the table next to me. There was a moment of silence during which I began to feel uncomfortable. Mom must have too because she started to say something. Dr. Wilson, who hadn't taken his eyes off me, held up his hand to stop her and asked where I went to school.

"In Norton, Massachusetts," I replied. "It's a boarding school." I was having a hard time looking him in the eye.

"I see," he replied. "Do you like it there?"

"I guess." I didn't know what else to say. I glanced up at Mom. She was taking the hint that Dr. Wilson wanted to engage me, but she didn't like being excluded. She always felt she could answer the questions people asked me better than I could, and most people let her.

Dr. Wilson seemed deep in thought. Finally, he reached out and took my chin in his hand, lifted my face so I had to look him in the eye, and asked, "What do you want to get out of this, Sarah?" He seemed very compassionate, but he also wanted a straight answer.

"I want to be able to wear heels and flat dress shoes like my roommate," I replied.

"I see," he said. He seemed to consider my answer. "Okay, jump down and come out into the hall with me." I didn't exactly jump down, but I followed him out into the hall. I didn't like being barefooted because I couldn't control my toes without support. They tucked under my foot, making it difficult for me to put the foot down squarely.

"Now, walk down the hall," Dr. Wilson said, "and then turn and walk back to me."

I didn't want to do it. Mom had followed us out into the hall and was standing with her arms crossed, watching nervously.

"It's okay," Dr. Wilson encouraged. "Go ahead." I felt his hand on my back, urging me on.

I started walking, my foot rolling under with each step. It was torture. My whole side was tense. When I know I'm being watched, the muscles on my left side overreact, making everything more difficult. As I started walking, all I could think was how bad I must look and how I'd look even worse coming back toward him. The worst part would be seeing it in his eyes.

When I got to the point where I was to turn back, I stopped and took a deep breath. My toes were being squished, and it hurt to put my weight on them. It was worse than usual because he was watching me. I tried to explain that, but he interrupted me. "No, that's good," he said. "That's what I want to see, the roll of your foot. Now, try to stand up on your toes."

I lifted myself on my right foot then tried to follow with my left. I could do it as long as my right foot carried most of my weight. "Now walk," he said. I managed with a quick limp, and my toes didn't tuck under as much as they had. Finally, after what seemed an eternity, I got back to him and could stop.

We returned to the examination room, and he had me get back up on the table so he could study my foot some more. My poor foot was happy to be off the cold floor and back in his warm hands.

After a few minutes, he stopped and turned to Mom. "Well, Mrs. Howell, I think we can help Sarah. I'd like her to come back and get some X-rays. Then, I'll be able to explain things more easily."

And that was the first of my many meetings with Dr. Wilson.

We went back two weeks later. It was the first time I'd had X-rays, and I found it interesting to be able to see inside my foot. As we looked at the X-rays together, Dr. Wilson repeated that while he'd never operated on a child with cerebral palsy, he didn't think it would be much different from his other operations. "Your foot rolls, Sarah," he explained. "We're going to try to fix that, and the way we're going to do it is by taking the flexibility out of your ankle. We'll do this by fusing the ankle bones so that your ankle won't roll." He said other things too, things about triple orthodesis, staples in my foot, a nail in my heel, and how I'd be in a big cast for ten days after the operation. It sounded like it might hurt, but I put the idea out of my mind and concentrated on being able to wear heels. It would be a dream come true. Mom and Dr. Wilson set a date for the operation before we left, but she didn't tell me.

There was no way for me to know what lay ahead. I'd never been through anything like it. I just wanted those heels, so I listened to what I wanted to hear and ignored the rest. Besides, Mother was excited that something could be done to make me look normal. I remember she thanked Dr. Wilson with her extra gracious smile when we were leaving. I also remember that he was very businesslike with her, not nearly as friendly as he was to me, and that it seemed to annoy her. I could tell because on the ride home, she said he was "very professional" and hadn't "minced any words." Riding along beside her, I decided I preferred being with my mother and another adult when the other adult was in charge, especially if he was giving me more attention than he was giving her.

Norman snuck me extra candy the day we returned for the operation. He seemed to expect us. Having been in a dorm with a lot of nosey, noisy girls all winter, I'd persuaded Mom to get me a private room. They gave me one on the eighth floor with a view of the East River.

That first afternoon, a kindhearted African-American nurse named Lucy came in and made me feel at home. Then, after Lucy left, a resident came to see me. He was fearsome cute. I can't recall his name, but I remember hanging on his every word. He told me I'd be getting a sleeping pill that night; then he asked if I was scared. Wanting to appear grown-up and brave, I lied and said I wasn't. "Oh yes, you are," he said, looking deep into my eyes. He was sitting on the edge of the bed holding my leg.

"Well, maybe a little," I conceded.

"You wouldn't be normal if you weren't," he reassured me. "But Dr. Wilson is a fine surgeon, and everything will go well. Do you have any questions?" I probably should have, but I couldn't think of any.

I didn't sleep much that night, despite the sleeping pill. They'd put a cot in for my mother, and she slept while I watched the lights on the East River. Dread had set in. When I wasn't thinking about the surgery, I fanaticized about being at the beach, or at home in my room, listening to the Beatles.

It was bright and sunny the next morning when they came to give me a shot. That was my breakfast. I was unaware of the effects initially, but when the nurses came in to shave my ankle, I realized I was very sleepy. Their voices were far away, in another world, and by the time they started moving me around, I was limp as a wet noodle. They put a funny-looking cap on my head; then it was "one, two, lift," and I was on a table with wheels. The lights in the hallway ceiling flashed by like headlights. I couldn't think about anything but the visual sensation—flash, flash, flash, and the vibrating table under me. There were no faces, just white gowns and shuffling feet. Someone put a hand on my shoulder when we stopped for the elevator.

I had a slight déjà vu about being at the mercy of strangers again and having no one to talk to about it. It was routine for them, but I was just a girl who should have been out playing with my friends. I should have been with the fourteen angels, sharing, laughing, and going home to our families at night. But instead, I'd been thrown into a world of uncertainty, all because I wasn't acceptable the way I was. The adults around me couldn't see beyond my cerebral palsy. They couldn't see that I had a special way of looking at the world.

The drugs continued to bounce my mind around. The images of the fourteen angels came and went, along with a vision of myself walking in high heels. I remember feeling that there were people around me, and they were saying, "You're normal now, you're normal now. You can come into the secret room and play with us. Just don't take off those heels." And then, the elevator bell rang and I jumped, and a hand was on my shoulder, and a soothing voice was saying, "You're all right, child."

"Nanny?"

"No, child, it's Lucy. We're going to take good care of you. Close your eyes and relax. It'll be over soon."

It was becoming harder to fight the drug. I closed my eyes. I could still hear voices and the shuffling of feet, but then even they blurred. I felt my left side relax. When I heard "one, two, and lift," I opened my eyes briefly; but it was as if my body belonged to someone else. My mind was all alone, without a body. "And over," I was on the operating table. Someone pulled my right arm down onto a board; and there were bright lights, hands above me, needles, small tubes, and machines. Someone put a mask over my face and instructed me to start counting backward from one hundred. I think I got to ninety-seven.

You're not aware of when you go out. It's not like falling asleep. I don't think there are any dreams when you're under anesthetic. All I know is what I learned later, which was that I was in surgery for most of the day. When I woke up in recovery, I had no sense of elapsed time and no idea of where I was. It wasn't like awakening from a night's sleep. You have no idea how long it's taken you to open your eyes, only that you're suddenly awake. I was awake and *very* uncomfortable.

There were nurses around me. One said, "I'm going to take your blood pressure."

I heard my voice. "My foot, my foot." I was frightened. I still didn't know where I was. I started crying. "My foot is tense . . . can't stop . . . What's wrong? What's wrong?"

"You're all right, Sarah. You're in the recovery room. You'll be here for a while. We're here to help you."

"Okay, okay," I replied breathlessly. Lifting my head, I looked down and saw the cast. My toes were sticking out of it, and they had blood-soaked cotton swabs between them. "Oh god, what . . . what's that?" I felt the most terrible panic. And then I fainted.

The afternoon passed with me slipping in and out of consciousness. My blood pressure dropped a few times, and I was aware of being moved to get it back up. I could sense it dropping. It felt the same way I imagine it feels to die. Everything slowed way down and became incredibly peaceful. When my breathing became shallow, I could tell by the voices that it was making them nervous. I didn't want to move, preferring to remain in my relaxed state, where my mind was completely empty. But they kept interrupting me. "Come on, Sarah, move your leg. Good. Now your arm. That's a good girl."

It was dark, maybe that night or early the next morning, when I was sent from recovery back to my room. I was awake by then and sick to my stomach from the anesthetic. On top of everything else, my right leg couldn't touch my left. Like a big sister, my right leg had always calmed and comforted my left, but the cast, which was thick and heavy, ran from the pad behind my toes all the way up to my crotch. So my poor left leg was alone and unconsoled. It quivered and twitched in its distress.

Mom was there, holding my hand. My fingernails dug into her skin. "Oh, Mom," I cried.

"What? Talk to me. What's going on?"

"I can't. I can't," I replied, gagging. I vomited again and lay completely exhausted. I could feel the sweat, tears, and spittle running down my cheeks. My saliva was yellow with bile from my empty stomach.

The nurse asked my mother to step aside so she could move in close and see what was going on. She took my face in her hands, studying me, then wiped it off with a washcloth and said, "Relax, Sarah, but look at me. Keep looking at me . . . Sarah?" I tried to relax and focus. She was trying to draw my attention away from my jumpy foot. "Deep breath. Breathe deeply, Sarah." My chest shook as I tried to breathe. "There now," she persisted. "Talk to me."

"My foot . . ."

"What about your foot? Are you in pain?"

"It's jumping . . . I can't stop it." I started to cry again.

"No, no, Sarah, stay with me. Talk to me."

"I can't . . . cross my legs. That's what keeps my leg still, touching it with my other leg . . . I'm going to throw up again . . ."

Lucy came in with some ginger ale. "Here, drink this."

"No, I can't." I leaned over with my hand covering my mouth, and the nurse grabbed the bedpan. My leg jumped and tensed, and I moaned and vomited, hanging onto the railing for dear life.

Lucy went to the end of the bed and took the toes of my left foot in her hand. "Shhh," she said. "We're going to get you something. Mrs. Howell?"

"Yes?"

"We're going to get Dr. Wilson and see what he can do."

Mom was in a situation over which she had zero control, and I could see it frightened her. She pried my hand off the rail and let me squeeze her hand as hard as I could. There were tears in her eyes, and her face was contorted by her effort to hold them in. At that moment, even though it was the worst time of my life, I felt she might really care about me. Then, another nurse came in and gave me a shot of morphine, and everything started to get dark. The last thing I remember was Lucy saying, "Don't worry, Mrs. Howell, everything's going to be all right."

When I came out from under the drug, my first sensation was my leg starting to jump again. It made me realize that my foot had literally been taken apart and put back together. The idea was too horrible to think about.

Dr. Wilson was by my bed, talking to my mother. "There were bound to be some unforeseen side effects, Mrs. Howell." I couldn't see him clearly. "Polio victims don't have the muscle contractions. This is new for me."

Mother came into focus. When she and Dr. Wilson noticed that I was awake, they moved out into the hall. Alone, I took stock. Waking up from morphine wasn't like waking up from sleep. In fact, it wasn't like I'd been asleep at all. Instead of being rested, I was exhausted and sick to my stomach. "Mom, please," I called, feeling I was going to vomit again. She came back into the room and got the pan, but all I could manage were a few dry heaves. When the worst of them had passed, I managed to get some ginger ale down. My throat was so dry, the bubbles felt like ground glass. I later learned that I'd been hypersensitive to the anesthesia.

"Hello, child . . . Mrs. Howell," Lucy said as she came back in. She was smiling, and for the first time, I noticed how large and white her teeth were. They were so bright—and her skin so dark by comparison that when she smiled it was as if she was turning up the footlights. I watched the pink palms of her hands as she checked my IV.

"I have a terrible headache," I managed to say.

"You're dehydrated, honey. But we're going to fix you right up." Mom appeared at the other side of the bed. "This will make her feel better, Mrs. Howell."

Mom sighed. "What about her leg? Will the morphine quiet it?"

"It should. We'll give her more as she needs it."

"Very well, Lucy." Mom walked over to the window. She had a Kleenex in her hand, and she looked worn out.

I was becoming conscious of my leg again. Between all that had gone on and how I felt, I was as frightened as I'd ever been. Lucy said, "I'll be right back," and went for more morphine.

I appreciated Lucy. Dr. Wilson hadn't expected the jumping muscles, but nothing seemed to surprise Lucy. She was a true professional in her starched white uniform with a bright smile and a distinctive, high-pitched voice. Plus you could tell she'd had a lot of experience with sick children and distraught parents.

"Here we go, Sarah," she said as she came back into the room with the syringe held high. She and Mom rolled me over. My backside was becoming numb to shots, and I barely felt a thing.

Moving to the end of the bed, Lucy said, "Let's get rid of these," and started pulling the cotton balls out from between my toes. Within a few seconds, the morphine started taking effect, and I closed my eyes and drifted free.

I don't remember how many days I had to have the morphine injections. It seemed forever. But one day I awoke and my left leg was no longer jumping. It seemed to have gotten used to being by itself. There were only certain times of the day when I got tense, and if Mom was there—she was going home to sleep by then, she'd put her warm hands over my toes to relax me. It became a routine, Mom in a chair at the end of the bed with her hands cupping my toes.

They made me sit up more and more. On my tenth day in the hospital, Lucy appeared with a wheelchair and said, "Sarah, child, we are going to get you up today." I cringed at the thought. By then, I knew that there was a six-inch nail running up through my heel into my ankle to fuse the bones. The end of the nail stuck out of the bottom of my foot, and I was terrified that I'd bang it on something. The whole thing gave me the creeps. "Don't worry, Ms. Sarah," Lucy assured me, "we know how to do these things."

She detached my IV, then had Mom stand behind the wheelchair. "Don't worry," she reassured us, "the break is on. It's not going anywhere."

An orderly came in, and he and Lucy lifted me up and slowly lowered me into the chair, placing my cast ever so gently onto the raised footrest. Immediately, the sweat started pouring off me. It made Mom anxious. "It's normal, Mrs. Howell," Lucy said. "She's weak and not used to moving. We'll just wait for a minute."

Mom patted my hand. Lucy went out to take care of another patient. It would soon be lunchtime. Mom brought out the menu while we waited for Lucy. I had no appetite, partially because I was in withdrawal from the morphine, but also because I was feeling isolated and depressed.

Where was Lucy? Mom ran down the menu. Everything sounded gross. "Jello? That sounds good. With whipped cream?" She said it with as much enthusiasm as she could muster. I made a face. "Guess not. Come, Sarah, there must be something on here. Aren't you hungry at all?"

"Tuna fish?" I looked up at her.

"Tuna fish?"

"Yes. I'd like a tuna fish sandwich on white bread."

She put the menu down. "Well, I suppose I could go down to the cafeteria and get one." Feeling victorious that she'd gotten me to speak and then agree to eat, she picked up her purse and started to leave. When she got to the door, she stopped and looked back. I could feel her eyes, but I didn't look up. It was just too much of an effort.

My smile and determination had always been a big part of me, but they were adrift somewhere, lost along the way. Perhaps they were back in Cleveland, before the child in me grew up. My life had been manageable back then. But now? Now, I was on fast-forward. I'd been alienated from my mother and father and sister and brother and sent away to school. And on top of all that, with my surgery, I was contending with a magnitude of pain beyond what any fourteen-year-old should have to endure. I'd dealt with the physical limitations at school, the humiliation of not being able to wait on tables, a plug horse, not to mention Meg and her friends. And right then, instead of sitting there in that wheelchair, I should have been out playing with friends and having a good summer.

In my mind, "I" barely existed. Where was I? Was I there? Really? Was I breathing? I put my hands out in front of me for the reassurance of seeing a familiar part of my body. They were pale and fragile. My right hand was stiff and sore from gripping so tightly when the pain hit. When I thought about the operation and the first few days afterward, it made me break down and sob. I took my face in my hands to comfort my poor head, and feeling reassured, it let go with the tears. Part of me was determined to cry through my sadness, and I wept until I was too exhausted to continue.

When I stopped and lowered my hands, Lucy was sitting in a chair in front of me. Embarrassed, I tried to wipe my face. She'd brought a wet facecloth, but in her wisdom, she'd decided to wait until I finished. When she smoothed the facecloth across my forehead, it was deliciously cool and soothing.

"Hold out your hands," she said. When I did, she took my weak, slight hands in her strong big ones, turned my hands palm up and laid a second facecloth across my wrists. The coolness seeped up my arms. "Why aren't you on the children's ward, Sarah?" she asked out of the blue. "You seem to like kids."

I didn't know. Lucy looked around the room, took a deep breath, and said, "I was down there—on five—for quite a few years, but I needed a break. It's hard watching them go through their operations. I'll go back. It's what I love . . . But you didn't answer my question . . ." She shook her finger at me and smiled, pretending I'd tried to put one over on her.

"I needed a break too," I answered. "I go away to school; I'm always with kids."

"That may be, Sarah, but this is no place to be without people your own age, especially since they're going through the same thing you are." I thought about it. "In fact," she said, warming to the idea, "I'm going to see that someone takes you down for a visit." Mom returned with my tuna on white. "Right after you eat your sandwich," Lucy concluded.

"Down where?" Mom asked.

"To the children's floor. I think Sarah needs to spend some time with kids her own age. She's strong enough."

Lucy went to get an orderly while I reacquainted myself with tuna fish. I didn't get the sense that my mother wanted me to go to the children's ward, but maybe Lucy was right. Looking around, I realized that I was getting a little sick of my room.

Mom followed the orderly as he pushed me to the elevator. I was getting used to sitting up, and to my surprise, it felt good having something in my stomach. None of us spoke in the elevator or when we got to the fifth floor. As we moved down the hall, there were kids flat out on tables, encased in full-body casts. Some greeted me, and I said hello back to them. I'd never seen anything like it. Despite all they'd been through, without exception, they made an effort to be cheerful.

Turning a corner, we came upon a girl on a table. She was in a full-body cast too, but it was strapped to the table, and the table was in an upright position so that she was standing up in her cast. "Oh . . . ," she said. Her face was contorted with pain. "Please. I want to get off now. I can't do it anymore."

I asked the orderly to stop. Mom didn't want him to, but I looked up at him and said, "No, wait," and he stopped. "What is it?" I asked.

"It's a tilt table," he explained. The girl had become frantic and was looking around and yelling for her nurse to let her down. She was so upset, she didn't even see us. "These kids have scoliosis," the orderly said.

"What's scoliosis?"

"It's when their backs are crooked. Some of them come in here looking like pretzels. They can't be left lying down all the time. It's bad for their lungs. So they have to be stood up, and it hurts after a while."

"How long do they have to do it? How long are they in the casts?"

"Anywhere from a year and a half to two years." He was matter-of-fact about it. I was becoming concerned about the girl. She looked as if she was being tortured. "We have a school here," the orderly went on between the girl's calls for help. "Sometimes, they can go home for weekends."

There was a small key, like the key on a windup toy, on the side of the girl's cast. When I asked what it was for, the orderly explained that they turned the key periodically in order to straighten the girl's spine. I couldn't believe what I was seeing. It was out of a dungeon, like the rack, obviously far worse than what I was going through. I had what my mother called "a slight curvature of the spine."

Two nurses came up. The girl was crying uncontrollably now, but they wouldn't take her down. Instead, they encouraged her to hang in there "just a little while longer." It was awful watching it. No wonder Lucy had needed a break. Looking up at Mom, I saw that she was upset by it too. When I didn't ask any more questions, the orderly moved on. Back in the elevator, Mom leaned against the wall in silence.

Back in my room, I spent the rest of the afternoon thinking about that poor girl. Lucy was right, I had needed to see that other kids were missing their summers too. In fact, they were missing up to two years of their lives. I was in awe of them and, at the same time, grateful that I didn't have to go through what they were facing.

I ate a lot of tuna fish sandwiches and began to regain my strength over the next few days. Mom came to visit every day, though I can't remember whether she went home to Connecticut or stayed in New York at night. I also don't remember my father coming to see me. I think he must have come because he worked right there in the city, but I don't remember it. I vaguely remember a visit from Dindy. I was so busy trying to handle the pain and medication and get well that a lot got by me. Strange, how you remember some things and people clearly, but others not at all.

Things got worse after I had my seizure. It was my first one. I had it while I was sleeping, and when I woke up and opened my eyes, I had no idea what had happened. I didn't even know where I was. It was night and Mom was there. Some nights she slept in my room on a cot. And she was holding my shoulders down, and she had a terrified look on her face. A nurse was holding my legs. The first thing I heard was Mom calling, "Sarah! Sarah!" I didn't know she was talking to me because I didn't know who I was. In fact, I didn't know *that* I was. I had some sensations, but I *knew* nothing. But as she shook me gently while calling my name, I gradually came back. It was extremely weird. I had no memory of being gone.

"Mom! What are you doing?" I demanded.

"You had a bad dream. You swung your leg around, cast, and all; and you tried to get out of bed. We had to wake you. How did you swing your leg around like that?"

I had no idea. All I knew was that I was experiencing a strange kind of exhaustion. All I could think to say was, "I was sleeping." I looked at Mom and the nurse for reassurance. It was a different nurse than I'd seen before. When I tried to lift my cast, I couldn't budge it. "See," I said. "I can't lift my leg."

"You did, though, Sarah. And you swung it around as if it was weightless."

The nurse saw that our conversation not only wasn't getting anywhere, but also was making me frightened. She came in past my mother, laid a wet hand towel on my forehead, and said, "It's late, Sarah. Go back to sleep and we'll discuss it in the morning."

We didn't though. We didn't talk about it again, and I didn't have another seizure in the hospital. I think they passed it off as a nightmare even though they couldn't explain why I'd been so strong. I had no idea I'd had a seizure, much less that I had epilepsy along with my cerebral palsy.

I have no memory of the next few days. Eventually, it came time to get my cast removed and replaced by a smaller one. I was looking forward to it. Not only was my cast heavy and awkward, but the nail sticking out of my heel had gotten caught on the wheelchair a few times, causing my leg to thrill and vibrate.

They took the nail out of my foot and gave me the smaller cast, and before long, I was getting around on crutches. I had to learn to go up and down stairs. The physical therapist told me not to put pressure on my armpits, but to carry my weight with my hands. Well, that was easier said than done. I could move forward all right. While my left arm struggled to move the crutch forward, I could depend on my strong right leg for balance. But going down stairs was very difficult. In the first place, it was hard to remember everything. Plus I still got tired easily, and my armpits were always numb. But the hardest part was carrying my weight with my hands. I could manage with my right, but my left just wasn't strong enough.

I eventually got the hang of it. I made adjustments, something I'd taught myself to do and was pretty good at. And I worked hard, something else I'd learned to do. Plus I was happy to be up and about, and I could feel myself getting better, which is always motivating.

And then one day, it was over. I thanked and said good-bye to Lucy, then another nurse escorted Mom and me to the lobby. They made me ride in the wheelchair. When Norman saw me, he said, "Hey, pretty girl," and stepped in front of me, stopping the wheelchair. He grabbed my nose and showed me how he had it in his fist. I was glad to see him again. After being enclosed in the hospital walls for so long, the outside world seemed strange and slightly threatening. The sun was bright, and everything seemed frenetic. So I appreciated Norman's sheltering bulk and innocent jokes during those first few minutes outside.

"Open your hand, now," Norman said. I was feeling shy, but I laughed as I held out my hand. When I looked up into his large, round face and black eyes, I realized Norman looked like a circus clown. He had exaggerated features and could make all kinds of expressions with his face.

"Remember your 'hello' candy?" he teased.

I didn't remember at first; it seemed so long ago. But it came back when I saw the bright candy wrappers falling into my outstretched hand. They seemed to fall in slow motion.

"Now, no offense, little lady, but I don't want to see you around here again. Your 'hello' candy is now 'good-bye' candy."

"My name is Sarah," I said, but he'd started back to hold the door for another child. He turned and caught my eye one last time though.

He winked and pointed his finger at me and said, "Pretty name for a pretty girl."

"Good-bye, Norman," Mom said, formally.

And then we were in the car again, on the sweet-smelling leather seats, and Mom was driving me home. At first, the traffic and people and huge buildings frightened me. I squinted and put my hands over my ears. I was also uncomfortable and not looking forward to spending the rest of the summer in a cast. But the farther we went, the better I felt. It was a nice summer day.

I've still got the nail and my ID bracelet. Dear Lucy, she was such a good nurse. She knew not to let herself become too attached, but at the same time, she was positively psychic about sensing when I needed support. And she knew exactly what I needed and how to give it to me. And then, in a flash, she was gone, and I never saw her again.

Bathing was difficult, but going to the beach was impossible. When it rained, Mom put a plastic bag on my foot to keep the cast dry. My skin under the cast dried out and got chaffed, and that made it itch unbearably. I made one trip back to Dr. Wilson that summer to have a walking cast put on. When they removed the old cast, my leg and foot looked like they belonged to someone else. The scars on my ankle were red and angry looking, and my foot was swollen. My muscles had gotten used to being protected by a cast, and it was a relief to get back into one. But it was nice getting rid of the crutches.

Stamford, Connecticut, 1963. Mom and Dad in the family room in our house at Tyler Drive. This was the year after Dad was diagnosed with cancer. Seeing Mother's arms crossed reminds me that I don't remember seeing them touch, much less hug each other. They slept in separate beds.

Stamford, Connecticut, 1964. Dindy was home from Connecticut College and Murray from the University of Pennsylvania. I was a lowly and handicapped high school student, whom Murray teased and Dindy distained. Despite his playful appearance, Murray was about to have his nervous breakdown.

Second Year: The Seizures

Before I knew it, the walking cast had been removed, and I was getting ready to return to school. Dr. Wilson had wanted me to keep the cast on longer, but we decided it would make it too difficult to get to class. The operation was successful except for one small spot that hadn't healed over. I wore a heavy shoe and elasticized wrap for support.

House in the Pines didn't start until mid-September, so I had a few weeks for physical therapy and learning to walk on my new foot. It was sore and still swollen, especially at night, and my ankle no longer had any give to it. It was like having a brace on my foot except the brace was on the inside. But at least my foot no longer rolled over.

"Watch out," Mom yelled nervously when I tripped on the first step up to our dorm. I was entering the eighth grade and would be in the same house as Ms. Johndroe, though no longer rooming with Lynn. The judgment had been made that Lynn and I spent too much time together, and that it might be best if we were separated.

"That did not feel good," I said, disgusted that I'd been so careless.

"You're going to have to be more careful." I think Mom was wishing I'd kept my cast on.

"I know, Mom."

My room was on the same floor as the first year, but this year I had two roommates instead of one. I didn't like it much, but there was nothing I could do. Besides, so much was about to happen to me that I would barely notice the girls. Today, I don't even remember who they were.

"This is a nice room, Sarah," Mom said, looking around. Dad was there too. He stood in the corner without saying anything, a concerned look on his face. I had the feeling he didn't want to leave me.

Mom was right though; it was a nice room, bright and airy with high windows looking out on the lawn and large elm trees. It was a beautiful fall day with a bright blue sky, and the leaves were beginning to turn. Some leaves clattered against the window in the breeze.

When I waved good-bye to my parents and they drove off, I realized again that I didn't want to be at the school but that I had no choice in the matter. Well, I thought, at least I have Lynn and know what to expect. Plus I wouldn't have to wait two weeks to call home.

The next few weeks were uneventful. Ms. Pierce seemed glad to have me back in her English class and my grades in all my classes were reasonably good. Of course Meg wasn't glad to see me. She seemed jealous of the attention I got from Ms. Pierce. I wasn't competitive in the slightest, just doing my work and trying to please my teacher. Ms. Pierce posted my printed papers on the board for everyone to see. She told the class that if anyone else could print that well, they were welcome to print their papers too. Meg didn't like seeing me praised like that.

Getting around was difficult, but I managed. It was hard being left out of hockey, but I tried to be as much like everyone else as possible. Ms. Johndroe, who had somehow gotten it into her head that I needed help going from the dorm to the main building in the morning, insisted on driving me. It upset me because I was trying to be normal, like everyone else. It also set a precedent that would have unfortunate consequences.

I went along, though I tried to avoid Ms. Johndroe around the dorm in the mornings. The whole thing put pressure on me, and it wasn't long before I had my second seizure. It came on at night. My roommates told me I got up and walked around, pulled at the curtains, and tried to yank the mattress off my bed. Of course, I was completely unaware of what I was doing. My recollection was that I'd been asleep, having a nightmare about Ms. Johndroe.

I remember them trying to wake me. I wanted to wake up, but most of all, I wanted to stop the shaking. When I finally opened my eyes, Ms. Johndroe was over me, shaking me. I sat up and looked around, still confused. When I was awake, Ms. Johndroe took me by the arm and all but dragged me out and down the stairs. Meg, Joan, and some other girls came sleepily out of their rooms to stare.

"What's with her?" someone asked.

"You should have seen her. It was as though she was crazy or something," someone answered.

"Yeah, she was all over the room. She tried to rip the mattress off her bed," a third girl added. I couldn't recognize their voices.

73

"Go back to bed, girls," Ms. Johndroe ordered. I was still in a daze. Was I dreaming? I stumbled, and Ms. Johndroe's grip on my arm tightened. Her roughness was waking me up.

I didn't know what had happened or what to think about it. It made me jump when the door to Ms. Johndroe's car slammed shut. I had the same sense of total exhaustion I'd had when it happened in the hospital. It was a job just to remember my name. Then Ms. Johndroe took my arm in her vicelike grip again and was leading me into another building. I heard mumbling and a door slamming, and suddenly I was alone in a dark room. As an afterthought, perhaps, someone stuck her hand in the door and flipped the wall switch. The light! Oh my god, it was like a strobe light firing a thousand times a second, directly into my eyes. I put my hands up then groped around until I found the switch and turned it off. Ah, unspeakable relief! When I opened my eyes, moonlight was streaming into the room, lighting up a corner. I shuffled toward it with my hand against the wall. When I got into the corner, I leaned back, slid down the wall into a sitting position, wrapped my arms around my knees, and hung on for dear life. I had no idea where I was.

The bandage was digging into the back of my ankle. I stretched my leg out in front of me. Still exhausted but steadily more awake, I tried to figure out where I was. I looked around, my eyes searching the room. There was a bed directly in front of me with neatly pressed sheets and a hospital table suspended over it. I was in the infirmary. But why? What was I doing there? What had happened and how did I get there? I heard a car being driven off and leaned over to the window to see if I could recognize it. It was Ms. Johndroe's car. What was *she* doing there?

I crawled over to the door and pulled myself up with the doorknob. When the door wouldn't open, I shook it. Thinking it might help, I turned the light back on.

"You can't come out, Sarah," a voice said from the other side of the door. The school nurse opened the door, slipped in, and stood in front of me. "Come, dear," she said. "You should be in bed."

"Why am I here?"

She took me by the arm in an effort to lead me to the bed, but I jerked it back from her.

"Please, Sarah, you must get into bed." She pulled out the tight covers and threw them back. Seeing nothing else to do and being so terribly tired, I climbed up on the bed. She pulled the covers up over me and tucked them in so tight I could barely move then turned and left, switching the light off again in passing. I sank down into the bed and was immediately overcome by tears. What had I done? Why wouldn't anyone tell me? Finally, without having moved, lying on my back and staring at the empty ceiling, I drifted off to sleep.

The next thing I knew, I was being awakened by "psst! psst!" at my window. Opening my eyes and looking over, I saw that it was Lynn.

"Lynn!" I yelled, relieved to see my friend.

"Shhh! Someone will hear!"

Forgetting about my foot, I jumped out of bed and crumbled against the windowsill.

"Watch out!" Lynn said. "You'll kill yourself."

"What's going on, Lynn? Why am I here? What did I do?"

"You mean you don't know?"

"Know what?" We were leaning on opposite sides of the windowsill, nose to nose through the screen.

"You were thrashing about, Sarah. Pulling your mattress off the bed."

"I was?" I was shocked and confused. "I don't remember . . . a thing."

"You don't? That's strange."

"I'll say. Do you suppose I had a nightmare?"

"Maybe." She thought about it. "Anyway, what I wanted to tell you is that Ms. Johndroe called a dorm meeting this morning and told us that you aren't the same as everyone else. She said we aren't to upset you."

"*Upset* me? I'm *already* upset!"

"Quiet, Sarah, or they'll catch me," she hissed.

"Oh great. So now I'm this weirdo too?"

"I gotta go," Lynn said, drawing back from the window.

"Lynn, wait!" I begged.

"I can't. I'll be late," she whispered back as she set off for the main house.

Hearing the doorknob rattle behind me, I scrambled back into bed. It was the nurse with my breakfast. "How long do I have to stay in here?" I demanded, ignoring the tray.

"Well, you seem all right this morning. But I'm waiting to hear from Ms. Johndroe."

"I don't want to miss my classes."

"I know. I'll come back as soon as I hear from her, I promise." And with that, she walked out. I suddenly realized I was starving.

Ms. Johndroe finally came to get me. After what she'd said to the dorm, I would have been happy to stay in the infirmary. But at the same time, I didn't want to miss my classes. I wanted to be with the other girls. But how could I? It was so unfair. What right did Ms. Johndroe have to say anything?

I got through my classes. No one called on me, and I surely didn't raise my hand. After classes, I went straight back to my room and stayed there, dreading the moment when I'd have to face the dorm.

Finally, Joan came into my room. She didn't knock; she just came in, looked at me, and said, "That was quite the experience last night."

I was afraid to say anything.

"What were you dreaming about anyway? It must have been something awful."

"I don't know. I don't remember."

"Has anyone told you that Ms. Johndroe is moving you downstairs, behind the kitchen?"

"No, I hadn't heard. How do you know?"

"Because I'm going to be your roommate."

"You are?"

"Yup. We get our own bathroom. That's why I volunteered, girl."

She plopped herself down on the bed, smiling, then she stuck her tongue out and whipped it back and forth. Joan was kind of loud and vain, always checking herself when she passed a window. She thought she was pretty good-looking. She was okay, I guess. She was French Canadian with black hair and dark skin, and she wore "in" clothes. But her loudness and big mouth took away from her cute figure and anything else she might have going for her. She got good grades though, and Ms. Johndroe liked her. And she was willing to be my roommate; that was in her favor. I was surprised because she was friendly with Meg. Having our own bathroom must have meant a lot to her.

I didn't like the idea, but there was nothing I could do. Later that night, when Lynn was helping me move, she told me the others were envious of Joan for getting her own bathroom, but that no one else had been willing to be my roommate. The girls stood back and stared without saying anything when we carried my things down the hall. All I could think was that there was new tension between us and that Ms. Johndroe had caused it. Why couldn't she just leave me alone and let things work themselves out? Little did I know that her obsession with me had just begun.

Once into the back room, I felt disconnected from the other girls, especially Lynn. I also felt way too close to Ms. Johndroe. It was scary because she was so unpredictable. There were no more early mornings with Lynn, planning how to avoid Ms. Johndroe's black car. From my new room, I had to pass through her bedroom to get to the front door. It didn't bother Joan because she could keep right on walking, out the front door and up to the main house. But I had to wait. I had to sit on the step and watch Lynn and the other girls go off without me, giggling and laughing, and then be driven up to the main house. Once there, I had to go in through Ms. Johndroe's office. I couldn't even go through the same door the others used.

Ms. Johndroe started calling me her "brown-eyed Susan." She watched me like a hawk. It made it impossible for me to relax and have fun. I had another seizure. It came on in the middle of the night this time too. Joan told me I jumped up out of my lower bunk bed and ripped the shades down. Poor Joan, she was up in the top bunk, but she still had trouble staying out of my way. Afterward, just as before, I thought I'd been asleep. And then I heard the same footsteps and felt the same grip on my arm as I was dragged out of my room and up to the infirmary. I was put in the same moonlit room; and I felt the same succession of feelings—dazed, terrified, and excluded.

The corner of that infirmary room became my friend. As I was coming out of my seizure, still unsure of what had happened or where I was, I retreated to it. And sitting there, looking out the window, I slowly figured it out. Whatever was wrong with me, it was recurrent. My first thought was the hope that they'd always put me in the same room.

Back under the Knife

I don't remember how many seizures I had that eighth-grade year. It was awful being in the back room, and I hated it when girls called me "Ms. Johndroe's pet." One afternoon when Joan and I were in our room and I had my shoes off, a girl named Robin came in and said something nasty and then stomped on my foot. There was still this place in my ankle where the bones hadn't grown together, and it was tender; and when she kicked me, it was so painful I collapsed on the floor, whimpering. My foot swelled up, and the swelling didn't go down, and eventually I was taken to New York to see Dr. Wilson about it. He said they'd have to reopen my ankle, cut off a piece of healthy bone, and screw it into the space that wouldn't heal. That meant more surgery, and that, in turn, meant I'd have to miss more school. My parents ended up suing Robin's parents. Boy, that made me popular. After that, Ms. Johndroe all but followed me around.

So I went back to the hospital. Norman was still working the door, and when he saw me, he pretended he didn't want me to be there. He shooed me off with the back of his hand and gave me some "go-away" candy, which made me smile; then, Mom and I went back up to the ninth floor.

I couldn't believe I was back in the hospital. I didn't want to be in a room with other kids. I told my mother I was tired of fighting and the look kids gave me, that I didn't want to have to deal it there too. So I was put in a room with a young woman who had had back surgery. Dr. Wilson was her doctor too. Having gotten there first, she'd taken the bed under the window.

As usual, I was shy; but Mom, who was good at socializing, started right in with the young woman. Her name was Marty, and she was really nice, and after a while, the three of us were talking easily. On the rainy afternoon before my surgery, Marty told us her story. She said she was a teacher and that one day, she'd walked out of her classroom and was going downstairs to the office when she'd fallen and—just like that—broken her back. She told us she'd been in pain for years until she couldn't stand it anymore.

She said she'd decided she wanted her life back. I could relate to that, all right. She said Dr. Wilson had been her last resort, that he'd operated, and it looked like she was going to make a full recovery. I don't remember where Marty was from or the name of her school; but I remember she had frizzy black hair, happy brown eyes, and a big nose. I think she was in her thirties. Mom said she liked Marty all right—except for her accent.

My operation didn't take long; but when I came out of it, I was again in a lot of pain, and my left foot was back in a cast. While I was recovering, I told Marty about my school and Ms. Johndroe. My mother didn't seem to be handling my surgery as well as she had the last time, and I could tell this frustrated Marty. One day when I was out in the hall in my wheelchair, I heard Marty tell Mom that it was bad for a mother to hide her feelings from a daughter my age. I leaned closer to the door to hear how Mom would respond, but she didn't say anything. Later, after visiting hours, I told Marty I thought she'd been brave to talk to my mother the way she had.

"Well," she said, "she needed to be clued in." When I snickered at that, she smiled, raised her eyebrows, and shook her head then balled up a piece of Kleenex and threw it at me. "Some people just don't get it, you know?"

"That's for sure." I was snuggling down in my bed.

The next afternoon, Mom had a surprise for me. Somehow she'd gotten three girls from school to come see me. They weren't even friends. Surprised wasn't the word for it, I was shocked. They stood at the end of my bed not knowing what to say. I tried to make myself sound perky, and I pinched my cheeks without them noticing so I wouldn't look so pale. I think I scared them. It was funny. It was a small room with no place for them to sit, and before long, they got the wiggles. They leaned against the wall and ran their fingers through their hair in an effort to look like they were enjoying themselves, but I could tell they were uncomfortable. They didn't want to be there any more than I wanted them there. When I asked how school was, they answered in unison, "It's okay." I asked what was going on as if I'd be part of it if I were there, but we all knew I wouldn't.

I went directly back to school from the hospital, wearing a walking cast. When I found Lynn and we were able to talk, she told me she was outraged about Robin stepping on my foot. We were sitting on the couch in the common room; and when Robin came through, trying to look invisible, Lynn pointed at my cast and said in a loud voice, "See what you did, Robin?" I was starting to feel sorry for poor Robin. My parents had gotten a settlement from her parents, a process Mom seemed to enjoy. Her parents probably gave her holy hell for kicking me, but it was all a bygone as far as I was concerned.

The problem for me was the effect my parent's lawsuit had on the school. In addition to being more protective than ever, Ms. Johndroe started broadcasting what she was doing so everyone would know. Not only did Ms. Johndroe become more protective than ever, she also broadcast what she was doing so everyone would know. Her behavior made me even more anxious, on top of which I had a few more seizures. It got so that they left me too confused and exhausted to do my schoolwork. Finally, when it became unbearable for everyone, Ms. Johndroe told my parents about "the nightmares," as she called them. To my surprise, it was the first they'd heard about them. I hadn't mentioned them because I just didn't want to talk about them, but I couldn't believe Ms. Johndroe hadn't told them. Maybe that's what she really thought, that they were just nightmares. At any rate, as soon as my parents heard about them, they arranged for me to get tested.

I went for the tests the summer between eighth grade and freshman year. They had me sit in a special chair while they put sticky stuff in my hair and stuck pins in my scalp. It hurt a lot. I remember the doctor. He was an old man, bald, with a halo of powder white hair. "Now hold still, dear," he said. "This is the last one." But I jumped anyway because the pins hurt. Tears rolled down my cheeks, under my chin, and down inside my shirt because I wanted to be a "dear" and not move. Pain was familiar to me by then, and I knew how to endure it. When it came on, I removed myself. I'd go somewhere else in my mind and just let it flow. One trick I had was that I'd focus my eyes on a spot about as big as a penny on the wall or ceiling, and the spot would turn dark and I'd make an imaginary circle around it, and then I'd follow the edge of the circle around and around. If the pain got so bad that I couldn't concentrate, I'd reverse direction and go around the other way.

That's where I was, circling my spot, when the doctor said, "There we go. No more needles." A minute later, when the nurse called my name, I had to make a conscious effort to leave the ring and bring my mind back before I could answer. When she asked where I'd been, I said, "Oh, nowhere." It's a private thing, how you deal with pain.

My hair was full of the sticky stuff, and some had dried on my forehead. The doctor came back into the room, bent over me, and smiled. He was a weird old bird who looked a little like a mad scientist, but he was supposed to be a leading expert on seizures. He pulled a table around to the side of the bed. On the table was a machine with needles that made scratch marks on a wide roll of paper. Back and forth the needles went.

"Now, young lady," the doctor said, "we're going to turn the lights out for a few minutes, and this machine is going to tell us why you're having these dreams." He didn't use the word seizure.

So the lights went out, and the machine hummed while it measured my brain waves. I tried to swallow, but my mouth was too dry and pasty. Unable to focus on anything in the dark, I shut my eyes. The prickles on my head wouldn't let me relax, but I pretended to be at Lynn's house in Rhode Island, playing with George. The test seemed to take forever, but eventually the lights were switched back on. As usual, the sudden change made me jump.

With the test over, we reversed the procedure and removed the needles and sticky stuff from my scalp and hair. It was slow going and only slightly less painful than putting them in. When the nurse was through, my head was sore, and I was dog-tired from fighting the pain.

"Take your time, dear," the nurse said when I tried to sit up. "How are you feeling?"

I thought it was a ridiculous question, but I answered, "Okay."

As I was getting off the table, I caught a glimpse of myself in the mirror. My hair was sticking up in spikes. The nurse led me into the bathroom, sat me in front of the sink, and gently moved my head under a stream of warm water running out of the high spigot. As the water soaked into my scalp, it stung then turned pale red in the sink. I closed my eyes and took a deep breath. Finally, the nurse turned the water off and wrapped a towel around my head. "There you go. All done."

When I stood up, I felt dizzy. The nurse eased me back down onto the chair, saying, "You'll be all right. Just sit for a minute." Then she left me sitting there and bustled around cleaning up.

My friend, Lynn, left for France that summer. Her father, a professor, was on a sabbatical; and he took the entire family. Lynn was enrolled in a French school. The combination of Lynn's absence and my diagnosis of epilepsy was difficult. They said I had petit mal, a mild form of epilepsy that often accompanies cerebral palsy. They also told me that my seizures would probably occur only at night and that I'd eventually outgrow them. I was put on a medication called Dilantin. The problem with the medication was that it was going to take time for them to zero in on the right dosage. In the mean time, I could expect more seizures.

Third Year Away

I was handling a lot. The worst part was going back to school without my friend, which meant I'd be even more vulnerable to Meg, Dudley, Tara, and Betsy. They were the ones who had started to close in on me at the end of my eighth-grade year. They followed me around and teased me every chance they got. It was because of all the special treatment Ms. Johndroe gave me. Lynn had been my buffer, keeping them at bay, and I wasn't sure I could manage without her. The only good part was that I'd be in the main house, away from Ms. Johndroe. Plus the dining room was below the dormitory rooms, which meant I didn't have the long walk up to the main house for meals.

I had become quiet. I was adjusting to the Dilantin, which made my gums bleed; and I didn't want to be noticed, plus I had to stay on the lookout for the mean girls. Plus at the end of every day as I drifted off to sleep, I never knew but what I was about to have another seizure.

My room was at the top of the stairs, and I had two roommates. One, a girl named Edith, was new. She was short but kind of pretty, with naturally wavy brown hair that framed her face and brought out her blue eyes.

As always, it was hectic arriving back at school and settling in. Girls and their parents were coming in or out of the dorms, dragging trunks up the stairs; and the returning girls were calling out to one another, then joking and squealing.

When some of the girls gathered at the top of the stairs outside my room, I went out to see what was going on. It felt strange without Lynn. I was alone and afraid of what might happen next. Someone said, "There he is!" Then, someone else asked, "Where?" and the first person pointed. They were looking down the stairwell. I made my way to the railing and looked over. Someone said, "I wonder what his daughter looks like."

"Whose daughter?" I asked.

"*His* daughter," Betsy said, pointing. "Look down there, in the hall."

My eyes followed her finger. It was Robert Young, from the television show *Father Knows Best*. I'd enjoyed watching reruns of the show with Lynn, and I immediately wished she were there to see him.

We couldn't see the daughter because fat Ms. Johndroe, who was talking to them, was blocking our view.

Betsy said, "Why don't they move just a little? Come on, come on. Sarah! Don't push!"

"I'm not," I shot back. "I want to see as badly as you do. Cool your jets." I pushed her against Joan, who was next to her.

"Hey, quit it," hissed Joan.

Just then, Robert Young's daughter stepped out into the open and shook hands with Ms. Johndroe. None of us said a word. We were too shocked. Robert Young's daughter was the nerd of the century. The white bobby-socked, saddle-shoed, pimple-faced girl shattered our illusions of Hollywood glamour. Her shoulders were hunched; and her skirt—which started up under her breasts, with a silver buckle between them—ran all the way down to her ankles.

"Oh my god!" Joan whispered, and we all started laughing. Ms. Johndroe heard us and looked up, which caused Robert Young and his daughter to look up as well. Caught in the act, we dispersed, but not before seeing the girl's thick glasses and Bugs Bunny mouth. She was the absolute opposite of her slim, good-looking father. And she turned out to be every bit as meek as she looked, keeping to herself and making few friends.

I remember that day because it was kind of a highlight for me. I didn't have Lynn, but I'd stood up to Betsy. In addition, the arrival of Robert Young's daughter provided comic relief. Perhaps she'd draw some of the teasing away from me. When we gathered for dinner that night, I temporarily forgot how much I missed Lynn.

The schoolwork was harder in the ninth grade. I rode, but it was the same old story: the horses were slow, and the riding instructor wouldn't let me try anything. Plus I had to endure Ms. Johndroe's relentless attention and phony, exaggerated concern.

One afternoon, during free time, I tried to join a group of girls in one of the larger rooms. Dudley, Joan, and Tara were sitting on the bed; and a girl named Clara Rosengarten was in the chair. They stopped talking when I entered the room, and I immediately knew coming had been a mistake. Dudley, who was the ringleader, started to chant, "Check it, check it," and Tara and Joan chimed in, and finally Clara. Then, they all got up and circled around me and yelled it in my ears. When I tried to get out of their circle, they pushed me back, and I fell against whoever was behind me. Then, as if that wasn't bad enough, Meg came into the room, broke through the circle, came right up to my face, and yelled, "Check it! Check it!" It was like she was flailing me with the hard consonants. I was stunned and confused, but I knew I had to get out. Without thinking, I pushed Meg with my right arm, sending her out through the circle. Following her, I made a run for the door.

Once out of the room, I ran back to my room, stiff leg and all. When I got there, I turned to see if they were following me. They were out in the hall, with their arms around one other, staring at me and laughing. As I stared back at them, they broke up and went back into their room. The last one to disappear, Dudley, yelled, "You won't get away next time, Sarah." She slammed the door behind her.

I stood there, hugging the door sash, my heart pounding and tears welling up behind my eyes. I went into my room and threw myself on the bed. My roommates weren't there. After a while, I wiped my cheeks and blew my nose. I didn't know what "check it" meant, and I didn't understand why they were picking on me. I hadn't done anything to them. Ms. King, our housemother, was in her room at the end of the hall. Hadn't she heard them? And assuming she had, why hadn't she stopped them?

That night, I had another seizure. Again, I tried to rip the mattress off my bed. Apparently, my dosage of Dilantin wasn't large enough. Edith was so afraid I'd swallow my tongue; she socked me in the face to snap me out of it. Betsy ran and got Ms. King, but by the time she arrived, I was sitting up on the edge of my bed, utterly depleted. As before, I couldn't remember my name. It seemed every girl on the floor was outside our room, staring in at me. Ms. King, who had called Ms. Johndroe, took me by the hand and led me downstairs. Ms. Johndroe arrived in her car and drove me to the infirmary, where I was taken to my usual room and crouched in the same old corner. I felt safer by myself, though I also felt like an animal who'd been cornered and had no escape. As I withdrew into myself, I also surrendered to my fate. Afraid to fall asleep, I stared at the wall. Why wasn't the medication working? It was so unfair. But then, slowly, my sadness turned to anger at the girls who had teased me. And at Ms. Johndroe. "No more, no more, no more," I whispered as I rocked back and forth.

I sat like that the entire night, and when the nurse opened the door the next morning, I threw the bedpan at her. When she ducked back out, the bedpan crashed against the door and clanged on the floor.

"Young lady," she said, "Ms. Johndroe will hear about this." I could tell from her voice that she was making an effort to control her anger.

"I don't care!" I yelled. "Do whatever you want. I don't care anymore."

"You don't appreciate anything that's been done for you at this school," she replied.

"Go away. You don't understand anything. Go *away!*" I got up, walked over to the door, and started pounding on it with the heels of my hands. Then I turned, leaned back against it, and slid down to the floor, sobbing. "You don't understand . . . You don't understand . . ."

The nurse told Ms. Johndroe, and I was left alone in the room the entire day. Afterward, my medication was adjusted, and I stopped having the seizures. But I didn't stop worrying that I might have another one. I stayed on the Dilantin until my early twenties, and even then, it took a lot of convincing to get me off it. The doctors were right though; I did eventually outgrow the epilepsy.

Over time, I learned who my enemies were and what kinds of situations were dangerous at House in the Pines. I was able to do it because I learned to trust my instincts. Like a wild animal, I learned to sense dangerous territory and people. I was quiet and cautious, and I trusted no one. I slunk around, avoiding certain girls, situations, and, above all, the headmistress. I'd decided that after all was said and done, Ms. Johndroe was sick in the head.

The fact was, I was feeling steadily more left out and becoming more withdrawn as a result. I didn't realize it as it was happening, but it was not a good situation for a fifteen-year-old.

"We Got You a Horse"

My mother was beginning to realize that it was unhealthy for me not to be doing sports. But despite my begging her to, she was still unwilling to take me out of House in the Pines. Instead, she decided that I should have a horse. She said that while the school could stop me from riding their horses, they couldn't stop me from riding my own.

Her announcement came during a phone call at the end of freshman year. The phone was in the hall, and Joan usually answered it. "It's for you, Ms. Johndroe's pet," she teased. When I took the phone from her, she pushed me. Pushing her back, I told her to get lost. "I'm going, I'm going," she taunted.

"We have a surprise for you," Mom said, with a hint of mystery in her voice.

I wasn't sure I'd heard her right. "A surprise? What is it?" When I heard my voice go up, I realized how much I'd been hoping something nice would happen. With Lynn away, things had gotten pretty bleak.

"We got you a horse, darling."

I was stunned. We'd talked about getting a horse and actually visited a few places. We'd gone to Meg Ferguson's farm and looked at her family's driving Morgans. But I was having enough problems with Meg, and I didn't want to get a horse from her. Besides, Mom had said their horses were too expensive. And then we hadn't looked any more after that. I asked where she'd found the horse.

"He's on a farm across the river from our house," Dad chimed in. When Dad had started thinking about retirement from his job in New York, he and Mom had moved from Stamford, Connecticut, to Rhode Island, where they'd rented a house on the Pawtucket River. I'd only spent part of the previous summer there, so I wasn't clear about the surroundings. I couldn't remember a farm across the river. "When can I see him?"

"This weekend," Mom replied. "I'll come get you."

A few girls had overheard snippets of our conversation and gathered around. Edith whispered, "See who?"

I put my hand over the mouthpiece of the phone and said, "I got a *horse*, Edith. Can you believe it?" I started jumping up and down and giggling.

"That's great." Edith seemed pleased for me. Edith and I had become closer since she'd punched me to keep me from swallowing my tongue. Her willingness to step in and act had made her proud of herself. "Talk, girl," she said. "Don't leave your parents hanging." When I started talking again, she turned to the other girls and announced, "Hey, guys, Sarah's parents got her a horse."

Meg must have heard because she appeared in the hall and stood with her arms crossed, staring at me. I watched her while listening to Mom tell me when she'd pick me up. I wasn't bothered by Meg. In fact, I looked right through her. All I could think about was my horse. *My* horse. Wow. I couldn't wait.

Finally, the weekend arrived, and Mom picked me up. When we got home, I called my new friend, Leslie, to share the news. She begged me to let her come with us. Before I knew it, Mom's Mercedes was throwing up a rooster tail of dust as she sped up the dirt driveway to the farm.

The farmhouse, at least two hundred years old, was badly run-down. There was very little paint left on it, nor on the barn next to it. Plus the property was a mess, with abandoned cars, trucks, and farm equipment scattered around. A few scrawny chickens stepped cautiously through the weeds, pecking at threadbare tires.

As we were walking from the car to the house, a boy emerged from one of the outbuildings with a sack of grain over his shoulder. He was shirtless and lean and tanned, with a shock of blond hair over one eye. "Oh my god," Leslie whispered. "*Who* is *that*?"

"Leslie!" Mom hissed.

"I don't have any idea, but I'm going to find out," I whispered back. The boy heaved the sack of grain up off his shoulder and onto the ground next to the henhouse door then stood up and turned to face us with his hands on his hips. Leslie and I were practically drooling, and he knew it. Leslie grabbed my arm. "Breathe, Leslie, breathe," I whispered, giggling.

But then it occurred to me that it was just a matter of time before the boy would notice my limp. Either that or my wandering eye. Because that's the way it always worked. It ruined the thrill and made me shy and inhibited. I was envious of Leslie. It didn't matter whether she moved or not. There was nothing to notice about her—except her beautiful, smooth skin, high cheekbones, green eyes, perfect teeth, and wheat-colored hair, which she wore back in a ponytail.

Leslie came from a nice family, part of the social set my parents had joined when they'd moved to Rhode Island. Like mine, her parents were summer people with a house in a part of Westerly known as Watch Hill. Standing next to her, I noticed—for the first time really—how pretty she was and how well dressed.

I tried to walk behind her, but it was no use. The boy glanced at my left leg, and then, when he looked up at my face and saw that I'd seen him noticing, turned to greet my mother. Well, that's that, I thought. He'll never look at me again. Leslie continued staring, kind of flirting by staring, but I looked down. I just wanted to see my horse.

Mom held out her hand and said, "I'm Mrs. Howell, and this is my daughter, Sarah, and her friend, Leslie." The boy started to reach out a muscled right arm, but thought better of it, drew it back, and wiped the hair out of his face instead of shaking hands. Mom's hand was left hanging. It was an awkward moment. The boy looked down at the ground in front of him, causing his hair to fall back over his face, and nudged a stone with his foot. He pushed both hands into the pockets of his jeans, sliding them lower on his hips and further exposing his underwear. "Carter's the name," he said, still staring at the ground. "I'll get my father." He was on his way by the time he finished saying it.

We waited for what seemed forever. I walked out past the house to the barnyard. Even littered with junk, it was a nice farm. Behind the house there was a dirt road leading down to some open fields. The fields, which were separated by ancient stone walls, ran down to the river in the distance.

There were two bay horses grazing nose to nose way off in one of the fields. I wondered if one of them was my horse. As I was studying them, Carter came around the house on another horse, riding bareback, and galloped off down the road toward the horses in the field. As he went by, I noticed that the horse he was riding, another bay, had a striking blaze on its forehead. It was thin, but appeared strong and smooth gaited.

The father came out of the house and introduced himself. "John Davis," he said with a farmer's economy of words. "My son will get Prince for you."

"His name is Prince?" I asked.

"Silver Prince," he said proudly.

My eyes returned to Carter. He'd opened it up and was in a mad gallop down the valley. He hadn't bothered with a bridle, much less a saddle, but he was able to control his horse with a lead line attached to his halter. He hadn't even fed the line through the horse's mouth the way most people do when riding that way. I'd never seen anything like it. I felt like I was on the movie set of *Giant*, watching James Dean. When I glanced at Leslie, I could see that she was awed as well. When Carter got to one of the gates, the horse dropped its hind end and stopped dead then sidled up to the gatepost so Carter could open the latch and gate without dismounting. Mr. Davis chuckled. He was obviously proud of the way his son could ride. No question, Carter made the stuck-up girls at school look like rank beginners.

Mr. Davis cut a handsome figure himself. I took a closer look as he watched Carter gather up the bays. He was tall and lean, with pale blue eyes, rosy cheeks, and gray hair under his baseball cap. You could see where Carter got his perfect skin.

As we watched Carter drive the horses up the road, Mr. Davis came down off the porch, over to me, and put his arm around my shoulder. "The one on the left, that's Silver Prince," he said. "That's your horse. The other bay is his half sister, Princess, and Carter is riding the sire to both."

I hung on his every word, studying Prince as Carter drove them up by us and into a small paddock. I walked over, no longer caring that Carter could see my limp. I had a horse, and that was all that mattered.

Leslie followed. "Look at him," she whispered, referring to Prince. "Oh my *god* . . ." She was referring to how thin he was, how his hip bones stuck out, and his coat was soiled and matted. But none of that mattered to me. As I looked at the eighteen-month-old stallion, all I could think was, *He's mine, all mine, no . . . matter . . . what.*

She was right though; both horses were in terrible shape. Their coats were dull and lifeless, and you could count their ribs. My eyes ran over Prince's body, from one bony contour to another. The manure was an inch thick on his stomach. When I glanced at Leslie, she seemed distressed, for me as well as the poor horse.

Mom put her hand on my back, urging me closer. She was either proud or trying to persuade me that she'd made a good choice. I went up to the rail fence, stuck my hand through, and said, "Come on, boy. Come on over." When Prince looked at me with curiosity, Carter glanced up at his dad, impressed that I'd gotten the horse's attention.

Prince had large eyes that were relaxed but alert. He shook his head, and his forelock settled to the side, revealing a star. It was the only white hair on his body. When he twitched his ears, I noticed that while their outsides were reddish brown like his coat, the insides were black. He had a black mane as well and black stockings on all four legs. His legs seemed well formed, given his condition. When he looked at me, his eyes were kind.

He decided to investigate the hand sticking through the fence and walked toward me, blowing air out of his nostrils as he came in to smell me. His chest was narrow, but he was still young. When he stopped in front of me, I reached in a little farther, but he stayed just out of reach. Then, after considering it, he stretched out his neck, touched the tips of my fingers with his nose, and blew hot air on my hand. I smiled, thrilled.

He came closer to investigate. He felt my hair with his upper lip, blew sweet, hot breath on my face, and just barely touched my cheek with his soft muzzle. When he was done, I looked into his eyes, reached up slowly, and gently rubbed his forehead.

It's unheard of to have such an instant connection with a horse—or for a horse to have one with a human. And we both knew it. We knew it was extraordinary, and on some deep level, we understood that it involved an implicit contract. I don't know how else to say it: We belonged to each other. I was going to change his life, and he was going to change mine. Our souls had met, and they would never part again. For me, the sense of it made it difficult to breathe. I knew why it was it so powerful. It meant that I'd never be alone again.

I crawled through the fence and stood next to him, rubbing his neck and ears. Carter was intrigued. He sensed our connection too.

"Well, would you look at that," Mr. Davis said, referring to how his son was watching me. I looked at Carter and smiled, and he came over and stood beside me. It was obvious what was going on with Carter. He was waking up to the fact that I wasn't just another little rich girl from Watch Hill.

"Nice job, getting him to come up to you like that," he said quietly.

"Yeah, I did, didn't I?" We both snickered nervously. Carter rested his arm on Prince's neck and looked me up and down, his blue eyes sliding over every curve of my body. It embarrassed me, and I shuffled my feet and looked away so I wouldn't have to make eye contact. He was so cute, I could feel my heart beating.

Mom felt the tension and, wanting to distract Carter, started in on how the vet was going to come the next morning to examine Prince. Mr. Davis agreed to have Prince waiting in a stall.

"Let's go in the house," Mr. Davis said. "I've got some things to show you."

I didn't want to leave Prince, but I climbed out through the fence. When I glanced back to reassure my new friend that I wasn't going to abandon him, he was watching me, ears up and eyes alert despite his dreadful condition. I moved my lips without making any sound, "See you in a little while," then followed along to the house.

Carter held the screen door for us. My mother went in first, followed by Mr. Davis. Leslie and I were staring at Carter, with the result that we tried to go through the door at the same time and bumped into each other. Mr. Davis snickered. He seemed well aware of his son's effect on girls.

The house was old and run-down, but it had the original wide floorboards and beamed ceiling. Mr. Davis led us into the kitchen and took his cap off. The room was pale yellow, and there was an old wood cookstove against one wall, with spices in a rack above it and a large harvest table with chairs around it. Leslie and I sat down. It was clear from the scratches and dents in the table that a lot of people had used it for a lot of things over the years. When Mr. Davis offered my mother a chair, she looked at it in such a way that he dusted it with his cap. "There," he said. "We don't get much time for housecleaning this time of year." I was annoyed at Mom. There hadn't been anything on the seat of the chair. Hadn't she been in the house before?

Carter disappeared upstairs. He seemed to be teasing Leslie and me with his comings and goings. Mr. Davis went into the living room to get some papers. "Mom," I whispered when we were alone, "haven't you been in here before?"

She leaned toward me and said in a low voice, "No, dear, your father and I came over to see the horse, but I didn't come in." Leslie was looking around, taking it all in while waiting for Carter to come back.

"Well, have you bought him yet, or not?" I asked impatiently.

"No, dear, we want the vet to look at him first."

"But Mom, you said he was mine."

"He is, Sarah. In due course. Calm down."

I tried, but it wasn't easy with Mom talking out of both sides of her mouth. I knew what the vet was going to tell her. I'd been around horses long enough to know that Prince was in wicked bad shape. The vet was going to talk her out of getting him. I slumped back in my chair, feeling both anxious and disappointed. When I glanced at Leslie, she was still looking around. She had a dreamy half smile on her face. Carter was the last thing on my mind at that point.

"Mrs. Howell," Mr. Davis began as he sat down with us, "this is what I wanted you to see." Mr. Davis seemed anxious about what the vet would say too—and he knew more than I did. He put some papers in front of Mom. They showed Prince's lineage. When I leaned over and read the papers, I was amazed. Prince's great-grandsire had been Broadwall Parade out of Broadwall Farm in Greenwich, Rhode Island. Broadwall Farm belonged to Meg Ferguson's family. What's more, the horse she rode at school was from the same bloodline. Oh boy.

"What is it, dear?" Mom asked.

"Yeah, you look like you've seen a ghost," Leslie added.

"Mom," I answered, jabbing my finger at the paper, "this is the same farm where we went to look at Morgans. I go to school with this girl, remember?"

Mom looked at the papers. "Why yes, Sarah, you're right . . ."

"Oh, so you know Broadwall Farm," Mr. Davis said, clearly relieved. He explained that Broadwall Parade had been the only American horse selected to perform with the Spanish Lipizzan stallions when they first came to the United States. I heard him out then asked how it happened that Broadwall Parade's bloodline had ended up on the Davises' farm. He explained that he liked driving Morgans and had been looking for a big-boned mare to pull a full-size carriage. He said he'd found one at the Fergusons', a retired brood mare named Silver Mae. Silver Mae, who'd mothered Parade, had come from out west somewhere and had been in her twenties when Mr. Davis had bought her. The Davises had bred her and gotten Silver King, the stallion Carter had ridden down the valley, and then Silver King had come of age and impregnated his mother—twice. And that's how they'd gotten Silver Princess and my horse, Silver Prince. Prince had been a mistake, actually, Mr. Davis explained. Silver Mae had been twenty-eight when she'd had him. It proved too much for her, and they'd had to put her down a few months later.

What a story! My mother goes out and finds a horse on this farm that no one has ever heard of, and she agrees to buy it for $175, and the horse turns out to be related to the horse Meg Ferguson has at House in the

Pines! Meg Ferguson, the biggest snot in the whole school! I couldn't help but think, *Oh boy, I could have fun with this*—assuming the vet doesn't talk Mom out of buying him.

The vet, Dr. Barrett, called us the following night. I couldn't stand it, so I picked up the upstairs phone and listened in. "Jane," he said to Mom, "that colt isn't going to make it."

"What do you mean?" Mom replied.

"The horse is so undernourished it's doubtful he'll survive. His growth is stunted, and one of his testicles hasn't descended. It should have by now, he's almost two. Even if he does live, I'm not sure I could geld him."

"Oh . . ." Mom said, clearly dismayed.

"Besides, Sarah couldn't take this horse to school," Dr. Barrette went on. "Not with those kids. They'd laugh her out of the barn. Let me find you a horse that's healthy and already trained." When Mom didn't reply, he said, "Jane?"

"But . . . it's too late," Mom said, in a desperate whisper.

"What do you mean?"

"You don't understand. She wants *this* horse. You should have seen them together. She feels—knows—that this is the horse for her. Her heart's set on it. Besides, I've committed to Mr. Davis."

"You what? Jane, I told you to wait."

"I know you did. But it's a done deal. Will you still help us?"

My heart was crying out in frustration and despair. I broke the connection and hung up lest I butt into their conversation. What did Dr. Barrett mean Prince might not survive? He'd make it, I already knew that. This horse wasn't going to walk into my life and connect with me the way he had, only to then disappear. I went back to my bedroom and sat on the floor.

After a while, Mom came up the stairs and into the room. "Were you listening in?"

"Yes." I got up. I was thinking I didn't want to go back to school. "Mom," I started.

"It's all right," she said. "Dr. Barrett's going to help us."

"Really?" I couldn't keep from grinning.

"Yes, he said that if this horse means that much to you, he'll do his best to get him into shape. He's going to start by increasing Prince's feed and putting him on a special grain-and-vitamins mix. Then, as Prince gets stronger, he'll worm and try to geld him. He said it will take all summer."

Seeing the concern in my eyes, she added, "Dr. Barrett told me to tell you to keep your spirits up and your fingers crossed."

I had to beg Mom to let me see Prince again before I went back to school. When we got to the Davis Farm, he was in a stall, having some grain. He raised his head to look out at me and immediately started coughing.

Carter came around the corner of the barn carrying another food bucket. "Dr. Barrett's orders," he explained. "I forgot to put it up." He filled Prince's bucket with the feed mix Dr. Barrett had ordered. The new mix smelled of vitamins. "Yeah, nasty," Carter said when he saw me sniffing. "What are you feeding him anyway?"

I didn't answer. Prince was still coughing, and I was concerned. He appeared to have a wad of grain stuck in his throat.

Carter caught on. "We have to rub his neck," he said. "Come on, help me."

We entered the stall, and I pushed up against Prince's neck from one side while Carter rubbed the ball of grain from the other. It finally broke up enough for Prince to get it down.

"I guess we better get this on," I said, referring to the grate that belonged on the bucket. It was a special bucket Dr. Barrett had brought to prevent Prince from gulping great mouthfuls. Dr. Barrett intended to give Prince up to fourteen quarts a day, and he knew that, starving as he was, Prince might gorge to the point of choking. Carter was ashamed because he hadn't put the grate on, but I didn't say anything.

I didn't care how much we had to do. Prince was mine, and I was going to take him to school with me the next fall, and that was all there was to it. When it came time for us to go, I patted Prince while whispering good-bye. Reluctant to break contact, I was resting my hand on his mane when Carter came up across from me, reached over, and put his hand on mine. It startled me, and when I looked up at him into those bright blue eyes, he pulled his hand away. Our hands had touched occasionally when we'd been massaging Prince's neck, but this was different, a *lot* different.

"Thanks for helping me," I said, for lack of anything else.

"Yeah, that's okay," Carter replied. We looked into each other's eyes again. After a brief pause, he said, "I didn't think you knew what you were doing when I first saw you."

"I know."

"We keep these horses thin because we show Silver King at the fairs," Carter added. So that was it. They were feeding Silver King all the grain.

It was Carter's way of telling me they didn't have the money to feed all the horses properly.

"There are no papers with this horse, you know," he went on. "My father waited too long to get him registered."

It was the most I'd heard out of Carter. "That's okay," I replied. "I don't care."

"You don't?" He sounded surprised.

"No, I really don't." It was the truth. As of April 14, 1964, Prince was mine, and that was all that mattered. Well, that and the fact that I'd met a boy who hadn't asked why I limped.

I saw Leslie again briefly before returning to school. We talked about Prince then Carter, and then the new rage, the Beatles. I loved their music, and it was nice to have something in my life that gave me a thrill. Leslie was crazy about them too, as were a lot of the girls at school. I had sort of an advantage in the situation because my father's secretary knew the *Life* photographer who'd photographed them when they'd made their first trip to New York, and she'd given me some pictures that no one else had. Having the pictures on my wall had gotten me some status at school.

Prince had a long forelock that hung down over one eye almost to his nose, and it made him look like the Beatles drummer, Ringo Starr. When I mentioned it to Leslie, she agreed, and we decided we should change his name to Ringo. It was such a perfect name for him; we broke up giggling when we came up with it. Since we were renaming things, we also decided that henceforth, we'd refer to Carter as the Bronze God.

Leslie agreed that it had been a great weekend. I hadn't talked to her about House in the Pines. She was a friend who liked me for who I was, and I wanted to leave it that way. She said it was too bad I had to go away to school, and I could tell she didn't like my mother. Seeing my life through her eyes made me realize more than ever what a bad situation I was in with my family.

I was anxious about going back to school because the teasing had become so intense. When I got there, I tried to keep my thoughts on Ringo, but the last five weeks of the year dragged by. Mom called with updates. Apparently, Ringo was putting on weight. I was crazed to get out of there and be with him.

Stonington, Connecticut, The Stanton-Davis Farm, 1964. this is were Ringo was born. Built before 1675, the farm was initially owned by Thomas Stanton, an Indian interpreter for the New England colonies. In the Revolutionary War, it was a provision farm, providing food for General Washington's army.

Stonington, Connecticut, the Stanton–Davis Farm, 1964. Carter Davis, a.k.a. the Bronze God, riding Ringo's sire, Silver King. You should have seen him without his shirt on.

"He's Got Heart . . .
and So Do You"

Finally, I was home for the summer. For the first time in my life, I was looking forward to it. I had Ringo, and that was all that mattered. Plus I was excited about seeing the Bronze God. I was turning sweet sixteen, I had a killer figure, and I knew it. My hair was short behind my ears and very dark with red highlights. I'd taken to wearing frosted lipstick along with black eyeliner and mascara. And miniskirts, of which I had a pretty good selection. My favorite was green with white polka dots. That was one thing about my mother: I never suffered for lack of clothes.

My parents had a little Boston Whaler with an outboard docked across the street from our house, and Leslie and I would hop in and shoot across the river to the Davis farm. We tried to look as sexy as possible when visiting Ringo. Leslie started referring to the Bronze God as TBG. She said the TB fast and put the emphasis on the G, as in TB-G.

Ringo was always glad to see us. He'd begun to fill out, and his coat was looking healthier. Dr. Barrett didn't want to move him until he was stronger. He said Ringo had every kind of worm known to horses, and he wanted to leave them all behind at the Davises'. Poor Ringo, it was hard to take at times, but I kept my spirits up and my fingers crossed.

Carter and his friend, Buster, hovered around when we visited, looking for opportunities to show off. I wasn't convinced that Carter liked me, plus Leslie had her hopes up. She and I spent hours brushing Ringo and leading him around in his new halter. Dr. Barrett warned me that when Ringo started feeling better, he might become difficult, but he was always good.

Carter went about his chores, most of the time with his shirt off. Mr. Davis came out of the house one day, said some cows had broken loose, and asked Carter and Buster to take the horses and go down to the lower pasture and get them back. They were only too happy to oblige as it gave them another chance to show off their riding. So Carter jumped on King and Buster on a workhorse, and off they went, lickety-split, waving their free arm and hooting like cowboys. Carter cut a fine figure on King.

Leslie and I went into the barn and were brushing Ringo when we heard hoof beats coming up the hill. I peeked out through a crack in the barn door and saw that the black workhorse was wandering around riderless. "He must have fallen off," Leslie said. She was trying not to laugh. When we went out, Carter came into view on King. He had Buster up behind and was driving two cows. I looked at Leslie, and we couldn't hold back the giggles. The boys dismounted and went into the house, and we didn't see them for the rest of the day. I guess they felt they had to regain their dignity before facing us. Leslie and I agreed that a little humility wouldn't hurt them.

One day, having gotten Ringo a bridle, I was sitting on a rock outside the barn putting it together. I'd been dropped off without Leslie that day, and Mom was going to pick me up. The sun was bright, and a warm breeze blew through my hair. It was one of those days that make you want to keep taking deep breaths so as not to miss any of the myriad smells of summer. The bridle leather was stiff such that I was having a hard time with the buckle, and I was concentrating so hard I didn't hear Carter come up behind me.

"Need some help?" When he said it, the sudden noise made my left side jump. The pieces of bridle in my lap fell on the ground, and I was embarrassed. "Whoa," he said, "I didn't mean to scare you." Carter squatted on his haunches and picked up the pieces. He did it gently, delicately, as if the woven reins might tear. "These are kind of Western looking for someone who rides English," he observed. He was looking at the reins in his opened hands, but then he looked up at me, and he looked *right* at me and didn't look away. His blond hair was down over one eye, and he had a short section of straw sticking out of the corner of his mouth. I was so startled that I forgot what we were talking about. Finally, smiling knowingly, he said, "So? What's the story with the reins?"

"They're English reins that happen to be braided, Carter."

He snickered, shook his head, and said, "Well, here, let me help you." He took the bridle out of my hands and pushed the reins through the rings on the bit. I could see the tendons moving in his hands, and the calluses, and the muscles working in his forearms. He maneuvered the stiff leather with ease, and all the while, he kept rolling the straw back and forth across his upper lip with the tip of his tongue. "Here," he said, handing me the bridle. When he stood up, he was closer than I'd realized when he was squatting. Neither of us said anything. He stood over me without moving, but when I didn't dare look up at him, he finally turned and walked away.

"Thanks," I called after him.

The exquisite moment had come and gone. I knew Leslie had had similar encounters with him. We shared our stories, discussing the minutest details. I was sure that in the end, he'd pick Leslie because he'd seen that there was something wrong with me. And yet, one thought nagged me. He hadn't asked why I limped. Why not? Everyone always asked. That was my one ray of hope, the off chance that he hadn't asked because he simply didn't care.

He was a mystery, the mysterious Bronze God, and he really got Leslie and me going. One day, he asked if we wanted to go on a hayride that coming weekend. Was he asking us *both* to be his dates? He said he'd call that night and let us know the details. Leslie and I were in the kitchen guarding the phone when it rang. She jumped up and ran upstairs to listen in.

"Hi, girls," he started. Oh god, Leslie and I thought simultaneously without being able to share the thought; he knows we're both on the phone! Not *too* obvious! He told us the time then said good-bye and hung up. Leslie came thumping back down the stairs, almost killing herself in the process.

"You were breathing too hard," I accused. "He heard you. *I* heard you!" I felt *so* embarrassed.

"I couldn't help it!" Leslie squawked. "I was out of breath from running up the stairs!" She started laughing, and I started in with her, and we grabbed each other and gasped and swooned over the Bronze God. We were going on his hayride, and it was going to be dark; and we were going to be sitting next to him, near him, close to him, but how close?

"Wait," Leslie said suddenly.

"What? What's wrong?" I asked.

"He asked both of us. Which is supposed to be his date?"

"I don't know. Maybe it's a group thing." She seemed satisfied with that idea, and we laughed and danced some more.

It was my first glimpse of being a teenager. My surgeries and all the teasing at school were no longer a part of my life. They just fell away, like a snake's dry skin. I was a new person. I had my horse, my friend, Leslie;

I'd met a boy, and he'd asked me—well, us—out. I was on cloud nine for the rest of the week.

The day before the hayride, I decided it was time to ride Ringo. Not a lot, just a little, to see if the tack we'd gotten would fit him. He was much stronger, and it was looking as if he might survive. His testicle still hadn't dropped, but Dr. Barrett was giving him hormones as well as the vitamins, and we expected it would.

Leslie and I took Ringo down to the field below the farmhouse. We'd made a little ring and were going to take turns riding. Leslie was a good rider. Her mother had performed in Madison Square Garden, and she'd seen to it that Leslie and her sister had learned early and well.

I rode first to make sure Ringo was strong enough. He seemed fine, and I trotted around and around. Out of the corner of my eye, I saw that Buster and Carter were watching. Ringo was full of beans, feeling his oats as they say. He kept breaking into a canter and then speeding up into a gallop, which was faster than I wanted him to go. It was my chance to show Carter that I could really ride. He thought I was good, but I wanted him to be totally convinced. So I sat straight but deep in my seat and talked to Ringo, snugging him up at the same time then loosened the reins and sliding the bit back and forth in his mouth. He'd only had a bit in his mouth a few times, but he got the message, slowed to a walk, and then stopped.

Leslie came over and said, "That was great, Sarah. You brought him right back." I glanced at Carter. He'd been on Ringo a few times with the halter, so he knew Ringo wasn't bridle broken. Leslie nodded in the direction of the boys and said, "They watched you the whole time. I think you *really* impressed them."

I looked down at my friend, smiled, and replied, "Yeah, and the hayride's tomorrow night."

I dismounted and gave Ringo a big hug. Leslie said, "He loves you already, Sarah." He shoved me with his nose. I could have sworn all three of us laughed.

When we finished, I led Ringo back to the barn and took his stuff off. I wouldn't ride him again for a while as Dr. Barrett felt it might strain his back. Carter had ridden him too early, and that plus his poor diet had probably caused the slight sway in his spine, up by his withers. Dr. Barrett hoped it would straighten out as he grew.

The day of the hayride, Leslie and I went through the usual teenage deliberations about what to wear. It seemed it would never be time to go, but at last we were getting into Mom's car and setting out for the Davis farm. As we got out of the car, Mom said she'd pick us up at eleven. When Buster appeared and said hello, I realized that it was the first time I'd heard him speak.

Behind Buster, out by the barn, Carter was up on the hay wagon with a group of kids. Neither Leslie nor I knew any of them. Mr. Davis was there as well, holding the reins of two big workhorses. The horses were stepping in place and tossing their heads and spittle, anxious to get going.

Buster led us around to the back of the wagon, and Leslie climbed up on. I was trying to figure out how to get up. Bringing Ringo back from a gallop to a standstill was easier than getting up a three-step ladder. Leslie looked down, concerned. I grabbed the sides, put my right foot on the rung, and pulled myself off the ground. I managed to get my left foot up on the next step, but since my left leg couldn't lift me, I had to do it all with my arms. And since my left arm wasn't very strong, my right had to do most of the work.

I tried to put my right leg on the step next to my left, but I hadn't left enough room for it. Just then, Carter's hand appeared in front of me. Leslie let out a little gasp, cleared her throat to hide it, and moved out of his way. Carter was waiting for me to take his hand, but I couldn't reach for him with my strong arm for fear my weak one wouldn't hold. Not knowing what to do, I froze.

Sensing what was going on, Carter grabbed my right arm. "Let go, I've got you," he said confidently. I let go, and his other hand grabbed my left wrist and pulled me up into the wagon. Between my anxiety and Carter grabbing me like that, my heart was pounding. I managed to make my way over to Leslie and get settled in the hay.

There were no introductions. When the wagon got underway, the other kids paired up and wiggled under the hay. Even Carter disappeared. Carter had a date? Leslie and I and one other boy were left out. Cupping my hands, I whispered into Leslie's ear, "What's going on?"

"I don't know," she whispered back. "But I'm not going under the hay, that's for sure." We huddled close and waited.

Mr. Davis was driving the team of horses. Looking back, he saw our discomfort. He also saw that the one boy who hadn't gone under the hay with a girl was edging closer to me. "Sarah," he said, "do you want to drive the horses?"

"Sure." I replied, welcoming the escape. Standing up, I said, "Come on, Leslie," and pulled her up with me. When he handed me the reins, Mr. Davis smiled and winked.

It was fun though we were crestfallen about Carter. But then, suddenly, he was behind me, and his breath was on my ear, and then his arms were around me, and he'd taken my hands in his. "Not too loose," he said. "You want to keep contact with their mouths." I glanced back at him and smiled. Oh, the way he looked at me. He looked into my eyes as if to say, "You're the one I want." Mr. Davis faded into the background. Leslie saw it too. Being my friend, she moved away from us. I couldn't believe it.

Ringo finally got strong enough to be moved. Our neighbors up the road had a barn, and they said he could board with their two horses and a pony that belonged to another neighbor. Ringo would be in a small stall, but that was all right; he was fairly small himself.

Ringo's testicle had finally descended, and Dr. Barrett was planning to geld him, but he wanted to wait for cooler weather when there'd be fewer flies. In the meantime, it was hard having a stallion in with the other horses. Ringo had grown, his coat was shiny, and he was becoming pretty frisky. I couldn't turn him out with the other horses for fear he'd pick a fight, so he stayed in the barn for the most part.

I took him to the beach whenever I could. He'd become strong enough to be ridden regularly, and sometimes I'd ride bareback. He loved to splash around in the water. I'd hang onto his mane and feel the power of his body as he smashed through the surf. When we came out, I'd dismount, and he'd stretch and have a good shake. Then, I'd lead him up into the dunes and sit, and he'd stand beside me, and we'd both stare out at the ocean. He looked at it just as intently as I did, and his alert bright, brown eyes took in the boats passing by. On windy days, his forelock and mane would blow around, making him look like a warrior prince.

I'd been told that walking barefoot on the beach was good for my foot, and that riding would strengthen my leg. Dr. Barrett said the salt water and exercise in deep sand would strengthen Ringo's legs as well, so we went to the beach as often as we could. We were helping each other get stronger, and he seemed as grateful to me as I was to him.

When I wasn't with Ringo, I was usually with Carter at the beach or a party. Word was getting around among his friends that he was dating a rich girl. His parents were pleased because they liked me, plus I think they felt it was good for Carter to get exposed to the Watch Hill kids. He stopped by almost every night, and when my parents gave me a sixteenth birthday party, he came as my date.

But there was a problem: he was hung up about his family. He didn't like the never-ending work on the farm, and he made it clear he intended to leave as soon as he could. I think his father worked him very hard. He was also hung up about coming to Watch Hill. He said it reminded him of what he wasn't. For me, where he came from was one of the best things about him, and I thought it was neat that he'd have the farm someday. I thought he was great just the way he was. Unfortunately, it didn't matter what I thought.

He ended up in the bushes with another girl. When I heard about it, I gave him back his ID bracelet, and he stopped coming over. I was heartbroken. I'd hear about him and miss him, but summer was drawing to a close and Dr. Barrett was going to geld Ringo, so I had other things to think about. As August passed, I thought less and less about TBG and his magnificent farm by the ocean. When I did think of him, I always ended up hoping he'd come to realize how special he was. As for me, well, he'd given me, a girl with cerebral palsy, a summer of sweet sixteen.

The thought of returning to school was scary, but at least I'd have Ringo with me. I thought it had been a good move on my parents' part, getting me a horse. Still, I was anxious because a small group of girls had been after me the previous year, and they'd become progressively more physical in their abuse. So I tried to focus on the good things. Lynn would be back from her year in France. We'd written to each other all year, so she knew I had a horse. She wrote that she couldn't wait to see him.

It was a cool, sunny September morning when Dr. Barrett went to the barn to operate on Ringo. My mother wouldn't let me go, which was hard for me, but Dr. Barrett said he'd call as soon as he was through. The night before, on my last visit, I'd left Ringo's halter on so it would be easier for Dr. Barrett to grab him. As Dr. Barrett said he would, Ringo had become hot tempered as he'd gotten stronger. In one instance, he'd bitten our neighbor on the chest while she was tending her horses. I think he was annoyed because she was trying to tell me how to take care of him. He didn't like her tone of voice, so he hauled off and let her have it. It got her to leave us alone, that's for sure.

Ringo may have been getting a reputation as a wild stallion, but he was always gentle with me. I was the only person he'd come to in the pasture, as well as the only one he'd allow to touch his head. He never even hinted that he might hurt me. And I certainly never hurt him. So I figured it might confuse him if I was there during his operation.

Dr. Barrett's house was across the road from Ringo's pasture; and sometimes, when I'd go over to play with Ringo, I'd see Dr. Barrett watching us out his living room window. I'd go over because I'd get to feeling sorry for Ringo having to be out by his lonesome. Our favorite game was hide-and-seek. I'd run around the field until I could duck behind a bush, and he'd look for me and not see me, and finally he'd come and find me. And when he found me, he'd arch his neck and tail and dance around as if it was all a gay surprise. Or if he knew where I was, he might fast trot across the field at me and slam on the breaks in front of the bush. And I'd step out laughing and say, "Ah, you found me. Now, it's your turn," and he'd spin around and let out a squeal and tear off to the other end of the field. And I'd kick up my heels the way he had, and turn and face him, and he'd look at me with his ears up. And I'd call, "Go, Ringo, it's your turn," and he'd drop his head and stomp his foot and blow hot air onto the dirt, making a little cloud of dust. And I'd stomp my foot too and run at him, and he'd take off behind the bush. I think he thought he was out of sight, the way I'd been, even though he was bigger than the bush.

Our communication was so complete and clear; it was as if we had our own language. When we were together, nothing and no one else mattered. After he'd put the bush between us, I'd run over and say, "I found you!" And he'd lower his head, and I'd pet him, maybe rub his forelock; and then he'd pull back, squeal, and gallop off again. We played hide-and-seek until one of us got tired. I was usually the one who quit first since I had essentially one good leg to use against his four strong ones.

I think Ringo knew Dr. Barrett was trying to help him. Everybody knew. He was Dr. Barrett's special project and, hopefully, his success story. And Dr. Barrett loved Ringo; everyone could see that too. Plus Dr. Barrett saw what a special bond Ringo and I had. He told people, "This whole thing is a miracle." So I knew Ringo was in good hands for his surgery.

It was a long morning—endless!—but the call finally came. I picked up the phone to listen in as Dr. Barrett told my mother about it.

"Well, I'm through," he said. "It went all right as far as I can tell, but he won't get up. I need Sarah to come up and help me." I hung up the phone, went down the stairs two at a time, and was past my mother and out the door before she was through talking to him, running as fast as my left leg allowed.

When I finally got to the barn, Ringo was lying on the floor of his stall. I looked at Dr. Barrett. "He won't get up for me," he said, "but I think he will for you." My heart was in my throat. Turning into the stall, I glimpsed the sun streaming in through the cobwebs in the open window. "Go on," Dr. Barrett encouraged, waving his hand. "Go right in with him."

I walked in, approached Ringo slowly, and took the cheek strap of his halter. "Easy, boy," I said quietly, consolingly. "It's all right, now." He didn't look up, but he whispered a nicker at my voice. I rubbed his ears. There was a startling amount of deep red blood on the floor under his tail. I took the lead rope, snapped it onto his halter, and said, "Come on, Ringo, let's go outside." When I tugged on the rope, he made a huge effort and was suddenly up on his feet.

"I thought so," Dr. Barrett said, relieved. "Well, come on, let's take him out."

With Dr. Barrett leading the way, I slowly turned Ringo and walked him out of his stall, down the concourse and out of the barn. He stumbled along stiff legged, groggy, and obviously very sore. When we got outside, we paused in the warm sun.

Dr. Barrett checked Ringo over from head to tail, taking his time to be thorough. As he ran his hands over Ringo's body, he said, "As you know, Sarah, a few months ago, I wouldn't have given two cents for this horse. I didn't think he'd reach full size, he'd had such a bad start. But I was wrong." He stopped and turned to face me. "He's got heart, all right, and so do you; don't ever let anyone tell you any different." He patted Ringo then reached out and patted me, as well.

He said he had to be somewhere and started to leave. When he got to the barn door, he turned and said, "Keep him walking on his lead for a few minutes and then turn him out. I'll check on him later." He was wearing his favorite hat, a battered and stained old Panama. As he stood there, he took it off, ran his other hand over his bald head then put it back on and pulled the brim down snug. Holding up his hand, he nodded and disappeared into the barn.

No one had ever talked to me the way Dr. Barrett just had. Others had complimented me, but I always felt they were just being nice. But Dr. Barrett and I had worked together; I knew he didn't say things he didn't mean.

I was also grateful for all he'd done for Ringo. I guess I kind of cherished him for that. He'd put a lot of time into Ringo because he wanted us both to succeed, and he knew we'd have a better chance if we could be together. I don't know if another vet would have understood and done as much.

As vacation ended and I started looking back, I decided it had been my best summer ever. I was sad about losing Carter, but happy to have Ringo. The thing about Ringo was that I felt safe when I was with him. Dr. Barrett had been right: it had been a miracle.

Fourth Year Away

Finally, the dreaded day arrived, and off to school we went. My parents arranged for someone to trailer Ringo up. He'd recovered completely and looked as well as he could, considering his start. He was still small for his age, but his eyes were bright, and his coat was lustrous. Plus anyone who knew horses could see that he had a huge heart.

It was mid-September, and I was entering my sophomore year. I'd gotten word that Lynn and I would be roommates again. We were assigned a bottom-floor room in a split-level dorm just below the main house. It was one of those buildings where you walked into the second floor on which there was a large living room and kitchen, and then had to go downstairs or upstairs to the bedrooms. There was only one bathroom per floor, but it was the nicest dorm I'd been in, plus it was close to the stable.

Our housemother was an elderly woman named Ms. Ditchett. I laughed the first time I said her name. Ms. Ditchett was a mousy little thing with blue-gray curls. She looked as if she'd taken off her curlers without remembering to brush out her hair.

It was cool and clear the day we made the trip back. We followed the trailer in Mom's Mercedes. I was worried about Ringo because he'd only ridden in a trailer once before and it was a long trip, but Mom let me ride with him the last leg and he did fine. I'd braided his forelock so he could see where he was going. I'd also spent hours grooming him so he'd look his best when he made his grand entrance at school.

As we rode along in the trailer, my thoughts drifted back to our trips to the beach and swimming in the surf. I could almost feel the water splashing on my face as I recalled crashing through the waves. I remembered how we walked home and I washed him down, and how he liked to drink straight from the hose. He seemed to know and accept everything about me, plus he was always glad to see me. And I thought about how, when I went down to bring him in from the field at night, he'd jerk his head up and his ears would snap to attention when he saw me, then he'd greet me with a friendly nicker. I called it his percolator greeting. And how he'd come running over and stop on a dime directly in front of me, as if he wanted to show me how agile he'd become. And how I'd turn and start for the barn and he'd come up behind me and nudge me, pushing me toward the gate. It always made me laugh. He knew it would. It was our private joke.

His requirements were simple, and so were mine. We both needed to be accepted, appreciated, and given a chance to prove ourselves. He seemed to be the only one who understood that. He never criticized or judged me; he was just there with his constant companionship and devotion.

As I thought about him, I realized that he was becoming my teacher and that I should pay attention because there was a lot I could learn from him. He could give me what the educated teachers and my mother hadn't figured out. My mother could have gotten me out of the school if she wanted to, but she'd chosen not to. It was easier for her, having me away from home. That way, she could go on pretending she didn't have a daughter with cerebral palsy. I was only sixteen, but I'd spent four years, a quarter of my life, away from my family. It had gotten so that it was actually awkward when I was home.

I stroked Ringo's neck. The trailer swayed abruptly, and he looked up at me. "It's okay," I reassured him, rubbing his head. He went back to munching his hay.

We were almost at the school. I thought about Ms. Johndroe and how being home for the summer and having all my experiences had helped me see how sick she was. Then I thought about the five girls who tormented me and how spoiled and awful they were. I was going to have to watch out for myself, but I was learning how to do it. I was used to not trusting people. Animals had always been my closest friends, and now I had Ringo. Rocking back and forth in the trailer, I slowly went inside myself, into my memories of all the good things that had happened that summer. It made me sad that it was all over. Ever attentive, Ringo lifted his head over the rail, lowered it to mine, and sniffed my face. He pushed me with his nose, the same way he did in the field, but more gently. He did it to make me laugh, and it worked. I was hugging his head as we turned into the school.

When Ringo smelled the other horses, he gave a loud whinny and immediately started sweating. He was excited, maybe a little nervous. When I backed him out of the trailer, a group had gathered to see the newcomer. It was much more activity than Ringo was used to. He stood, feet firmly set and head high, looking around.

Someone said, "Oh, he's cute." I stroked his neck and talked to him then led him into the barn. He'd never walked on concrete, and the sound of his iron shoes startled him. His head flew up. "It's all right, Ring," I reassured him. "It's just your own feet. Come on . . ."

Ms. Keaner was there ahead of us, looking Ringo up and down. "What's *his* name?" she demanded in a booming voice.

"Ringo."

"Ringo?" she said. "What kind of name is that?"

"It's the name I gave him."

"Well, young lady, my papers say his name is Prince, and I think he looks like a little prince, so that's what I'm going to call him."

Well, I thought, what a nice greeting, you old bag. Have it your way. I have my own horse now, and no one's going to tell me I can't ride; for all I care you can call him the Aga Khan.

Ms. Keaner showed us to Ringo's stall. The barn had been repainted, the same white with green trim, and the iron bars between the stalls were a shiny jet black. Outside, in the afternoon sun, the fences were bright white against the lush green pastures. The sweet smell of fresh hay was wafting down from the loft.

Ringo and I spent the first few weeks getting used to things. The five girls who liked to torment me were in my dorm again. I was hoping to see my name on the riding list if, for no other reason, to get away from them.

I finally made it. Lynn saw it and told me. She was happy for me. She thought Ringo was great. So I hurried down to the stable, and everyone was outside, either riding or waiting for her horse to be saddled. Eventually, Ms. Keener led Ringo out. She was holding his reins up high, under his chin, and tight, and occasionally she'd jerk on them. When she did, the bit snapped in Ringo's mouth, hurting him and making him jumpy.

"Let go of him," I said angrily. "You're holding him too tight. He doesn't like it." I stepped forward and reached for her arm.

"He tried to bite me, Sarah," Ms. Keener said, indignantly.

I had her arm, and I wasn't about to let her yank the reins again. "Give him to me, Ms. Keener," I said, glowering at her. The girls were watching this face-off, wondering who was going to back down. Ringo pranced around on the end of her arm.

"He's been nasty, Sarah, and I need to make sure he's not going to do anything," she said firmly.

"He'll relax if you give him to me," I said.

She gave me a funny look but handed me the reins, whereupon Ringo immediately quieted. As she watched, looking back and forth between Ringo and me, it dawned on her that I just might know what I was doing. The truth seemed to seep into her head. I could actually see her attitude shift. It went from dismissive of what I represented to open to and perhaps even respectful about who I might be as an individual. "Well, go on then," she deferred. "Take your horse; time's awasting." Turning to the other girls, she said, "Well? What are you staring at?"

"We need our horses," they explained.

"All right, hang on; I'll get them" she replied.

I mounted up and started for the ring, sitting tall and proud because I could feel the others watching me. As we walked along, I realized that it was because of Ringo that I'd spoken out. I'd stood up for him where I might not have stood up for myself.

Our first ride was a good one. Ringo was spirited and quick, but I kept my balance and sat my saddle. I wanted the girls to see how well I could ride when I was on a real horse. As it turned out, we made the drill team.

The most amazing thing about my relationship with Ringo was that in the thirty years I rode him, I fell off only once. It was early on when I was teaching him to hunt, and he refused a jump. But that was the only time. That's unheard of, considering how long we were together and how often I rode him. And it wasn't just due to my horsemanship. Such a thing only happens when the horse makes an effort to protect the rider. That was the magic, the reason I believed Ringo was my guardian angel.

I was a girl who couldn't depend on her family for support. Girls are supposed to have their families; and when they don't, some of them, the lucky ones, find outside angels to help them. And I found Ringo. I sort of created him, and then he created me. He came to me out of my need, and I appeared for him out of his. I've always thought we both were aware of it, even as it was happening.

My relationship with Ringo came from a place, a neediness that few people ever experience. And because of our relationship—because we acknowledged the neediness and actually did something about it, I understood things about life that other people don't understand. Ringo and I were able to help each other because we were completely open and accepting of one another. Very few people achieve such closeness, such a union, because very few people are willing to open up—to themselves, never mind someone else.

Ringo and I merged more than ever that year. I still hung around with Lynn, but otherwise I wasn't very social. I seldom spoke unless spoken to, and most people didn't reach out to me.

My foot had started rolling over again, so my mother made another appointment to see Dr. Wilson. I knew what that meant. I'd assumed I'd had my last major surgery, but I understood that I was an experiment for Dr. Wilson and that his ankle fusion hadn't worked as well as he'd hoped. I could also feel the tendons in the inside of my ankle tightening, pulling my foot over. In addition to those problems, my toes needed fixing.

Dr. Wilson was more serious this time. When I walked up and down the hall, I could feel the roll. I had on flats that I'd been able to wear since my ankle fusion, but it had become increasingly more difficult to keep them on. "It's the tendons," Dr. Wilson explained to my mother. "They're pulling the foot over. There's no other explanation because the ankle is solid."

"So?" my mother replied. "What's the next step?"

"I believe a tendon graft may do the trick. The tendon on the lower inside of the leg is pulling that ankle over. I want to take out some of the tendon on the outside of the leg and use it to lengthen the tendon on the inside so the pull will be even."

He spoke with conviction, but he wasn't convincing me. An operation meant I'd miss more school, which appealed to me, but it also meant I'd be separated from Ringo. Dr. Wilson said it couldn't wait until summer because my foot was rolling so badly. I was worried about Ringo, how he'd manage and behave with the likes of Ms. Keener if he couldn't see me every day.

I went back to school to wait for my surgery date. Mother talked with Ms. Johndroe. My marks were good enough so that Ms. Johndroe thought I could keep up. She said my teachers would get together and figure it out. I asked Lynn and Prim Bullock to watch out for Ringo, and they said they would. The good news was that I'd be away from Meg, Dudley, and their buddies, who still delighted in teasing me. They thought they were *so* cool, even though they made me want to barf. I was glad I hadn't told Meg about Ringo being related to one of her horses. It gave me something to look forward to.

It was a difficult time for my family. The previous spring, believing the three children would be away at school the following fall, Mom and Dad had rented an apartment in New York. But then Murray got himself suspended from college and, as he was about to go in the army, had a nervous breakdown. Mom and Dad had him committed to Payne Whitney in Manhattan. So it ended up that Dad was working in New York, Mom was manning the fort, and Murray and I were in separate hospitals. Dindy was in college in Connecticut, a three-hour train ride away.

Murray had slit his wrists. I found out about it when I called home. Mom told me the police had come to the house and taken him away in a straitjacket. She said it was my father's fault. My reaction was, cripes, first she horrifies me; then she makes me sad by blaming it on Dad. The whole thing disgusted me. As far as I was concerned, it was her cold, overbearing nature that had been the major factor in poor Murray's breakdown. She had the same attitude toward Murray that she had toward me, the same attitude that had kept me at House in the Pines. No one else's feelings mattered; our job was to do what pleased her. And if you didn't, it was as if she was neatening her house, and you were just another tchatchka. The whole thing made me withdraw from my family and pour my energy into my relationship with Ringo.

New Friends

Dr. Wilson insisted that I be on the children's floor this time. I didn't want to, but I didn't argue. I was put in a big room with three girls. They were very friendly. When I entered the room, each one introduced herself, and the two who were reasonably mobile—one on crutches, the other in a wheelchair—came forward to greet me.

The only name I remember was of the girl who could barely move. Her name was Kathy. Whereas the other girls were roaming around the room, chattering and giggling, Kathy sat quietly in her bed. She was small and had beautiful shoulder-length hair, which was the darkest blue-black I'd ever seen. All three girls were nice and forthright, but Kathy was somehow the purest. Maybe it was that she was injured more severely than the others, and thus in greater pain. Or perhaps it was her appearance. Whereas the others had scraggly blond hair and teenage pimples, Kathy had lustrous hair and clear, fresh skin.

All three girls had polio and had endured numerous operations. Their legs were covered with scars. They were hoping to be able to walk one day, but it wasn't sure that they would. The two girls who could get around gathered at my bed as Mom unpacked my things. They were different somehow, like me I suppose.

"Welcome to our humble abode," one of them said with a grin. The other girl shook my hand. I smiled at her then turned to acknowledge Kathy. Her beauty drew me to her.

"I'm Kathy, Sarah," she said, holding up her hand. When I took it, she held on for a moment.

"Hi," I said. "How did you all know my name?"

"We asked," they said, laughing, and I was immediately caught up in their good spirits. It was clear that they'd been through a lot. There had been no real childhood for them, only the harsh, minute-to-minute reality of pain and frustration. Most people would have been overwhelmed by what they'd been through, yet they were able to laugh about it. I guess you could say they'd grown up fast.

114

We spent that first afternoon talking about their operations, hopes, and dreams. In their dreams, they imagined themselves standing straight and tall in long gowns, greeting people in receiving lines, or being announced, then gliding down a long staircase on their father's arm. One imagined a handsome prince who would come forth and invite her to dance and how she'd walk to the dance floor with him, then glide and twirl the night away.

"What color would your dress be, Kathy," I asked, wanting to hear more.

"Maybe blue, and how about you?" The others laughed at her rhyme.

"Yellow for me," I replied. "Yellow has always been my favorite color."

"Why is that?" one of the other girls asked. She was sitting on my bed with me. The other girl was in her wheelchair between my bed and Kathy's.

I knew why I liked yellow, but I'd never shared it with anyone. It was a simple thing, but I'd not talked about it with friends, not even Lynn. But my friends weren't like these girls. My friends hadn't had to dream about walking down a flight of stairs in their favorite dress. I'd dreamed about it plenty of times. In my dream, I wore high heels and was happier than I'd ever been. "I like yellow because it's a happy color," I answered.

"Yeah," the girl in the wheelchair said.

"With your dark hair, you'd look good in yellow," the one on my bed said.

"You really think so?"

"Oh yeah," they said together.

We looked at each other. "Do you guys always say the same thing at the same time like that?" I asked, laughing.

"It's because we've been in this room together for so long," Kathy replied. They all nodded, and the four of us laughed together.

I'd gotten so caught up in their good spirits, I hadn't noticed that Mom had left the room. When Kathy saw me looking around, she said, "She'll be back. She probably went to talk to your doctor." When I looked at Kathy and she looked back at me, I had the sense that she understood a lot. To understand things the way she did, she had to be open to the truth, and it takes great courage to be open to the truth when you're so badly crippled. Perhaps that was it, that Kathy was unusually open because she was so brave. We all knew the reality of our situations. There was no time for pretending. Nor was there any time for competition, for who was prettier or had the best figure. Those issues didn't even exist. We had a higher priority. It was to accept exactly what was going on, be completely honest about it, and laugh as much as possible. Kathy, by her example, was showing us the way.

It was what had been missing from my life. Since Nanny, Ringo had been my only source of total acceptance. But now, for a short time, these girls were completely open to me, inviting me to be my own true self. They operated on the principle of "what you see is what you get," so "take me or leave me." In that sense, they were the exact opposite of the foolish girls at school.

Or my family. For me, the saddest part of my disability was my family. No one in my family, neither my brother nor sister, nor mother nor father, could accept me as I was. My mother saw that I got along with the three girls in my room, but she didn't understand why. And she couldn't join in and laugh with us. She could smile and be friendly, but she couldn't really let go. She had to remain standoffish, above it all.

Kathy picked up on it. That night, when the other two girls went off to watch a movie, Kathy and I stayed behind. Kathy had brought what seemed like her entire bedroom with her, including her stereo. We listened to some of her records. I was drifting in and out of sleep, and Kathy was listening to her music, so we didn't talk much. I had visions of being in the ocean with Ringo, clinging to his mane as his strong, warm body swam next to me.

I awoke the next morning to be given a sedative; then, they cleaned me up and took me to the operating room. I recognized the sensation of the flashing lights overhead in the ceiling of the hallway, like streetlights going past, and again felt like I was entering some kind of twilight zone. People's voices grew farther and farther away, and then I couldn't hear anything at all.

When I awoke, back in my room, there was violin music playing. Kathy had put a record on for me and was peering in through the bars on my bed, watching and waiting for me to wake up.

"Listen," she said when I opened my eyes. "Isn't this beautiful? If you really listen, the music will replace your pain." I looked at her. She smiled and took my hand. She'd made the Herculean effort to get out of bed, into her wheelchair and across the room to sit next to my bed. The music did seem to relax my leg. Or maybe it was the combination of the music and her holding my hand.

Kathy was another angel who'd come to help me. Like Nanny and Ringo, she completely accepted me. Plus we had the kinship of our trials and the ways we dealt with them. She reminded me that I was disabled, but I could accept it from her because she understood that having a disability meant that you had a special way of looking at the world. She and my other roommates had that same way of looking at the world. It was a gift, that detachment. It enabled us to transcend our trials, to the point where we could even laugh at ourselves.

We cared about the simple things, the simple day-to-day tasks, because they were what we had to deal with. We couldn't overlook or avoid things; we couldn't skip steps. The simple tasks were there, staring you in the face, saying, "Deal with me, deal with me," and you had to. Things like Kathy getting herself over to my bedside. There was no time for such things as who was smarter or funnier or prettier. It wasn't important what so-and-so might think of my limp. Those things were unimportant, a waste of time. When I thought about going back to the superficiality of House in the Pines, it made me want to bolt. My time with Kathy and the others just reinforced how misunderstood I was, and how poisonous it was for my spirit.

Over the next few days, I had an interesting conversation with Kathy. It was the kind you go in and out of over time. It started out by our agreeing that our handicaps kept our common sense intact. The logistics of trying to get ourselves around physically seemed to help us figure our lives out. As we talked, I began to feel a deeper, no-nonsense self emerging. It was a good self and I respected it. In addition, I sensed that the process of affirming this newly discovered part of me was affirming of all of me.

I talked about Ringo; and as I did, I realized that he also had that inner self, that no-nonsense core. In opening to him, I was opening to his essential strength; and as I opened to his strength, I also opened to my own. I had the sense that he was aware of all that. He couldn't speak, of course, at least not my language, and he probably wouldn't have explained it that way if he could; but I felt he appreciated what I was learning from him. The feeling comforted me, and I promised myself that I'd always stay the way I was with Ringo. I'd go to him and into myself, and together, we'd survive House in the Pines and everything else life presented.

As I was thinking about these things, I was also telling Kathy about the school and how the kids and teachers were constantly pointing out my disabilities. It was a great help, a great unburdening to be able to talk with her that way.

"Why don't your parents take you out of that school?" Kathy asked me one afternoon when the four of us were together in our room.

"My mother says there's no place else to go." I looked around at their faces. All three had expressions of disbelief.

"Oh come *on*, Sarah, you don't really believe that, do you?" one of the blond girls asked. I was in bed, and she was slumping on her crutches next to my bed.

Kathy turned her wheelchair around so that she was facing me head-on and proceeded to tell me about her school and how everyone treated her just fine. It was a private school, a good one, I guess, because she loved it.

As I listened to the girls, my doubts about my mother resurfaced. The intuitive part of me that I was just discovering was telling me it was another wake-up call. If my brother had tried to commit suicide, maybe Mom wasn't doing all she could for her children. Maybe it was simply easier for her to leave me where I was. As I thought it, I came to accept the idea as true. I also knew that I'd gone along with her habit of not accepting a daughter with cerebral palsy. I'd adopted her attitude that it was socially *in*correct. But this new take on things was difficult for me because I was young, and a part of me still needed to believe my family loved me. They love me, I reasoned; it's just that, unlike Ringo's, their love was conditional.

"My mother felt she was lucky to get me in anywhere . . . ," I heard myself say, "because a lot of cerebral palsy children are thought to be retarded." That was it: Mom thought I was retarded. I was startled to hear myself blurt it out. In some ways, the three of them were better off than I was. They had a known disease that cripples, plain and simple, but there was no epilepsy involved, no spasms that make you look retarded.

The conversation ended with everyone agreeing that we felt normal the way we were because, in my case, I'd been born with my disability, and in theirs, they'd forgotten what it was like not to be disabled. One slight problem for me was that little was known about cerebral palsy, so I didn't know what to expect. But it wasn't a big problem because I didn't spend a lot of time thinking about the future. Most of the time, I was too concerned with right now to worry about later.

When I returned to school, I lost touch with my hospital roommates. If you're out there and read this, you girls, now women, know that I remember our time together. It meant the world to me.

I had to deal with a cast at school, getting around and managing snow and ice, but the healing wasn't as bad as before because there were no bones involved, which meant I went straight to the smaller walking cast. Wearing walking casts had become second nature by then. I could almost dance in them.

I made my parents drive me by the pastures and barn before they left for home. Ringo was in one of the fields; and when I got out and called to him, his head shot up, ears pointing and eyes wide, and he tucked his bottom and sprinted over. When he got to me, he searched my face, looking, listening, and sniffing. His whiskers tickled me when he checked me out. I patted his nose, rubbed his chin, and kissed him in my favorite spot, just behind the corner of his mouth. His breath, always different depending on the season and his diet, was fresh grass sweet, a welcome homecoming for my senses. After satisfying himself that I was really back and safe, he jerked away, squealing with glee, and kicked up clods of dirt as he high-stepped down the pasture.

Ms. Johndroe picked up where she'd left off, stifling me with her special treatment. And of course, my five tormentors picked up where they'd left off as well. Riding would get me out of my dorm and away from them all, but I had to wait. Lynn made an effort to stay close to me, but it wasn't always possible. I tried to stay in my room when she wasn't around.

One afternoon, some of the girls decided to take advantage of the fact that I was alone. They came into my room, and two of them grabbed my arms and walked me backward onto the bed. On my back, I struggled, but it was useless.

They were laughing. "Look at you now, Ms. Johndroe's pet," one yelled in my ear.

"Got the pencils, Meg," Dudley hissed.

"Oh yes, I do," screeched Meg, holding them up for me to see.

My eyes widened. "No, don't!" I screamed. But I couldn't stop them. While the two who'd grabbed me held me down, two others shoved the pencils down inside my cast. The pencils hurt, but I could manage the pain. My greater concern was that the points might reopen the incision. I struggled so hard the sweat poured off me. Finally, using every ounce of strength I could muster, I sat up, leaned toward one girl, and bit her on the arm. When she jerked back, I leaned the other way and bit another girl. Screeching and at bay, they withdrew. But the damage had been done. A heap on the floor, in shock and gasping for breath, I sobbed as I tried to jimmy each pencil up and out of my cast.

When I finally left my room, Tara was waiting for me in the hallway. "If you tell anyone, you're dead," she whispered.

There was one pencil I couldn't get. I could touch it, but it was wedged in, and I couldn't pry it out. After a day or so, during which I tried every chance I got and with increasing frustration, it had chafed the skin raw. When it became intolerable, I told Ms. Johndroe. I said I'd lost the pencil in the cast while trying to scratch my ankle with it. She seemed to believe me, but the school nurse couldn't get the pencil out either, so I ended up having to return to the hospital and get the cast replaced. When the people at the hospital cut the cast off, they saw all the pencil marks and scratches and immediately understood what had happened. They didn't speak to me about it, but one pursed her lips and said, "Hmmm." They cleaned and sterilized my entire ankle and foot before putting on the new cast.

I withdrew more than ever after that. One day, lonely for Ringo, I went down to his pasture and climbed up on him. I still had my cast on and wasn't supposed to be riding, but it was worth the risk to feel the sense of freedom I got just sitting on him. Ringo was the only one who could give me that feeling of independence during those difficult days. Without him I don't know if I could have made it through. He was the only thing, the only one I really cared about. I don't remember thinking about my mother and father, and certainly not my brother and sister. The teasing was getting to me.

I didn't dare tell anyone, even Lynn, how I'd been attacked or how horrifying it had been. I loved our room, and I tried to concentrate on making it nice, or on the special times I spent with Lynn and a few of the other girls. Along with Ringo, those little things enabled me to keep myself together. When I was alone, helpless and afraid, I became scattered or fragmented; but when I was with my friends or Ringo, I felt together or whole.

My parents gave me everything I wanted and a lot I didn't want. They'd given me Peanuts and Joe-Joe and Ringo, but they'd also given me braces and surgery and House in the Pines. That was the thing. To my mother's way of thinking, I had everything a girl could want. The problem was, my mother wasn't me, and she didn't see things the way I did.

One afternoon in our room, I was standing, staring into our closet at my clothes, and Lynn was sitting back on her bed, trying to talk me into trimming her hair again. Snapping the scissors in the air, she said, "Sarah, hel-lo." Her voice was high-pitched, both whiney and teasing.

I turned and looked at her. "Did you know that my mother got me an incredible charm bracelet?"

"A . . . what?" Lynn said, wondering what I was talking about.

"You know, a charm bracelet, with everything in your life on it?"

"Like what?" Lynn asked, sprawling across her bed.

I walked toward her, thumping the floor with my cast, and flopped down on her bed beside her. Pulling her pillow out from under her, I stuffed it under my arm, settled down on it, and stared up at the ceiling while imagining the bracelet.

"It's gold, and it has my dog, Fundy, on it. It also has some gold coins."

Lynn was staring at the ceiling with me as if the bracelet was up there. "Wow, that's cool," she said. "What else?"

"Well, the best part is Ringo. He's on it, with the date that I got him. And, oh yes, there's a tiny silver heart. I think it belonged to my grandmother or something."

"That's really neat," Lynn said, looking at me and smiling.

"Yeah, it is, isn't it?"

"Your parents are good about stuff like that. Look at your clothes for God's sake!"

It was true; I had beautiful things. It was Mom's thing.

Lynn held the scissors up in my face. "You promised."

"Yeah, yeah, I know. Give them to me." I'd been trimming Lynn's hair since the seventh grade. She sat up and turned around, and I got myself organized and started brushing her long brown hair. "Remember, if I do this, you have to hold my cast out of the water while I take a bath tonight."

"I know, I know." She laughed and gave me a cuff on the knee.

Hanging out in our room on quiet afternoons like that, we were like sisters, real family. My brother and sister weren't real. I talked about them to anyone who would listen as if they were real, but they weren't. In the things I said and the way I talked, I created a caring brother who discussed things with me and played with me and a sister who thought I was special. I made up stories about the times we spent together. The stories were true. The events really happened. They just didn't happen the way I related them. The interactions between Murray and Dindy and me, all the dialog and stuff, that was all made-up. Away from home, I had the perfect family, the one that went with all the beautiful clothes. The pretending was a big part of my life at House in the Pines. It kept me going, especially when I couldn't ride.

Ringo was the only thing I didn't make up. I didn't have to because he was real, and we were real and how we felt about each other was real. Ringo kept me grounded, kept me from spending too much time in fantasy land.

Meg continued to taunt me. I'd hear her, just within earshot, telling other girls that I was a loser, and so was my horse. When I finally told her that Ringo was related to her horse, I thought it would shut her up, maybe bring her down a few notches, but it didn't work out that way. She said it was ridiculous to think Ringo was related to her horse, and that I'd obviously made it up. We ended up yelling at each other. The problem was that she had her whole group supporting her, and they'd been to her farm, whereas I had only Lynn, who knew nothing.

I must say, though, after the incident with the pencils, Meg and her biddy buddies never laid a hand on me again. I think they knew they'd gone too far. We yelled at each other, and occasionally there might be a sneak shove, but that was the extent of it.

It seemed every time I tried to stand up for myself, the school would panic, and I'd end up in the infirmary. Meg never got sent anywhere. It wasn't fair, and it drove me crazy. It got so bad, sometimes I felt my head was going to burst. I'd literally sputter. As spring vacation drew closer, I was actually looking forward to going home.

A New School

Mother saw the change in me. It wasn't good. I was quiet and stayed by myself. Either that or I hung out with Ringo. I couldn't see much of Leslie because she was in public school, which was still in session; and besides, I didn't know any of her friends. My mother became so concerned that she started looking into other schools for me. Of course, she didn't tell me she was looking. At the end of summer vacation, when Ringo and I went back to House in the Pines, I assumed I'd stay there until I graduated.

I don't know why my parents were so secretive about it. Perhaps they didn't want me to get hurt if nothing worked out. But a few weeks later, when they picked me up to go home for a weekend, they told me they were actually taking me to Vermont to look at another school. I was so shocked I became hysterical. "What do you mean?" I demanded. "I'm going home for the weekend. You didn't tell me about this." I started crying. "I don't understand. What's going on?"

I finally got myself under control. "Okay," I said, staring straight ahead. The car was suddenly silent. But I couldn't let it go. I looked at Mom again and asked, "Why?" My voice cracked. "Why now? I don't understand." I didn't want them to send me to another school, one that might be even worse than House in the Pines. "If you're going to take me out of school, can't I live at home? Please?"

"No," my mother said, shaking her head emphatically. "That is out of the question."

"My grades are good enough," I pleaded.

"They are good, Sarah, but we've been through this. It's just not possible."

I didn't have the energy to rehash that old argument. An appointment had been made for me to have an interview at the Woodstock Country School, and we weren't going to miss it. I looked at my father, but he wouldn't look back or even say anything. It was a two-hour ride to Vermont, and I resigned myself to spending the time staring out the window.

"This school is coed, Sarah," Mom said after a while. "That might be kind of fun." She smiled at me in the rear view mirror. But I had nothing to say. I was in my shutdown mode, the state in which I'd been spending more and more of my time the past year. Well, except when I was with Ringo. I felt lost and afraid most of the time, and Ringo was the only one who could snap me out of it. When he wasn't around, looking me in the eyes questioningly or shoving me with his nose, I could lose it pretty easily.

When we finally entered the drive at Woodstock, the first person I saw was a boy with hair down to his shoulders. He was wearing blue jeans and what my friends and I called stomp boots. I could barely believe my eyes. A girl caught up to the boy, and together they entered the main building. The girl was also wearing jeans, but hers had gaping, ragged holes in them. What kind of place was this? My mother was willing to send me to a school where the kids looked like this? It was the opposite of where I'd been. At House in the Pines, we had to wear skirts and keep our bangs above our eyebrows.

I stepped out of the car somewhat sheepishly. I'd recently had my cast removed, and my leg was stiff, and it all made me self-conscious. The main building was a renovated old barn, quite a change from the grand house with pillared entrance at House in the Pines. I didn't know what to make of it all, but my heart was racing.

We sat down in the waiting area. Other students came into the building or down the hall and past us on their way out. I studied their faces in an effort to get a sense of the place. When some looked back at me, checking out the newcomer, I looked down. My parents and I didn't say a word.

After a while, a big man with a kind but wrinkled face came down the hall and into the waiting area. "Hello, Mr. and Mrs. Howell," he said, "I'm David Bailey, the headmaster. Sorry to keep you waiting." My parents stood up, and he shook their hands; then my mother sat down again. The time was coming when he was going to look at me.

Another man joined us, and Mr. Bailey introduced him as Peter Sauer, head of Admissions. The two of them looked at me in my chair and, seeing that I was too shy to get up, knelt down on either side of me. Mr. Bailey shook my hand and then continued to hold it in his large, bony hands. My head down, I froze. I couldn't bring myself to look at him. Mr. Sauer crouched down on the other side of me, but I was determined not to talk. I wanted Mr. Bailey to let go of my hand.

Mr. Bailey told me that he and Mr. Sauer knew about the treatment I'd received at House in the Pines. Then, Mr. Sauer added that he had asked Ms. Johndroe for my school records, not realizing that she didn't know I was looking at other schools, and that she had gotten angry—"out of control" was his term. He said he'd called her a second time for my records, but she still hadn't sent them; and when he'd called a third time, she'd said they'd been lost.

"I guess Ms. Johndroe feels that if she can't have Sarah at House in the Pines, she won't let her go anywhere else," Mr. Sauer said to my parents. They were shocked, of course. So was I, and frightened too.

"You should have told her, Mom," I said. They were the first words I'd spoken, and everyone stared at me. I looked around. What was going to happen to me? I couldn't help it, I started to cry.

Mr. Bailey, who'd gotten up by then, saw how upset I was and lowered himself back down next to me. Mr. Sauer reached out to touch my hand, but I pulled it away. "None of this is your fault, Sarah," Mr. Bailey said. "Ms. Johndroe is not a well woman, and your parents and I are going to see that you are removed from that school."

"You don't have to remove me. I can't go back," I sobbed.

"It's all right, Sarah," Mr. Bailey said with a firm but gentle voice. "The decision has been made to accept you here at Woodstock without your records."

I could tell Mom was pleased. She straightened herself out and started in with her usual social niceties. But she was also uncomfortable. After all, she'd put her daughter in the hands of a crazy headmistress, and Mr. Sauer had exposed the fact. I was gratified to hear the truth, but at the same time, I couldn't help but wonder why she'd waited so long to find another school.

"Sarah, from now on, please call us Peter and David," Mr. Bailey said. "We're on a first-name basis here."

Mom told them about Ringo and me. When he heard the story, David looked at Peter and said, "There's the answer. That horse is what's kept Sarah going."

"Absolutely," said Peter.

"Let's get on this right away," David said to Peter. "So Sarah and Ringo can come next fall."

They had moved away from me in their conversation, but I listened to every word. *All right,* I thought, *but if you think I'm going to trust you guys, you're nuts.* Before we left, they showed us around the campus. David continued to try to make conversation with me, but I wouldn't play. With all that had gone on that day, I didn't feel I could trust anyone but Ringo.

In what seemed a last effort to break the ice, David said that no one would know I had cerebral palsy unless I told them. We were standing in the driveway, about to leave. When he reached over to pat my shoulder reassuringly, I pulled away.

House in the Pines had done its damage to me, but at least I knew my enemies. Even though it was awful, I'd found a way to survive. I didn't want to be thrown into a situation where I didn't know anyone because it was the unknown that was the real enemy. Compared to the unknown of Woodstock, I was safe at House in the Pines.

I don't know if I'll ever be able to forgive my mother for leaving me in Ms. Johndroe's hands all that time. I do know I'll always live with the memories. The worst ones were the things that happened when I had my seizures and was dragged through the night to the infirmary before they'd even stopped. I was in the hands of people who didn't really care about me, didn't know what was going on, and could easily have caused me even more brain damage.

As the year at House in the Pines came to an end, word got around that I was leaving. Lynn was disappointed, but I was too numb to think about her. I had no feelings, except for Ringo. He was the only thing that stirred me in any way. I was shut down—in limbo.

Ringo is my only memory of that spring. Talking was no longer part of my life. I had few friends. The only time I laughed was when I was with Ringo. Only Ms. Pierce praised me for my improved grades. Thanks to Ms. Johndroe, most of my peers and teachers put me down. I lost all my confidence. When people looked at me, I felt they saw me as incompetent, unable to do the things they could do. Except for Ringo. He thought I was the sun and moon together.

When I went home for the summer, Mom tried to be positive about the new school. She talked about how, because the school was a working farm in the country and more relaxed than House in the Pines, I might find it easier opening to people. I tried not to listen to her because I didn't want to think about going away again, especially to a new and unknown place. So instead of thinking about it, I focused all my energy and attention on Ringo. We took long rides, lay around through steamy summer days, or went to the beach to swim and watch the sunset. Sometimes, when I hosed him down, he'd shake and get me wet. Or the stream of water would tickle him and he'd jump around and kick up his heels. At the beach, walking next to him at water's edge, I occasionally lost my balance and would fall against his warm, solid body. He was always there, always gentle and supportive, although he wasn't above a little horseplay. In all the times he nudged me with his nose, and he could really push me around, I don't recall ever being knocked down. He was a happy guy. I could almost hear him laughing as he plopped his front hooves down into the water and splashed through the surf.

Sometimes when we were alone and I could let him run free, he'd tear around and show off. "Hey, wait for me!" I'd yell, and he'd stop dead in his tracks, the lead rope hanging down from his halter and the waves splashing against his legs. He never ran off. He'd gallop away, but then he'd stop and look back at me and twist his head in a playful way as if to say, "Come on, let's GO!" And I'd run to catch up, and I might say, "Thanks for waiting, old pal, old buddy." And he'd sniff my face, and I'd blow a puff of air up his nose. He liked that a lot. I think he was talking to me, and when I blew up his nose, I was talking back. Then I'd grab the lead line, and we'd go off to the dunes when I could get back up on him. He knew the routine. He'd stand next to a cut in a dune, and I'd get above him and jump on his back. When we went to the beach, I almost always rode bareback with nothing but his halter and a lead line as a rein. That way, I didn't have to saddle-soap the tack so often.

That summer confirmed how close Ringo and I were. I came to feel he'd be with me no matter what, even if we were separated or he died. He didn't just help me go on, he forced me to. Every moment I was with him, he sparked and affirmed the part of me that people were trying to crush. When we'd finally gotten home from school, I'd been hanging by a thread emotionally. He knew it, he could just tell, and he knew exactly what I needed in order to get through it. Many times when I was riding or we were playing, I'd pause and stare off into the distance, not thinking about anything, just spacing out. For a few seconds or minutes, I'd be without care. It was a huge relief. I didn't have to be the little girl, Little Sarah. Oh my god! I'd forgotten that escape; it's been so long since I've been there. But I'm feeling it again as I write this. It's beautiful, as if I'm no one, no thing, nothing. *I* ceases to exist, and because she doesn't, there's no longer anything to worry about.

That space or state of mind that I got into with Ringo was an emotional resting place. It's strange to be writing about it, to be putting the sensation into words. In that state of all eyes and no Is, I'd sometimes sing. Singing comforted me. My one claim to fame at House in the Pines had been that I'd made the school chorus.

My mother tried to encourage me musically. At one point, when I was in junior high back in Connecticut, she bought me a dulcimer. It was after I sang a solo in a school concert. I got a standing ovation when I sang the gospel hymn "Nobody Knows the Trouble I've Seen."

Mom jumped on the idea that I might have a talent and took me to see Joan Ritchie, the folk singer. We went to Ritchie's home, and she introduced us to her grandfather who'd made my dulcimer. He played it for us, with a bamboo stick pressed on the chords, then strummed it with a turkey feather. Mom thought my left hand might be able to hold the bamboo stick and move up and down the arm of the dulcimer without too much trouble. She may have been right, but I was too busy surviving to take up a musical instrument. I put the dulcimer in my closet and left it there.

At any rate, I liked remembering the night I sang the solo while walking the beach with Ringo. I liked remembering how the audience all stood up and clapped for me, and how I'd felt accepted. It was the same way I felt on the beach, singing with Ringo—perfectly normal. But the instant I went back to the house, I felt different and alone again.

Summer flew by like a dream in the night, and before I knew it, I was packing my bags to go to Woodstock. I was very much in my own world. I don't remember if I visited Lynn that summer. I think I saw a little bit of my pal, Leslie; but she had other friends whom she'd known longer than me, plus the novelty of my having a horse had worn off.

In an effort to lift my spirits, my mother came up with an idea for some fun. She had a friend, Mrs. Moore, who owned a massive Rolls Royce. So Mom decided that Mrs. Moore would drive us up to Woodstock, and I'd wear blue jeans and an old T-shirt, and on the way, we'd pay one last visit to House in the Pines.

"Mom, are you for real?" I asked. "So we get there, then what?"

"Well, let's see. How about this: You get out of the car and light up a cigarette." I had taken up smoking that summer; it was forbidden at House in the Pines. "We'll time our arrival to coincide with mail call when everyone's milling around outside."

I was incredulous. Was this *my* mother talking? "What will Mrs. Moore think?" I was warming to the idea.

"I won't tell her everything. I'm just going to say that you want to see your friend, Lynn." There was a twinkle in her eye and mischief in her voice.

I was sitting on the bed with a folded pair of pants in my hands. Mom was standing in front of me waiting for my decision.

"Let's do it," I hissed, conspiratorially. And with that, I got up and looked for the worst pair of blue jeans I could find, a pair like the ones I'd seen on the girl at Woodstock. This was good, a good plan. I pulled on the jeans and stood in front of the mirror. Turning to the side, I smacked myself on the butt and screeched, "Yes! Perfect!"

When the day came, we started off early to make sure we got to House in the Pines for mail call. Mrs. Moore and Mom carried on a conversation in the front while I sat in the back clutching my flip-top box of Marlboros. House in the Pines had been in session for a week, so I knew there'd be lots of mail from parents, especially those who'd just dropped their kids off for their first time away from home. And lots of mail meant lots of girls standing around reading it.

The ride seemed to take forever. I spent some of the time looking out the window or playing with my cigarettes, but then I started to watch my mom as she interacted with her supposed friend, Mrs. Moore. I couldn't believe what a schemer Mom was. It wasn't like her to take revenge against an establishment institution like that. In fact, the whole thing was a little freaky. But as we rode along, I began to realize that bad things had happened to me at House in the Pines. Bad things had been done to me; I actually had been abused. Mother's little plan was her way of helping me get past it. While she couldn't admit to making any mistakes, herself, she could blame the school. Well, half a loaf is better than no loaf at all.

As we approached the school, my heart started beating faster, and I could feel the familiar ache starting up in the back of my eyes. I was squeezing the Marlboro pack, all but crushing it. How was I going to survive in another school? I hoped Ringo would arrive at Woodstock at the same time we did. I leaned forward to ask my mother about her arrangements for him.

She reached back and patted my hand. "Everything's under control. Ringo will be dropped off at the barn. Bruce Fairweather said he'd be there to receive him. So he'll be settled in his new stall by the time we arrive."

Bruce and Emily Fairweather ran the barn and riding program. We'd met them during our visit.

"Well, here we are," announced Mrs. Moore as she drove onto the House in the Pines campus. "Looking forward to seeing your friend, Sarah?"

My heart was in my throat. It was weird being back, especially since I wasn't staying. I'd spent four years of my life there, but in a few minutes, it would all be over for good.

"Answer Mrs. Moore, dear," my mother said.

"Oh yes, Mrs. Moore, I am."

I showed Mrs. Moore how to get to the parking lot beside the main house; and sure enough, as we pulled in, there was a crowd of students milling about. Suddenly, for a brief second, I wished I was with Mom and Dad in our car instead of with Mom and Mrs. Moore in that big Rolls Royce.

Mrs. Moore turned in her seat and peered at me through her half-glasses. Her eyes were an imperious ice blue. My mother and she had been college roommates, so I'd been seeing her at our house for years. She walked with a cane due to a bad hip. She was a well-dressed woman with silver hair and pleasant enough, I suppose; but I found her frightening, especially when Mom and I were conspiring behind her back. I knew she wouldn't approve.

I sat for a moment, not knowing what to do. "Well?" asked Mrs. Moore. "How do we find your friend?"

"Hattie, there's something Sarah must do first," Mom said. "Go ahead, dear, do your thing." She waved me out of the car.

I climbed out of the Rolls, paused until everyone saw me then took out a cigarette and lit up, puffing deeply to get it going. I wanted to look as relaxed as possible, but it wasn't easy what with Mrs. Moore complaining. "Jane," she said critically, "how can you let her do this? It's not right. I don't want to be a part of this."

"You're not a part of it, Hattie," Mom replied. "This is something that Sarah wants to do, and only she and I know why."

Mom was right. It was something I *had* to do. I called to Prim who was towering over the others, then leaned against the car in my torn blue jeans and crumpled T-shirt. I was a little cold, but I wanted to give them the full effect. Prim looked over, wasn't sure who she was seeing at first, then did a double take.

"My god, it's Sarah!" she screamed.

"What has she got *on*?" someone asked.

Meg stepped forward, staring at me. I took another long drag, blew smoke at her, and waved. The satisfaction was exquisite.

Prim ran toward me and was immediately followed by others. They went right past Meg, bumping into her as they came. Ms. Cushie, the teacher who called the names for mail call, looked as if she was seeing a ghost.

Prim hugged me, and before I knew it, I was answering a million questions. "You can wear anything you want there? And smoke?" she asked, touching my clothes in disbelief.

I drew back against the Rolls, took another drag, and smiled. "That's right. You should see the place. It's beautiful. And there are boys, and some of them are extremely cute, and you can call the teachers by their first names."

"Unreal!" someone exclaimed.

Meg had come over and pushed her way to the front. "I never heard of such a place."

I took another drag on my cigarette even though it was beginning to make me sick. "Yeah, well, believe it, Meg, because it's true. I'm on my way there right now."

Unable to come up with a good response, she could only shake her head.

"But you know what the best part is?" I said, going after her. "The best part is that I won't have to look at your piggy little face anymore." I started to laugh. The group oohed and aahed and twittered. I was willing to say anything because I was safe; and I knew that finally, after all the teasing and torture, I would never have to deal with this snobby lamebrain again. At last I was free of her and her little band of nasties. She turned on her heel and walked away. I don't think anyone at the school had ever talked to her like that, and there was absolutely nothing she could do about it.

The others moved in closer. In the distance, I saw Lynn come out of the study hall. She started over, and I put out my cigarette and made my way through the group to meet her. We hugged.

"Why?" she asked. "Why did you leave?" I could see that she was on the verge of tears.

"I had to, Lynn." I was feeling sad, too. I couldn't believe I was leaving my sweet friend, forever probably. I could tell she didn't understand, but I was in no shape to explain it, certainly not in front of all those people.

Ms. Cushie came over. "This is not fair to the girls," she said, clearly irritated. "What are you doing here like this?" She was Russian and had difficulty with her English. "You know smoking isn't permitted on campus."

"But I'm no longer a student here," I replied.

"I know that, but it's a shame to see you end your time here this way. It's . . . cheap." And with that, she turned and walked away.

When I turned back, expecting to continue talking to Lynn, she was gone too. She probably felt betrayed. And maybe I did betray her a little. It made me sad. As things turned out, I wouldn't hear from Lynn again until I received a wedding invitation from her some years later.

The group was being called in for lunch. None of the teachers had come over to say hello; but suddenly, out of nowhere, Ms. Johndroe appeared. She came up and stopped and gave me a cold stare. When Mom saw her, she got out of the car and came around to her. In a gesture of conciliation, Mom reached out to touch Ms. Johndroe's arm, but Ms. Johndroe stepped back as if afraid of the touch. Mom was going to say something, but I guess she decided against it. Certainly Ms. Johndroe wasn't going to take the lead. She turned without saying anything and continued on to the dining room. It was the last time I ever saw her, too.

Prim broke away from the group and came back. She still had that friendly, beautiful face that I'd first seen in the study hall four years before. She put her hand on my shoulder. "Great to see you, Sarah." She'd been brave to come back for a final good-bye, and I could feel her sincerity. "You're lucky you're getting out of here. I hope I survive this place." She smiled.

"You will," I reassured her. "You're strong, Prim."

"So they really let you smoke at this school?" she asked, devilishly.

I nodded.

"Cool."

"Prim!" called Ms. Cushie. "You are to come along immediately, young lady, or there will be tardy marks in store for you!" And with that, Prim gave me a quick, awkward hug and set off to join the others.

Alone, I turned back to the car. Without thinking, I reached my arms up and looked up into the sky. The tops of the tall pines were swaying gently in the breeze. I turned a full circle then another, arms out and head back, taking in the clouds. I was no longer part of House in the Pines. I was rid of Meg, but I'd also lost my friend, Lynn. Where did I belong?

Who wanted me? Anyone? Home? No, no one wanted me at home. My new school? Maybe.

Being on the campus and seeing the girls tipped me into a combination of sadness and anxiety. I knew the school, the people and the rules. As bad as things were, it was all known and understood. What was going to happen to me? I wanted to sink deep inside myself where no one could find me, where I'd be safe. The idea soothed me. Yeah, and I'd only come out for Ringo because Ringo never stared at me critically or spoke harshly. If I only came out for Ringo, I wouldn't have to figure out who my enemies were. I wouldn't get caught off guard. And I wouldn't be alone in there either—at least not the way I was alone with other people.

Ringo knew what it was like to be starved and neglected. We were both starving when we met. We'd had to learn to take nourishment from each other. I had few words for him at first. We just had a feeling for each other, a faint rhythm or harmony between us. For some reason, we cared about each other and each other's pain. We took care of each other to make each other feel better. I wasn't a person to him. I was more like another horse. Except that I could take care of him. He could look after me like a stallion watching over his mare, yet at the same time, I was the one who brought the food and care to him.

"Sarah," Mom said sharply.

"What?" I stopped and faced her.

"Come now. Get in the car. We have to go."

"Oh, right. We have to go." I mimicked her then laughed. "Did you see their faces, Mom? It was great, wasn't it?"

"Yes, it was, dear."

I got into the back seat and went deep inside and remained there for the rest of the trip. The scenery went by like flash cards, and I got lost in the motion. Who was I now? I rested my head against the window and looked down at my lap. I could feel my heart beating. *I must be alive*, I thought. Where was my friend, Lynn? Where had she gone? I was too numb to cry. I wanted to sink even further into myself where no one would find me. Was it safe there? I didn't know, but I was going there anyway.

Before I knew it, we were pulling into the Woodstock School. It was 1965, and I was to be a junior. The car stopped at the main building. I looked at the building, but I didn't want to go in. Mom and Mrs. Moore got out of the car, glad to finally be there. "Come on, dear," Mom encouraged. "Let's check in."

I opened the door and got out without paying much attention. We entered the building. I was so removed that I was unaware of who was there or what we were doing. I just went through the motions. I think we signed in or registered or something.

I must have been standing in the way of traffic because a student bumped into me. "Hey, Jack," he called to another boy.

Seeing me, Jack said, "Look, a newbie!" He nodded a greeting and laughed as he went past. His long hair was flopping, and his boots were clomping.

"Can't talk," Jack said to the first boy, "but she's kind of cute."

"Don't mind them, Sarah," said the lady at the counter.

Mom grabbed my arm and pulled me up to the counter. "You're being spoken to, dear," she said as pleasantly as she could. I was amused by the fact that I was embarrassing her. I looked up at the lady who had a comforting expression.

"It's all right, Mrs. Howell," the lady said. "Everything's new, but they catch on fast."

Mrs. Moore had become anxious, what with her cane and the kids running up and down the hall, so she'd returned to the car. Mom was frustrated, but she was too focused on getting me settled to talk about it. I felt a little discombobulated, but it was all right because I'd withdrawn and was safe inside. I certainly wasn't going to ask anyone for anything. I'd just keep going through the motions until I could get back with Ringo.

We started to leave the main building. Out of the corner of my eye, I saw the lady walk over and talk to another adult. I sensed they were talking about me. Then I realized that the other adult was Peter Sauer. He held up his hand, cutting the woman short, and started toward us. "Mrs. Howell," he said somewhat excessively, "how nice to see you again."

"Oh yes, Mr. Sauer," Mom said, shaking his outstretched hand. "We're *so* glad to be here. We were just on our way up to the dorm."

"Of course," Peter replied. "May I have a word with Sarah before you go?" He put his arm around my shoulders and guided me away from her.

"Why, certainly," Mom answered, nonplussed.

I was out of it. When Peter stopped me then stood directly in front of me, all I could do was stare down at my feet.

"Sarah?" he asked gently, trying to get me to look up at him.

I didn't respond. I was concentrating on the patterns in the tiles on the floor.

He reached out and gently lifted my chin with the tips of his fingers. When I had no choice but to look him in the face, the forced intimacy made me gasp for air.

"It's okay," he reassured me. "Really, it's okay." But I didn't trust him. Too much fear. I could barely breathe.

"Sarah, I can't recall whether David and I talked to you about your cerebral palsy, but I want to make sure you understand this: No one in this school—and I mean not one student—is going to know about your handicap unless you tell him." He waited to see if the message was registering. I nodded ever so slightly. "The teachers know," he went on, "but that's as far as it goes." He studied my face. "Do you understand?" He sighed with the effort of it all. I looked away then back at him. "Go ahead up to your dorm now," he concluded. I didn't waste any time getting away from him.

"What did he say, dear?" Mom asked impatiently as we walked out to the car. I got into the back and shut my door. She got in the front. Turning to face me, she asked again, "Well, what did he say?" I looked at her. She wasn't going to let it go.

"I don't know, Mom. Welcome to the school, something like that."

"Could you be more precise?" She persisted.

"Mom, please, don't do this to me," I yelled, stomping my feet on the floor of the car.

"Jane, may we please simply go to the dorm," pleaded Mrs. Moore.

"Yes, Mom. I want to find Ringo." She turned to the front, and I sat back in my seat.

It was a short ride up past the playing field and through the pastures to the girl's dorm. The dorm, called Owen Moon House, had once been a private home. It had white clapboards and black shutters, was set in the side of the hill facing the road, and had elaborate gardens running down to a magnificent, stone amphitheater. Mrs. Moore drove up to the front door and Mom and I got out and went in.

In the front hall, we were met by the housemother, Chris Magreal. She was a round woman with dyed, reddish hair in a bun. My first reaction to her was that her dyed hair was in sharp contrast to her aged face. She had on a long, purple dress or skirt with a matching top, and a shawl around her shoulders. I thought her getup a little strange. Her hand outstretched, she welcomed us into the living room. It was long, with a couch at one end and various chairs scattered around—none of which matched. I realized that I'd seen the room on our initial visit but had completely forgotten it.

"Call me Chris," the woman said. Her eyes were beady, but not unkind.

For some reason, I thought about the living room at House in the Pines where I'd sat so many times with Ms. Johndroe. It had a grand fireplace, matching high-backed chairs, and long curtains that dressed the windows nicely. I looked for curtains in this room, but there were none. Didn't they have any money? What was the story with this place?

Chris made small talk with Mom. I didn't say anything. While I could tell it irritated her, Mom didn't dare comment on my silence.

"Please, I mean it, call me Chris," the woman said to Mom. I could tell Mom didn't approve of the first-name stuff. She wasn't having much success putting on that social smile of hers.

"I'll show you your room, Sarah, and then you can bring your things in." Chris turned and started for the door leading back to the students' quarters. Rearranging her shall, she led us up the stairs. Her movements seemed very deliberate. The floorboards were wide, and there were no rugs or any pictures on the walls. At the top of the stairs, the floors creaked so loudly that I wondered how long it would be before someone fell through.

To the right was a bathroom with a green linoleum floor. It was okay, I guess. The double doors on the left were to my room. Ms. Magreal grabbed the handle on each door and threw the doors open. I thought it was strange to have these kinds of doors in such a place. She acted as though this was to be the grand entrance to a ballroom. Slightly off balance, she stepped into the room.

Before us was a fairly large room with five beds in it. There was a beautiful long-haired, blond girl lying on one of the beds. She sat up as we walked toward her. She looked at me with the largest blue eyes I'd ever seen. My first thought was that she was a young Mia Farrow.

"Sarah, this is Stephanie Farrow," said Ms. Magreal. I nodded, and she gave me a half smile. I found out later that she was Mia Farrow's younger sister.

I stood there, feeling increasingly self-conscious. Stephanie wasn't very talkative. We stared at each other.

"All right," Ms. Magreal said as she led us through another door. The new room, my room, was a closed porch. We went down one step. My bed was on the left under a row of windows. The windows continued around three sides of the room. My roommate was on the right side of the room lying on her bed. She had taken the two dressers and put them back-to-back in the middle of the room. There was no question as to which side of the room was to be hers.

Ms. Magreal clearly understood what had been done, but didn't confront the girl. "Jennifer," she said, "this is your roommate, Sarah." Jennifer looked at me and said a cool hello. "This is Jennifer's second year at Woodstock," Ms. Magreal added by way of explanation.

"How nice," Mom said.

I didn't like the setup. The room was cold, and I had to open the door and go through a room with five people in it to get to the bathroom. And on top of everything else, it appeared I had the roommate from hell.

"Jane! Jane!" Mrs. Moore called up the stair well. "The man is here with Ringo. What should I tell him?"

I shot out of the room; raced down the stairs past poor, well-intended Mrs. Moore; and on out the front door. The trailer was in the drive. I went straight to its side door and opened it. Ringo stuck his head over the edge of his stall; gave me a muted whinny then, seeing the barn and smelling the other horses, raised his head and snorted. His eyes were bright and his ears up.

I was so glad to see him. His forelock was bunched over one eye. "Hi, boy, did you have a good trip?"

"He was good, young lady," said the hired man. "I think he knew he was coming to see you, he loaded so fast."

I gave the man a quick smile then put my full attention on Ringo. I was glad to see him. I hadn't realized how alone and anxious I'd been feeling until right then. After all, I didn't know who was going to be mean to me, who was going to be nice, how to defend against the former, or whether or not to trust the latter. Just making eye contact was too risky for me. They might laugh at me or shove me. It was better to look away and stay inside myself. But now that Ringo was here, I could look into his face and see love and acceptance. It gave me the courage to trust again, which was a huge relief.

Mom came out to find me hanging onto Ringo's neck while he nuzzled and smelled me. "You go ahead up to the barn with Ringo, Sarah," she said. "Mrs. Moore and I will get your things." I was happy to oblige. "The only time I see a light in that girl's eyes," Mom said to Mrs. Moore, "is when she's with her horse." She started for the car. Mrs. Moore watched Ringo and me for a moment then followed along.

I unloaded Ringo and led him up to the barn. He seemed happy to be there. Bruce and Emily Fairweather, the barn managers, came out and greeted me. They assigned Ringo to the first stall on the left. It was a nice old Vermont barn with wide floor planks and exposed beams. The tack room was half the size of the one at House in the Pines, and had no heat or fancy bridle holders, but it was certainly cozy. Ringo was alert, taking everything in, walking in circles in his stall, looking out the side window then hanging his head out into the aisle. Then it was back to sniffing the water bucket then another circle. I stayed in the stall with him, not wanting to leave. If I went out, I'd have to talk to Bruce or Emily. I didn't want to do that, but I knew I had to unload the trailer and put Ringo's gear away.

I left the stall as quietly as possible. Bruce and Emmy were down at the back of the barn. Out at the trailer, I started gathering gear.

"Here you go, miss." The nice man Mom had hired to trailer Ringo handed me the bridle. I smiled, picked up the saddle, and headed back to the tack room. As I entered the barn, the man slammed the back of the trailer. It startled me.

Bruce and Emily came into the tack room behind me. I was looking for a free bridle holder, but there wasn't one. "We can do something about that," Bruce said.

"I'll get another holder," Emily offered. "And I'll put his name on it, so no one else will use it."

I turned, almost dropping the saddle. "Here, let me take that," Bruce said. "It can go over here on this mount where you can reach it."

I stood there, not knowing what to do next.

"Sit," said Emily.

"What?" I heard myself say.

"Sit down," she repeated, sliding a rubber bucket toward me with her foot. I turned the bucket upside down. The rubber caved in a little with my weight. I cleared my throat.

"He's Morgan, all right," said Bruce.

I looked up at Bruce. He had that weathered outdoor look, plus he was handsome with a pleasant smile. His hair was short and sort of stood on end like a crew cut. His hands looked like they'd done a lot of hard work. Emily was next to him. Her hair was light brown, long, and braided down her back. Her eyes were blue, her skin soft and pale. They both wore jeans and jackets that had seen better days. There were no riding uniforms at this school. I pictured Ms. Keener as I looked at these two smiling faces before me. Did Ms. Keener ever smile? I had to stop thinking and respond to Bruce's observation. I looked at the floor. "Yes, he's Morgan. He's my friend."

"I can see that," Emily said. "He's wonderful." They seemed interested in Ringo, so I told them a little more about him.

"You can feed him before breakfast then come back and take him down to the pasture before classes if you want to," Bruce said.

"Really?" I said.

"Yes, the pasture across from the main building will be his."

Wow, his own pasture where I could go out and visit him between classes.

"Well, I'm going to head out." I got up and nodded good-bye. Outside, I thanked the driver. He said he'd stop and talk with Mom before starting home. Standing close to him, I realized how big he was. As he walked away, he cast a huge shadow on the ground. He turned and said, "Oh yes, the rest of your things are over there, miss." He pointed to the entrance to the barn. He was wearing both suspenders and a belt, but there was no way his pants would fit over his belly. He hoisted them up over his tiny bottom before climbing up into his truck. I suddenly wished that Ringo and I were going back to Rhode Island in the truck with the nice man.

When I'd put the rest of Ringo's stuff away, I walked over to his stall and pressed my forehead against the cool bars. He raised his head. He was munching a mouthful of hay. When he drew in close to sniff me, then exhaled, his breath was deliciously sweet.

Bruce and Emmy were behind me, watching. "Don't worry about him," Emmy said. "We'll be here."

Back at the dorm, I said good-bye to Mom and Mrs. Moore and watched them drive off. I couldn't cry because, basically, I couldn't feel. When the Rolls disappeared, I turned like a robot and went to my room to unpack.

More girls were arriving, and the dorm was busy. Jennifer got up and left the room without a word when I walked in. We never even looked at each other, which was fine with me as I wasn't into talking right then. I unpacked as fast I could and went back up to the barn. It was late in the day, and I wanted to feed Ringo myself. I'd brought our grain from Rhode Island—which he was used to—and I was worried that Bruce and Emily would fail to see it and feed him theirs.

"Hey there, take it easy," Bruce said when I wheeled around the corner into the barn. He had a bucket of grain in his hand. When he acknowledged that it was for Ringo, I grabbed the edge of the bucket and peered in. "Don't worry," he said, smiling, "it's your grain. We'll change him over to ours gradually over the next few days." I nodded. "Here," he said, shoving the bucket into my chest, "you feed him. You can feed him morning and night if it will make you feel better." Halfway down the barn, he turned and added, "Just be here early, before seven. Without fail."

I stood with the bucket still against my chest, waiting for some snide remark or put-down, but there wasn't one. Another stall door opened and shut. The horses were restless, and some kicked at their stall walls. Ringo slammed his entire body against his door in his impatience. It woke me out of my daze, and I took his grain into him. His head was in the bucket before I could get to the feed bin.

"Hungry, aren't you?" I said. Bruce dropped a pitchfork of hay outside the stall. I brought it in and shook it out in the corner opposite Ringo's feed bin.

"When you're through, I'll show you about the water," called Bruce. There were no other students in the barn. I left Ringo and went over to Bruce, and he handed me a bucket with Ringo's name on it. "Here, take this," he said. "It's his bucket, and no one else will use it. All the privately owned horses have the same."

"There are other students with their own horses?" I said.

"Oh, you finally feel like talking, eh?" Suddenly, I was embarrassed. "There are two horses arriving next week. They belong to a brother and sister who go here." He walked me over to the water tank and explained how we kept it full. I filled Ringo's bucket and put it in his stall. "You better get a move on," he called. "You don't want to be late for dinner." I didn't want to leave, and certainly didn't want to be with people. Bruce reminded me that I could come back to the barn after dinner.

The dining room, offices, and many of the classrooms were in the main building. Called Upwey, it was a huge converted barn which had once been the center of Upwey Farm. As I started down the path from the dorm, I could see that the quarter-mile walk down the hill would be a bit dicey in winter. It was all downhill, which meant uphill coming back. Tree roots stuck up like veins on the path, and I tripped a couple of times. With ice, it would be treacherous. The paths at House in the Pines flashed through my mind. They were all paved and lit, whereas here I was wandering through dark woods on bare, rough ground. Squirrels were running here and there gathering nuts for winter.

I was halfway down when I realized that thus far no one had asked me why I limped, much less criticized me. Bruce had let me wander around and look at the horses without asking me what I as doing. You couldn't even go in the barn at House in the Pines without Ms. Keener pouncing on you with questions and orders. But here, for the first time, I was being left alone, given some space. I still didn't trust it, or anyone, but at least I noticed it.

I entered the back door of the main building. It was a small hallway, filled with noisy students. I avoided all the faces and looks, particularly the boys'. I had no experience with going to school with boys and no desire to start sitting in a classroom with them. I pushed through the crowd toward the dining room. It was filled with wooden tables and benches. Students and teachers were all going in at once. Feet were shuffling on the linoleum floor, and second and third year students were greeting one another for the first time since returning.

"Hey, man. How ya doing?" one boy said to another. They pushed past me in an attempt to get seats together. This first night, we could sit wherever we wanted. I didn't know where to go. Seeing an empty place on a bench, I went for it and sat down. The kitchen was straight ahead. Pots and pans were banging, and large bowls of mashed potatoes were being set out in a square opening into the kitchen. A male teacher at the head of our table asked two students to get the food. He called them by name, so I guess they weren't newbies. I didn't want to look up at anyone at the table, but the teacher made me. He was probably in his thirties, with sandy hair—layered straight back on the top of his head—and a beard, which was neat and trim. He wore casual clothes and had a strong, compact body. I was forced to look up because he asked me my name. I was the closest newbie to him, I guess. Looking at him, I was convinced that if I said two words, I'd be teased by everyone at the table. "Sarah," I said as quietly as I thought I could get away with.

"Did you say Sarah?" he asked, leaning in toward me.

"Yes," I said. I guess he thought he was onto something, maybe a way to embarrass us all, because he asked everyone at the table to introduce him or herself. It was clear from their level of nervousness, which the newbies were. Especially poor Elizabeth. She was tall, pale, with high cheekbones, pale blue eyes, and shoulder-length dark hair a little on the frizzy side. As she stuttered her introduction, I noticed that she had a slightly turned-up nose and big, white teeth.

Kim was the other newbie at the table. She was short with long hair pulled back off her round face, rosy cheeks, and a stout body that looked strong. I later learned that she was a serious dancer.

"Well, you new students—Sarah, Elizabeth, and Kim—I'm David."

The food tasted a lot better than it looked, but I wasn't hungry. I pushed things around on my plate, wondering what David would say if I didn't eat—and what the others might do because of what he said.

Seeing that I wasn't eating, David leaned forward and said, "It's okay, you don't have to eat if you don't want to, Sarah." I glanced up at him and then immediately back down at my plate. Thoughts raced through my head. Did I hear him right? Was this some kind of nasty trick? I caught Elizabeth's eye to see if I could tell, but she just shrugged. My body was tense and I wanted to leave the table, but I hung on.

Finally, at another table, David Bailey stood up and said a few words. He was greeting everyone, but I wasn't paying attention because I was numb. I wasn't sure I could make myself stay in my seat. It wasn't that anything so bad had happened, but that something was about to happen. The anticipation was sometimes more than I could manage.

When we were finally excused, I was one of the first ones out of the dining room. I jammed down the hall and pushed my way out the door, only to find myself standing alone in the weak light of the single bulb over the entrance. Out across the parking lot, I could see that the path to the girls' dorm was in complete darkness. What should I do? Just then some girls came out of Upwey behind me and started for the path. They had flashlights, so I let them lead the way. None of them said a word to me. It was as if I was invisible. I stumbled along in the dark behind them until we got to the dorm then continued on up to the barn. Once safe in Ringo's stall, I stayed there until it was time for bed.

Ms. Magreal had changed her clothes and was parading around in an even stranger outfit than the one she'd been wearing. Her hair was slightly messy, and she seemed a little frantic. When, reluctantly, I went to my room, my roommate, Jennifer, was already in bed. She sat up, perched on one elbow, and said in a firm voice, "I want you to know that it is really going to irritate me if you come in late and wake me up." I'd calmed down since dinner because I'd been hanging out with Ringo, but her manner made me feel alone and numb again.

Jennifer was waiting for a comment—she seemed as if she wanted to fight with me—but I didn't respond. I had yet to say one word to her. I got half-undressed, climbed into bed, turned my light off, and lay on my back, hands folded on my chest, stiff as a toy soldier. The door into the adjoining bedroom was shut, but I could hear the girls talking and laughing. In our room, the darkness enveloped me. It made me feel like someone had thrown a bear rug over my head—claustrophobic but, at the same time, relieved to be separated from awful Jennifer. In the safety of the darkness, the tears finally came.

Suddenly, as the tears subsided, I felt I couldn't stay in the room another instant. Sitting up, I wiped my eyes and looked around. My bed was under the window, and when I tested the latch, I found that I could open the sash far enough to squeeze out onto the roof. The window squeaked, and Jennifer rolled over. I froze, knowing it would be a mistake to wake her.

I crawled out and crept down the roof on my butt and heels. The edge looked to be about three feet off the ground. Though I lowered my feet as far as possible before pushing off, I still landed like a sack of potatoes. Pain shocked my body, but I knew from experience that it was due more to fear than actual injury. After a brief check, I scrambled up and started for the barn. As I was going around the corner of the house, I looked back to see if I'd made a clean getaway. Sure enough, Ms. Mageal was in the upstairs hallway window, watching me go.

I stumbled for the barn, my heart pumping. I'd thrown on some clothes in the dark, but I hadn't finished tying laces or tucking things in. I must have looked a sight.

I crept over to Ringo's stall, let myself in, whispered hello, moved up to his head, and gave him a hug. I think I woke him up. Then, I leaned back against the wall and walked down it with my shoulder blades until I was sitting in the straw. I wrapped my arms around my knees, buried my face in the space between them, and moaned like a baby. Ringo understood. He tried to push my head off my knees with his nose. When I gave in and lifted my face, he slapped his lips at my hair and the collar on my shirt.

"So, Ringo," I said after a while, "you certainly seem settled in." He was so sure of himself, so relaxed. I ran my fingers through his forelock and rubbed his head. He liked to be scratched on the forehead, up and down between his eyes. In fact, he liked it so much he'd lean into my hand and jerk his head up and down to enhance the effect. "You're so silly," I whispered, laughing. When he'd had enough attention, he searched around for the last of his hay and stood, head lowered, munching it.

I was cold but couldn't leave, especially since Ms. Magreal had seen me sneak out. "I've really done it now," I whispered. But a part of me didn't care. I was with Ringo, and he was keeping whatever was left of me intact.

Sometime before dawn when I couldn't stand the cold any longer, I crept back to the house. I tried to climb back onto the roof below my window, but it was no go. The cold had sapped my strength. After a few failed attempts, I decided to sneak in the front door. Well, wouldn't you know, Ms. Magreal was there waiting for me. She must have been sitting by the door because she opened it as I was reaching for the knob. I was afraid at first, but when she didn't say anything, I walked right past her and up to my room. You can bet my lips were sealed. Months later, I learned that David Bailey and the faculty knew the whole story of what went on that first night.

Despite getting to sleep so late, I woke up in time to get back to the barn by seven as Bruce had instructed. The barn was busy with horses stomping, snorting and squealing, and Bruce and Emily bustling about with their chores. "You're right on time, Sarah," Emily greeted me. "He's waiting for you."

I grabbed Ringo's bucket and grained and watered him. While he was eating, I brushed him and put his halter on. Emily came over with a lead rope. "You know where you're going?"

"I think so. The pasture across the road from Upwey, right?"

"Right. Well go ahead then. Be careful crossing Route 5. I'll bring down some water. Don't worry, he'll be fine."

I led him out of the barn and down the dirt road past the dorm. In the woods, girls were chattering like squirrels as they made their way down the path to breakfast. The air was crisp and cool, and the foliage brightened as the sun came up. Ringo, ears up and eyes bright, registered everything we passed. I gave his lead line a lot of slack so he could look around and sniff the dirt. He snorted, blowing circles of dust off the gravel.

When we got to the pasture, Emily was already there. She'd set a bucket of fresh water against a post just inside the gate. I opened the gate and led Ringo in, and immediately I could feel his excitement. The second I unhooked his lead line, he coiled and took off up the hill. You wouldn't think a horse could run that fast.

"That's a fine horse, Sarah," Emily said as we watched him sprint. I was proud of him. It was as if he knew he was handsome, and enjoyed showing his stuff. His antics made me smile. "How old is he?" Emily asked, leaning on the gate.

"About four and a half. He should be a little bigger, but he had a bad start." It was important to me that Emily knew that I knew Ringo was small for his age. "He's catching up though," I added so she'd also know he'd be getting bigger. I always enjoyed talking about Ringo, probably because he was the one subject about which I knew I was an expert.

The bell rang in Upwey. "Oops. Better get going," Emily said. I crossed the street then paused and looked back before going in. Emily was watching me. "Don't worry," she called. "You can bring him back up to the barn after lunch." When she missed my nod, she added, "Do you understand?"

"I understand," I called back.

As I entered the dining room for breakfast, I was wishing I could have stayed out with Ringo. It wasn't until someone put a plate of scrambled eggs in front of me that I realized how hungry I was.

Elizabeth was at my table again, but we didn't speak to each other as we were separated by other people and too shy to speak across them. Besides, I was too distracted to reach out. But she caught up with me in the common room after breakfast. I was standing at the front window looking across the street at Ringo. He seemed content, standing in the warming sun, munching long grass. I wasn't aware that she was next to me until she spoke. "Hi," she said, almost obsequiously. "I'm Betsy. We've been at the same table."

I looked at her. Didn't she remember that David had made us introduce ourselves and that I, therefore, knew she'd been at the table? "I know," I said. "Hi."

"Is that your horse?" she asked, looking out at Ringo.

"Yes."

A pause followed. I wasn't going to say anything. "So is this your first year here?" she persisted.

"Yes."

The bell rang, signaling the beginning of classes. My first class was English with Peggy Bailey, the headmaster's wife. By coincidence, Betsy was in the same class. Scared, I sat in the corner, praying I wouldn't get called on. Mrs. Bailey looked at me once in awhile, but she didn't ask me any questions. It was like we had a secret that was so secret that we hadn't even discussed it.

It was the same with all my classes that first morning. I didn't offer to talk, and no one tried to make me. It was a relief because I felt that if I could remain silent and apart, I wouldn't be as vulnerable. When the bell rang ending the last class, I went straight to the dining room, knowing that as soon as lunch was over, I'd be back out with Ringo.

When we were dismissed, I ran down the hall, out the front door, and across the street. He was off in the field, but he looked up, saw me coming, tossed his head, and started over. As I was opening the gate, I heard the Upwey door slam. Looking back, I saw that Betsy was still dogging me.

She looked both ways and started across the highway. "Can I walk up to the barn with you?"

"Sure, I guess." In one way, I didn't want her to walk with us, but in another, it seemed all right. She seemed lonely and lost too, and she didn't have a Ringo.

As we walked up the dirt road, she said, "My family's from Pittsburgh, but we also have a nine-hundred-acre farm in West Virginia."

"Wow," I said, thinking she must be rich.

"My grandfather built the main house. There's also a farmhouse and log cabin. The only easy way to get to the property is over a suspended bridge. I really like it there."

"You're kidding!" I said.

"Nope. You'll have to come see it some time." She seemed proud as well as warm. I told her I was from Rhode Island.

"What made you come to this school?"

"The headmistress at my other school was crazy, and my parents had to get me away from her," I said.

"Are you for real?" Betsy's voice went up.

"Why? Why are you here?"

"I wasn't doing well in my school either. But I didn't want to come here," she replied.

"Neither did I."

She asked about my limp. At first, I wasn't going to tell her. I was going to make something up the way I usually did. But there was something about her that made me trust her, or maybe *want* to trust her. So I told her the truth. She was very interested. As I told her about it, I remembered that Peter Sauer had said it would be my choice whether or not the students knew. And here was Betsy, being as nice as could be to me about it. That's when I realized how the school's taking that position had given me some control over my relationships, a tiny bit of power. It caused a little spark of hope to flare up, but I didn't let it get too big. Immediately, I went back to thinking about Ringo and the afternoon ride ahead of us. I was planning to take him exploring.

Emily was in the barn. I put Ringo in his stall and went to get my saddle.

"We have a horse for you, Betsy," Emily said.

"I've never ridden. Well, once or twice," said Betsy,

I decided to saddle Ringo at the cross tie instead of in his stall. "You can come with me if you want," I offered as I led him past Betsy.

"All the school horses are gentle," Emily encouraged. "Plus they'll go anywhere you want."

"Well . . . all right," Betsy decided.

"You have two hours before classes resume, right?" Emily asked.

An older sway-bellied mare was brought out, and Emily and I showed Betsy how to saddle up. Then, with Ringo and me leading the way, we went on a long trail ride. I gave Betsy some pointers about riding, and she was grateful. All in all, it was a fun afternoon and the start of a good friendship.

Having a friend made a lot of difference. When I couldn't be with Ringo, I could pal around with Betsy. She became less shy to the point where she'd actually raise her hand and speak in class. I wanted to be more like her in that respect, but I just couldn't bring myself to do it.

The evenings in my room were hard as I really hated my roommate. Chris Magreal made me a present of a heavy blanket to take when I went up to visit Ringo. It was amazing to me that the school was letting me spend the nights with my horse. No one said anything about it, one way or the other, but Bruce and Emily actually started leaving a light on for me. I had never heard of a school treating its students like that. There was absolutely no pressure from anyone. I had never felt so free. Not only that, but because I felt so free, I began to want to reach out to other people. The only problem was that I didn't know how. How do you start trusting? How do you look at people and know they won't hurt you? It seemed too risky. People had let me down so badly. They'd seemed to be listening to me; but then, suddenly, they'd do something mean, and I'd see that they hadn't really been paying attention at all. Why would Woodstock be any different? Part of me was sure it wouldn't be, but another part, a quieter part, kept reminding me that they let me go up to the barn to visit Ringo every night.

The days turned into weeks. Halloween came—we had a big party for it—then we started talking about Thanksgiving vacation. I still wasn't raising my hand in class. In one of my classes, across from Ringo's pasture, I spent the whole time gazing out the window at him. My teacher could see what was going on, but he didn't say anything, at least to me.

I'll tell you how much that teacher indulged me. One day when I got to class, a boy had taken my usual seat next to the window. So the teacher, Bill his name was, asked the boy if he'd mind doing him a favor. And when the boy said sure, Bill explained that he'd forgotten some papers up at his apartment. Would the boy mind going up and getting them for him? And the boy was happy to get out of class, so he got up and left. When he was gone, Bill pointed at me, said, "You," jabbed his finger at the vacated seat, said, "Go," and when I got to the seat, jabbed his finger at the seat again and said, "Sit."

I sat down and that was all that was said about it. Had he really forgotten his papers? I didn't think so. I thought the whole thing was very cool. And as I sat there watching Ringo, I thought, well, I guess the teachers are going out of their way to make me feel accepted.

Another thing happened that confirmed it. It was in biology class with John Pierce. One day, out of the blue, he started harping on how stupid horses are. And he went back to it the next day and the day after; and every time he started in on them, he'd look at me, kind of challenging me. Well, I ignored him for a while, but one day when I wasn't paying much attention, I reacted without thinking and said, "Horses are smarter than a lot of people I know." It was the first time I'd said anything in the class, and I guess everyone was aware of it because my statement was followed by absolute silence. Mr. Pierce looked at me, and a slight smile crept over his face. He was obviously pleased, but I felt tricked. I felt my cheeks flush.

I stood up, knocking my chair over—which only made things worse—and bolted out of the classroom. Fighting to hold back the tears, I ran down the hall and out of the building. Upwey was quiet because classes were going on, and the fire door shook the whole building when it slammed.

I went out into the middle of the playing field at the south end of Upwey and was standing there with my hands on my hips, kicking dandelions, when the door opened and John Pierce came out after me. He came right out into the field, which caused me to turn my back on him, grabbed me by the shoulders, and whipped me around to face him. I didn't know what he was doing, but his determination was scary.

"Let go!" I yelled.

"I knew there was a human being in there!" He yelled right back at me. "Look," he said, gasping, "I know what happened to you at your other school. But it wasn't your fault!" He paused to catch his breath. "You are *not* going to be pressured or teased here. So why don't you just *stop* being afraid." He let go of me, stepped back, and added in a softer voice, "Because—believe it or not—you really *are* safe here."

It was what I'd been avoiding, the truth that I was safe and respected, and it made my body shake and my eyes fill with tears. God, would I ever stop crying! It was more than I could handle, and I almost fainted. He grabbed me and held me against him, and well, I don't know, maybe he stumbled, whatever happened, we went over. He didn't let go of me though. We got our legs straight, and we lay there on the soft ground, and he kept hugging me as long as I kept sobbing.

Later, when I thought about the incident, it occurred to me that if he'd let go of me at that moment, I would have seeped down into the earth like water and disappeared forever. That's how I'd felt, and he seemed to sense it because he held me until I felt stronger. "It's okay, Sarah," he kept saying. "It's all right."

When we finally got up, we were a little muddy and at a loss for words. Walking back to Upwey, he said, "You can skip the rest of class."

I just looked at him.

"Go on, wash your face and then sit in the common room."

I hadn't felt such strength in an embrace for a long time, maybe ever. It went right to my core and instantly lightened my load. When we got to the door, I stopped, and he went around me and opened the door. As I went by him, I could feel his warmth and understanding. It was the first time I'd really noticed his appearance. I'd smelled his smoke. He smoked a lot, one cigarette after another while teaching, and kept a coffee can on his desk for his butts. I'd always thought it was kind of gross, but I decided maybe it wasn't so bad. He also had a deep, gentle, yet assertive voice. Plus he was the rugged outdoor type who wore leather work boots, heavy wool pants, and bright flannel shirts. He was so big I'd been frightened when he'd come out of Upwey after me, but he'd turned out to be a gentle giant.

He put his hand on my shoulder and asked, "You going to be all right?" The afternoon sun was shining off his bald head.

"I think so." It was odd, saying it. I'm not sure I'd ever thought, much less owned, that I was going to be all right.

He held the door for me, and I stepped inside. Then, for some reason, I turned back, smiled, and said, "Do you ever wear a coat?"

He laughed. "Nope." Then he pointed his finger at me and winked. As we walked down the hall, he started whistling a tune. I'd heard him whistle it before—it was one of his favorites. I knew it, but I could never quite come up with the title because he'd changed it somehow, sort of made it his own.

His students were standing in the hall outside the classroom, waiting to hear whether or not they were going to have to do more work. "Okay, gang," he said. "Back inside." He nodded to me to get on with my business, and quietly shut the door.

I walked down the hall to the ladies' room—thank goodness it was empty, stood in front of the mirror and splashed cold water on my face. The Vermont well water was sweet and cold. I dried myself, went to my cubby for some books, and settled down on the common room sofa.

The common room ran across the barn from front to back and was large enough to accommodate the entire school, some 120 students plus faculty. I liked it because it had a huge fireplace, couches, stuffed chairs, and booths with tables like a restaurant. You could sit and talk, or just do homework. The windows along the front and rear walls were small and square, and the floor was a dirty red linoleum. The room tended to be dark, but it was our, the students', space, warm and cozy.

Too distracted to read, I got up and moved to an old stuffed chair in the corner by the fireplace. No one could sit next to me there, plus I had a better view of the rest of the room. There were a few students around, mostly boys. One stared at me. I knew he was a senior and that he had a reputation for nastiness. It made me uncomfortable.

"What are you looking at?" he asked, as if picking for a fight.

"Not at you, you jerk," I replied, glaring at him.

"Newbies aren't supposed to be in here now, newbie." He got up and was coming toward me when a male teacher happened into the room.

"Eh-eh, David. This is not social hour. Sit back down," the teacher said.

I smiled and shook my head. Whoever he was, David wasn't anyone I wanted anything to do with. He was short, probably even shorter than I, and he had zits. His only saving grace was his long black hair. I curled into the corner of my chair and spaced out. I must have drifted off because when the bell rang, I jumped.

Betsy entered the common room, saw me, and came over. "You okay?" she asked. "I thought you had biology last period. What are you doing here?"

"It's a long story. Do you want to ride this afternoon?" She nodded enthusiastically. "Good. I'll tell you about it then."

We headed for the dining room. "You're a bit of a mystery, you know?" Betsy said. "The way you're so close to Ringo, yet keep your distance from people?"

"Yeah, I know," I replied. "But when I explain it, you'll understand." Betsy and I were becoming friends.

That afternoon, I told her the whole story. It was easier to talk while I was up on Ringo and we were walking along through the woods. Betsy listened even as she kept her attention on her horse. We rode forever it seemed, walking where we had to but trotting and cantering when we could. Betsy was getting the hang of it. On the way back, we stopped at the South Woodstock Country Store and got some oranges. It was a great fall day, and I felt free, almost happy. John Pierce had enabled me to put House in the Pines behind me once and for all, to finally let it fade away. And in its place, I had a beautiful Vermont valley and a school that was relaxed enough to let a teenage girl find her own way. I had time, space and freedom. Whatever I asked for, they agreed to, whether it was fixing Ringo's stall or changing roommates. Plus I had my new friend, Betsy. We became inseparable so much so that when I decided to change roommates, we chose to live together.

We were so excited about the prospect; I decided we should talk to Chris Magreal. So one night, we made our way to her apartment at the other end of the dorm. Her door was open, and when we looked in, there was a glass of red wine on her desk. "Is she supposed to drink in the dorm?" I asked Betsy.

"Shhhh," Betsy hissed. "She'll hear you."

"But I don't see her."

"I hear her. Hear her breathing?"

"Oh, yeah." We tiptoed into the room. Wherever Ms. Magreal was, we didn't want to disturb her. Suddenly, there was a snort, and she sat up from her prone position on the floor. Betsy and I jumped and tried to back out.

"Wait, girls," Ms. Magreal said, mustering her most authoritative voice. She grabbed the edge of her desk and pulled herself up. Her bun was off to one side of her head, and her eyes were bloodshot and darkened with smeared mascara. She waved her arm, trying to get her shawl back up on her shoulder. Her nightgown strap was slipping too. I reached in and hiked it back up then gave her a hand with her shawl.

"Thank you, dear," she said, with as much dignity as she could muster. "I wasn't expecting guests this late. But it's all right, of course."

I started in about my wish to change roommates, and then Betsy and I explained how we wanted to room together. We had a plan for how the various changes might be achieved, but it was a bit confusing for poor Ms. Magreal. It was all Betsy and I could do to keep from laughing.

She went along with it though. Well, she said it was fine with her if the other girls would agree. So we left her with her wine and set off to negotiate it all, giggling as we stumbled down the hall. In the end, Jennifer kept our room as a single, Betsy's roommate moved in with another girl downstairs, and I moved into Betsy's room with her.

Betsy's room was bigger than my old one, plus the bathroom was right across the hall. But the best part was that Betsy and I could talk at night. We liked to shut the lights off and listen to the Righteous Brothers. Betsy had a fearsome crush on a senior. She liked to daydream about him while listening to "You've Lost That Lovin' Feelin'."

I'd started noticing boys, but I still wasn't talking to any. Actually, I was becoming more aware of everything. Betsy told me I no longer walked around with my head down. I didn't talk much in class, and my grades weren't great, but I was happier and that was a lot. The school had given me a sense of freedom that I'd not experienced before. Also, for the first time since grade school, back when I was one of the "fourteen angels," I wasn't being judged every time I turned around.

There was one incident with a senior, a girl named Barrett. It involved my cerebral palsy. Barrett was as weird as they come, tall and thin with a beak of a nose like the Wicked Witch of the West. She would come into the dorm kitchen and stroll around in nothing but underwear. And she was built like a string bean, not a curve anywhere. And her hair, straight to her shoulders, was neither brown nor blond, but a dull mousy gray.

I'd told only a few people about my cerebral palsy, but I couldn't hide my limp. My encounter with Barrett happened one afternoon when Betsy and I were on our way down the root-riddled path to Upwey. Barrett and a few of her friends passed us going in the same direction. I was ahead of Betsy, and they pushed in ahead of me so close that I nearly tripped. Well, I could forgive that. Anyone can be rude if they're being rambunctious. But when Barrett started imitating my limp, well, that was a bit much. Betsy and I looked at each other and shook our heads. But Barrett wasn't about to stop, and before long, her friends were all giggling about it.

"Gee, that's really mature, Barrett," I said. She was taken aback by my challenge, probably because she had no idea of all I'd been through at House in the Pines. What she was doing was nothing compared to pencils in the cast. "You must have a *lot* of imagination to think something like that up."

She turned, gave me a dirty look, and was about to reply; but before she could come up with anything, I gave her an exaggerated wink. Nonplussed, she continued on down the hill without saying anything.

When they were out of earshot, Betsy put her hand on my arm and stopped me. "How did you get the nerve to even *talk* to a senior like that?"

"Are you kidding?" I replied. "That was nothing. *She's* nothing."

I started to continue on, but Betsy wouldn't let go of my arm. "Wait a minute," she persisted. "What happened to you there?" Her expression revealed her concern.

"Oh man, Betsy, it's another long story," I said.

"So? I'd like to hear it."

"Really?"

"Well, yeah, really."

So I spent that afternoon telling her about my four years at House in the Pines. It was a cold, bright winter day, too icy to ride, so we walked the dirt roads. Betsy was intrigued. She asked a lot of questions, and her admiration seemed to grow with every answer I gave. She was a good listener, and I told her as much as I could remember, even about my friend, Lynn. In fact, I told her she reminded me of Lynn because she was so kind and thoughtful. We walked all afternoon, returning as the sun was disappearing from the valley.

There was a last class scheduled just before dinner, and when we entered Upwey, the hall was busy with students. We made our way to our cubbies to get our books. My class was Ancient history, and when I pulled out my large textbook, some of my papers came out with it and fell on the floor. I bent over to get them, but Betsy beat me to it. Telling Betsy about Lynn had made me remember my old friend, and I was missing her and feeling bad about not being in touch. I guess my conversation with Betsy had put me in a pensive mood. I loved my friends, partially because I'd spent so much time without any. So after helping me get my papers back into my cubby, when Betsy put her hand on my arm and looked into my eyes, well, it really touched me. There were students all around, so she wasn't about to say anything; but for a fleeting moment, as our eyes met, everything stopped. Everything stopped because her eyes were telling me she cared, and I could feel it.

"Sarah," she pleaded, "you must tell David Bailey what Barrett did. This is not House in the Pines. He'll do something, I know he will."

"Okay, I will. I promise." It took everything in me to keep from crying. Because Betsy knew that even though I could handle Barrett, it was tough for me. She knew what I'd been through, she cared, and she didn't want me to have to go through it again.

When class was over, I decided Betsy was right, that I really did have to stand up for myself. Besides, I'd promised I would. So I headed for David's office.

When I opened the door, David welcomed me like an old friend. I could tell why. It was in his face. He and every other teacher in the school had been waiting for me to reach out and show some initiative, so they could get behind me and support me. They'd respected me enough to wait for me to do it, and their faith was affirmed when I walked through that door.

After standing to greet me, David waved me to the visitor's chair and settled back in his desk chair. The smell of smoke hung on his clothes. He was a chain smoker, and it was ruining his health. His chest heaved just trying to get enough air to talk. Still, he continued to smoke. I guess he couldn't stop. He leaned forward and put his hands on his desk, palms up, inviting me to begin. I sat up in my chair. He smiled.

"Barrette Andrews," I said.

"Yes," David said. His voice was breath in the form of whisper.

"She pushed in front of me on the path, then mimicked my limp." There, I'd said it.

David leaned back and put his index finger to his lip. I wasn't sure whether he was signaling me to be quiet or just thinking. He had a pained look on his face.

"I'm not a tattle tale," I said, just in case. "It's just that I can't go through this again at this school."

"What did you say to her?" David asked.

I told him what had happened and what I'd said. When I finished, he sat up and slammed his big, bony hand on the desk. The speed and force of his movement startled me.

"Good for you!" he said, as loud as his voice would allow.

"What?" I started to laugh.

He rummaged in the side pocket of his jacket for his cigarettes, got the crumpled pack out, gently drew out a bent one, and lit up with a safety match. When he exhaled, he blew the smoke out of the side of his mouth away from me. "I've been meaning to talk to Ms. Barrette about a few things, Sarah. I think you may consider this matter taken care of." He spoke slowly and deliberately, with obvious effort. Taking another drag, he squinted, but he didn't take his eyes off mine. "It's been good for the students to be exposed to you. I can see that. Especially Betsy. You two seem to have become friends."

"Yes, we have."

He considered that. "You have a special spirit, Sarah, and I like it, and I see it coming alive in Betsy."

I tried to understand what he meant. I wasn't aware that anyone had ever seen me that way before. Well, maybe Dr. Barrett, Ringo's vet, but no, he'd only seen my strength. David was talking about that strength, but also about my determination to have fun along the way. He was referring to that combination of toughness and playfulness. It was interesting because the minute I saw that he'd seen that in me, I started to acknowledge it. And the minute I began to own it, I felt as if I was climbing out of a hole. I was energized to keep climbing. And down behind me, steadily farther back in the dark hole, was the way I used to be based on my experiences at House in the Pines.

Ever the gentleman, David got up again to walk me to the door. When I looked up into his weathered face to thank him and say good-bye, he put his hand on my shoulder and winked with both eyes. I smiled. Then he took one last puff on his cigarette, cupped it with his other hand to prevent the ash from falling on the rug, caught the ash when it dropped, carried it back and dumped it in his ashtray.

Back in the hall, I went looking for Betsy. She wasn't far away, and when I saw her, I could tell from her smile that she'd been waiting for me. It was Friday, which meant there would be a dance in the common room after dinner.

Barrette Andrews never bothered me again. Nor, for that matter, did anyone else at Woodstock. Well, there were the usual nasty remarks from the jerks, but everyone had to put up with their nonsense.

Betsy and I continued to hang out and enjoy the Vermont countryside. We rode as much as we could. There was no end to the back roads and open fields, but I do think we covered most of them.

I also made friends with a girl from New Jersey, Debbie Carman. She was kind of a know-it-all, but I ignored that part. She had a lot of energy and she knew how to do things. For example, she helped me train Ringo to pull a sleigh. The sleigh was back in a corner of an old outbuilding, under a lot of unused farm equipment. Bruce dragged it out, then found an old harness which we saddle soaped and refit for Ringo. The collar was a little big, but it did the job.

Betsy came to watch, but she didn't stay because she wasn't crazy about Debbie. Besides, she'd made some other friends, and she hung out with them when I was with Debbie.

I spent a few weeks walking behind Ringo, holding the long reins and giving instructions. There was snow on the ground, which was good because he was a forward-moving horse, and it would have been hard holding him back on bare ground. When we decided he was ready to pull, we started him on logs to get him used to the noise behind him. At first, he thought there was something chasing him. But being of good Morgan stock, he learned quickly.

He didn't like Debbie either, though. I don't know what it was about her, maybe a falseness, or perhaps her bossiness. Whatever it was, it caused him to put his ears back whenever she was around. When he did, it frightened her, and she showed her fear. I don't know, maybe it was simply that frightening her was fun for him.

She tried to overcome her fear. One weekend, when I had to go home but she was staying at school, she asked if she could take care of Ringo. It turned out to be a bad idea. When she was in his stall brushing him, he backed her against the wall so that she thought he might squash her. Bruce was in the barn, and when she called, he came and rescued her.

"Your horse tried to crush me," she said accusatively when I got back.

We were going into the barn. I'd just completed a long bus ride from Rhode Island and was exhausted. I went over and looked in on Ringo to be sure he was all right then said, "What were you saying?"

"I was brushing him, and he deliberately pushed me against the wall. I couldn't get out of the stall." She was genuinely upset.

Bruce came over. "It's true," he added. "I had to go in and force him over. He threatened me too. Not a lot, just testing. I think he knew you weren't around."

When I looked at Ringo, he looked away as if he didn't want to hear about it.

"We'll have to be careful from now on when you're not here," Bruce continued. "You two have quite the bond."

Debbie looked at me. I knew she was jealous of my relationship with Ringo, and I suspected that it was that jealousy he sensed and didn't like. She had an attitude, and it came across in her tone of voice, and it was a little hostile, perhaps dangerous. I'm sure Ringo picked up on it. I think he sensed that it was fear-based and that fear might cause her to do something foolish. At any rate, from then on, Debbie stood back whenever I worked with him.

Finally, the time came to hitch him to the sleigh. Debbie talked me through it. It was exciting for me though Ringo seemed pretty relaxed. When he was all hooked up, I stood back and said, "So? Now what?"

"We get in, silly," Debbie replied. But then she said, "Oh no, wait a minute," and walked around in front of Ringo, her reddish hair blowing across her face. She was really thin too and kind of a tomboy. "He should be facing the open gate, but I don't want to try to turn him from inside the sleigh."

"Okay," I said, motioning to her to go ahead and lead him around. I kept a snug hold on the reins. When Ringo got turned so that he was staring out through the open gate, he understood. And understanding, he wanted to go.

"Get in," Debbie bossed me.

"What about you?"

"I'm coming. Hold him in!"

I jumped into the sleigh, fumbling with the tangle of reins "Whoa, Ringo!" I ordered. He stopped, though he stomped in place.

Debbie jumped in the other side. "Ready?" she asked.

"Yeah," I giggled gleefully.

"All right. Loosen your reins and tell him to walk at the same time."

I gave Ringo his head and let the reins slide through my gloves as he took it. And as he took it, I commanded, "Walk." He stepped forward, encountered the inert pull weight, backed slightly, and jerked us off dead still. Suddenly, we were sliding.

The sleigh wasn't much to look at. Its runners were low and didn't curve much, and the body was also low and square, with a single seat across the front and an empty space behind. It was a nice color though—a faded barn red that showed up against the snow.

That was the first of many sleigh rides. Betsy and a number of other students joined us though we wouldn't take more than two passengers at a time. We'd slide along, and Ringo would lift his tail and step smartly, and we'd laugh and call out to people we passed. Sometimes we acted like a bus service, stopping for walkers, then taking them wherever they wanted to go. Ringo, who always loved having a job to do, thought it was great fun.

Our next project was teaching Ringo to pull a skier. Betsy even joined in on this one. Debbie introduced us to it. "It's really fun, Sarah. You attach a rope to the girth on both sides."

"How long is the rope," Betsy asked.

We were all standing at the edge of the soccer field. Ringo had his saddle and bridle on. A tall boy by the name of Reilly ran across the field, dragging a rope. "Here," he gasped as he stomped up through the crusted snow. Betsy and I looked at each other. It was clear that Debbie had already planned the adventure. Well, I thought, the sleigh rides were fun; we might as well try it.

Reilly and Debbie seemed to be friends, but that was the first time I'd spoken to him. He handed the rope to Debbie.

"Hi," I said.

"Hi," he answered with a goofy laugh.

"Hey," I said, "you're the one who took the picture of Ringo coming over the bridge."

"True enough." He was very smiley, with sandy-colored hair that fell over one eye.

"Well, let's get started. Reilly, go get David," Debbie directed.

"Why do we need another person?" I asked.

"You'll see."

Reilly went off to Upwey to get David. I watched Debbie as she attached one end of the rope to Ringo's girth.

"Okay," she said when it was knotted. She went behind Ringo and pulled the rope snug. I followed her, still not understanding what she was doing. "Now," she said, walking around to the other side of Ringo's head, "we tie this other end of the rope to the other side of the girth . . ."

The rope lay in a big loop in the snow behind Ringo. "We need David because David's going to do it first. David always goes first. He'll hold onto the rope. And you will get on Ringo and pull David around the field. Get it?" She was obviously excited by the idea.

As Debbie explained it, David was skiing across the soccer field toward us in kind of a skating motion. When I recognized him, I turned to Betsy and said in a hushed voice, "Oh shit, it's *him*!"

"Who?" asked Betsy, great consternation in her expression.

"The guy I told you about, the guy in the common room that day, the guy . . . I . . . called an asshole!" I hissed the last part while pulling Betsy to the other side of Ringo, out of sight of David.

"How did you manage to do that?" Betsy whispered, pulling on my jacket.

"I told you. He thought I was staring at him, and he got up and came toward me like he was going to kill me or something."

"You didn't tell me you called him as asshole!" Betsy's voice went up.

"Shhhhh!"

Debbie came around Ringo with David. "What's going on?" she inquired.

"Hey, I know you," said David. "You called me an asshole."

"Yup," I said, nodding like a klutz. "That would have been me."

"Does this mean you're going to pull me into the woods or something if I do this?"

"No. But I can't make any promises for my horse." I took Ringo's bridle and drew his head around so he'd get a clear look at David. Ringo took one look and laid his ears back.

David backed off. "Hey, forget this," he said.

"Come on, David," Reilly encouraged. "Don't be a chick, chick, chick." He started dancing around in the snow, flopping his arms and squawking like a chicken. We all laughed.

Thus challenged, David wasn't about to back down. So I got on Ringo, and he grabbed the rope, and I gave Ringo a cluck and flick of the reins, and off we all went. When we were halfway across the field, cantering smoothly, I looked back; and sure enough, David was coming along behind.

It worked out fine. Ringo didn't pull David into any trees, and David didn't say anything nasty to either Ringo or me. After that, until there was no more snow, Ringo, Debbie, Betsy, and I continued to give sleigh rides and pull skiers.

As the snow melted, I learned something about my new environment. Because the weather warms up before the ground unfreezes in Vermont, there are actually five seasons, with the additional one occurring between winter and spring. It's called mud season, and for good reason. The combination of melting snow coming down from above and frost coming up out of the ground make mush like I'd never seen before. On a muddy road, especially where the soil has clay in it, it can suck the boots right off your feet. It didn't stop Ringo, but then, nothing stopped Ringo.

And then suddenly it was May, the school year was drawing to a close, and I was on my way home. I hated saying good-bye to Betsy, but we pledged to write. We knew we'd be roommates the following year, so that was some comfort. I don't know how but I passed all my courses. My grades weren't good, but they were all right. But the important thing was, I was feeling better about myself.

I'd gone through the second half of the year with a few crushes on boys. One, in particular, caught my eye. He seemed out of place, perhaps because he was a real preppy. He had blond hair and dressed very neatly compared to the other boys. He didn't wear faded jeans, never mind jeans with holes in them, plus he wore polished loafers instead of boots. As a result, he was needled by a lot of the kids. They called him Pretty Boy. "Hey, Pretty Boy," they'd tease in a singsong voice, "can we borrow your washer-dryer today?" In Upwey, he'd retreat up the stairs to the drama loft when he saw them coming.

I thought he was really cute, but he didn't notice me. He was interested in a girl, Axey Noyes, who'd arrived from Washington DC in the middle of the year. Axey, who thought she was the bee's knees, flirted with Pretty Boy, whose real name was Jameson Parker. They spent the nights together in the common room. In the morning, you'd see them, spooning on the largest couch together. It didn't look very comfortable, but I wished it were me lying there instead of Axey.

The closest I got to Jameson was in drama class. We were in a play together. My heart would pound like crazy when we were on stage at the same time. Sometimes, he'd catch me staring at him. I remember in rehearsal one afternoon, he was sitting across the aisle from me while I was watching him, and he got up and came and sat with me. I thought I was going to die. And he said, "You know, you're really cute." And my face turned beet red. And I thought, what am I supposed to say? I really like you, Parky? Oh my god. What a jerk I am! I wanted to leap out the window.

He was staring at *me*! Oh, those blue eyes and blond hair! It was the same feeling I'd had with Carter Davis. "How old are you?" he said with a smile.

"I'm seventeen, almost eighteen. I'll be eighteen in July," I answered, hoping it would make a difference.

"I thought you were younger than that." He stood up, reached out, and took my hands, pulled me up in front of him, and kissed me on the forehead. His lips weren't on my skin very long, but it seemed like eternity in heaven. If there were other people around, I was oblivious to them. After kissing me, he looked me in the eyes again, still holding my hands, and said, "You know, I want to experiment with sex, and Axey is the kind of girl that I can do that with. She's been around."

"I'll say." Did I really say that? Oh my god, what a jerk I was!

He continued, "But if I wanted to just be with someone, you'd be the one I'd want to be with."

Part of me knew it was a total line; another part thought it was the sweetest thing I'd ever heard. Anyway, just then Axey came running up and started pulling on his arm, and he went off with her. What was he saying? That I was too sweet to have sex? Was that it? But he was a senior, and school was about to end, and I'd never see him again. I could *try* to be nasty!

As things turned out, I did see Parky again, though it was many years later. He became an actor with his own show, *Simon and Simon*. I saw it on TV one night. There he was, with those same blue eyes and sweet smile. I was happy for him. He'd wanted to be an actor, and he made his dream come true.

*The Woodstock, Country School, Woodstock, Vermont, 1966–1967.
My friend, Debbie Carmen, driving Ringo in the school sleigh. It
was only the third time Ringo had been in harness.*

Watch Hill, Rhode Island, 1967. Galloping on empty beach in winter.

In Love Again

That summer before senior year, it was hard to believe I had only one more year of school. In the beginning, I missed Betsy, but she wrote me wonderful letters from her family's farm in West Virginia. It sounded like a place I had to see.

We were able to stable Ringo in the same beautiful old barn he'd stayed in when he first came from the Davis Farm. There wasn't much grazing land around it, one pasture that he had to share with the neighbors' two horses and a pony, but it worked out all right for the most part. The neighbors, a family by the name of Phelps, were nice people. They had seven dogs and at least as many cats.

Nancy Phelps, the mother, had been a Miss Reingold in the '50s. She was still attractive, with a great figure and striking blue eyes that were accented by her thick gray hair. Hubbard Phelps, her husband, was tall, dark, and handsome, but he could be difficult.

The barn we shared actually belonged to another neighbor, but that didn't stop Mr. Phelps from being very particular about how things were done. For instance, he insisted that his horses be pastured separately from Ringo. It was a pain, very time-consuming, to the point where my mother decided we should find Ringo his own pasture.

It was early in the summer; and I was sitting on our porch with my pal, Leslie, catching up on the events of our school years. We'd just discussed how strange it was, being in classes with boys, and I was about to tell her about Parky when Mom came out of the kitchen door. "Sarah," she announced, "I have a solution for Ringo." She seemed proud of herself. "We'll make a pasture behind the garage. It's just the right size for one horse."

"That's a great idea, Mom." The three of us walked out to the garage and surveyed the small section of land behind it.

"He won't have much grass," Mom reasoned, "but at least he'll be out all day." Then, after a pause, she added, "I'm sure Mr. Phelps will love the idea."

"Sounds good," I agreed.

"Trust Ringo's grandmother to figure things out," she said, smiling. Mom appreciated Ringo for the companionship he'd given me. Plus I was living testimony to the benefits of riding. At the end of my seventeenth year, I was healthy and strong.

"Mrs. Howell, telephone," Maria called from the house. Maria was a small, round Antiguan Mom had hired to cook for us that summer.

"I have to run, girls," Mom said over her shoulder. "I'll talk to Hubbard."

"What about the Halls?" I called after her. "Will they let us have a horse back here?" The Halls owned the house we lived in.

"I'll talk to them too. Not to worry." The kitchen door slammed behind her.

It didn't take long to run a post and rail fence around the field. It was a stylish pasture for a stylish horse, and it was great having Ringo so close. We got back into the habit of playing together. He remembered our hide-and-seek game as if we'd never missed a day.

Dr. Barrett came one afternoon to give Ringo his shots. It was nice to see him again. When he arrived, he stood watching Ringo, and all he could do was shake his head. After a few minutes, he said, "I can't believe it, Sarah. Will you look at this horse. He is absolutely beautiful." Ringo had developed a sleek, dark mahogany coat and a black mane that fell in waves across his neck and upper shoulders. His chest had filled out, his legs were sturdy, and his rear end was charmingly dappled. He stood looking at us with his ears up as we watched him, and it was hard to tell who had the brightest twinkle in his eyes, Ringo or Dr. Barrett.

"He's going to be good sized, Sarah," Dr Barrett said as he walked out to Ringo. "He has good bone mass. See how big his knees are?" He took Ringo by the halter. "Yes, sir, I bet he'll be at least sixteen hands." I couldn't tell whether Ringo was happy to see his old friend again, or it was just Dr. Barrett's manner. "I can't get over this," Dr. Barrett carried on. "I knew after a while that he'd survive, but I didn't think he'd catch up so fast. How old is he?"

"Four."

He gave Ringo a pat on the neck; then, I held Ringo while he walked around to check his hind end. "How about shoes, does he keep them on?"

"Not really. He twists the rear shoes off."

"Well, I'll tell you right now, that isn't going to change. He does what we call a rope walk, which means he twists his hind feet slightly when he raises them. It's the result of poor nutrition when he was a foal. But if that's all we have to deal with, we'll be lucky." He checked Ringo's feet. "His frogs are full and healthy. They're a horse's shock absorbers. Good ones mean the horse will stand up over distances." He walked back to Ringo's head and reached into his pocket. Ringo put his ears back a little and jerked his head up slightly.

"Ringo," I scolded him, "it's okay."

Dr. Barrett drew a card out of his pocket. "Here," he said, handing it to me. "Hot shoeing is the only way to go, Sarah. You have to fit the shoe to the hoof, instead of the other way around. And Frank Page is the best blacksmith I know. Tell him I sent you."

I said we'd call Mr. Page.

"Good. Now for the shots." And with that, he headed for his car.

"Ringo," I whispered, "you'll soon be set for the summer."

The hot shoeing worked like a charm. Mr. Page hammered out clips that came up over Ringo's hooves in the back to hold his shoes on. It was fun watching him put the shoe in the fire, bring it out red-hot then hammer it into shape on his portable anvil.

There was a lot going on. I rode every day, and Leslie and I went to the beach a lot. When I wasn't with Ringo, there was an active social life. Watch Hill had a lot of summer residents. Most of the families had teenagers, and Leslie's parents seemed to know all of them. I knew quite a few kids from the previous summer, but I was steadily meeting more. In addition to the regular beach parties, the beach club was one of my favorite places to ride, so Ringo and I became a familiar sight. He was stronger and in good shape from pulling in snow, and I could ride him for three or four hours at a stretch. It was great to see the sand and breaking waves running off into the distance and be able to canter for a mile or two with the salt water splashing out ahead of us then back into our faces.

Murray and Dindy were home for part of the summer, but I have little memory of what they did. I do recall that my brother had some college friends visit for a weekend, and that I found them attractive and entertaining. I liked sitting around listening to them, especially John Benjamin. John would put his arm around me and tell me I was pretty.

My brother was back at the University of Pennsylvania and doing well. His grades had come up, and he'd been elected president of his fraternity. In addition, when he was home, he no longer allowed Mother to walk all over him. He'd learned to keep her at a distance. It made me happy to see him doing so well. I especially enjoyed watching him horse around with his friends.

I'm not sure what Dindy was doing, but I remember she liked to ride Ringo. She wouldn't really ride him the way I did, but she liked to get on him bareback and walk him around. We were strikingly different looking, Dindy and I. She was quite beautiful with her bleached blond hair down to her waist and her clear blue eyes. I, on the other hand, was as dark as she was blond, and I wore my hair short. Plus she was short waisted and had a bustline, whereas I was long waisted and flat-chested. And our presentation was completely different. Whereas she wore very little makeup and was partial to earth-colored slacks, I wore dark eyeliner and liked bright miniskirts. But despite our appearances, she was the more sophisticated. I was down-to-earth. I thought our differences made us quite the dynamic duo.

We were a nice-looking family. Girls were always after my brother. His thick, curly hair and six-feet-four-inch frame drew them like flies. I fit into this family, physically, which is to say I had the looks and the clothes. But I sure wasn't included. My physical disability made it awkward for Murray and Dindy to relate to me, and Mom certainly didn't help. This became clear when I realized that Murray didn't have the slightest idea of how to talk to me. It was the same with Dindy, but at least she made an effort. Murray simply didn't talk unless he had something specific to clarify or resolve. Once in a great while, he might try to make small talk, but he wasn't very good at it. It didn't help that we'd spent so little time together since going off to school that we'd become virtual strangers. Realizing all this, I felt, well, at least I can be around them for a little while before we go our separate ways.

My father was only home on weekends. He still worked in New York and stayed in the apartment Monday through Friday. He was soon to retire, at which point he and Mom planned to buy a home in Watch Hill for their summers and build a house in Florida for their winters. I remember hearing them talk about it, but it all seemed too far in the future for me to think about. I was about to become eighteen, and was having a great summer, and I didn't want to be distracted.

The best part was that I was no longer afraid. The most important thing that Woodstock had done for me was to leave me alone. They didn't make a big deal out of my disability. The faculty's forbearance and the beautiful Vermont countryside had replaced House in the Pine's oppressive structure, as epitomized by Ms. Johndroe's iron hand, and it was an unbelievable gift. In one school year, I had gone from being paralyzed by fear to being so relaxed that I could actually laugh with strangers. David Bailey knew how much emotional catching up I had had to do. He knew the first priority was to get me to trust because once I did, I'd move forward. My grade average for my first year, my junior year in high school, was a D, but that was all right. In David's mind—and mine too—I was ready to be a senior despite my grades. The Woodstock Country School had allowed my determination to shine through, and as it did, I'd become stronger. When I got home at the end of the year, I was clearer about how my mother liked to draw me into conversation, get my guard down, then say something hurtful. As a result, I was better able to deflect her and avoid the put-downs.

I wasn't clear about the details, but I always felt Mom had been a big part of why Murray had slit his wrists. So I was glad to see he'd learned to keep her under control. Dindy was another story. She was still struggling with Mom. She wanted to break away from her, but to a greater extent than Murray and me, she also wanted to please her. And she depended on Murray for guidance and support in her relationship with Mom, so they were close. I felt Dindy didn't want me to come between Murray and her, and Murray didn't care about me one way or the other. Accordingly, I pretty much left them both alone.

Leslie and I liked to walk around Watch Hill at night. There was a great place to buy ice cream cones, and we'd get our favorites—pistachio for Leslie and coffee for me—and walk and lick and talk about boys. It was on such a walk that Leslie told me about Richard.

"Sarah," she said out of the blue, "there's this guy who's interested in you."

"Really? Who *is* he?"

"His name is Richard Skarrow."

"You've never mentioned him. How do you know him?"

"Well, I don't really know him. It's my friend, Kathy, who knows him."

"I've heard of her." Then, in a whisper, "Isn't she a townie?" "Townie" was what we called the kids who lived in Westerly all year round. Westerly was about five miles inland from the summer community of Watch Hill.

"Well, yes, she is, which is why I wanted to talk to you," Leslie said. "Kathy didn't feel like she knew you well enough, and I wanted you to know. See, Richard's a townie too. And he thinks you're really cute and, he wants to ask you out."

"He does? Oh my god." I started to laugh. We were on the sidewalk in front of some stores that were closing, and there were a lot of people going by. Leslie pulled me into the alley. She obviously wanted to tell me something, but she was laughing so hard she couldn't get the words out.

"Come on, girl," I said, pulling on her arm. "What's wrong with him? Has he got zits or something?" I started laughing too, which just made Leslie worse. She laughed so hard her eyes teared up. We'd look away from each other and try to get ourselves together, but every time we looked back, we'd burst out laughing again. Passersby were staring at us.

Finally Leslie burst out, "He's black!" As she spit it out, she spun away in hysterics, bent over, and staggered sideways.

"Black?" I yelled. Leslie tried to put her hand over my mouth, but I pulled it away. "What do you mean?"

She managed to stand up. Wiping her eyes, she said, "What I mean is that he's Italian."

"Leslie," I said, "that's not black!" I gave her a friendly shove.

"No, I know, but he has black hair and dark skin."

"And you know this guy?"

"Well, only through Kathy. I've seen him around with his friends. They hang out in the parking lot . . ." She pointed across the street. "Over there. That's how Richard saw you."

"I guess I never noticed them," I said.

"Well, duh. They're Italian townies, with their own group of friends. But I know you've seen them. Richard drives a 1955 blue and white Chevy."

I did remember the car. With its mag wheels and loud muffler, you couldn't miss it. "Oh yeah," I said. "I think I know who you're talking about. He has a different girl every time I see him. Hasn't he taken Carol Baker to some of the yacht club dances?"

"Yes, that's him."

"Hmm," I said, trying to remember him. "He's not bad."

"Yeah, well, so what do you say? Do you want to go out with him?"

"Sure, why not, I'll give it a try."

Word got back to Richard; then, word of his reaction was sent back through Kathy to Leslie, and Leslie to me. It was that he'd call me Thursday after work. I was nervous but also excited. Thursday afternoon, I spent hours in my room, trying on clothes. I wanted to look really good. I had an assortment of pants and blouses strewn all over my bed when the phone rang. Mom answered just as I got to the phone. After saying hello, she paused and then said, "May I ask who's calling?" I could hear a deep voice; and then Mom said, "Just a moment, please," covered the receiver while mouthing "It's Richard," and handed me the phone. She had a smile on her face, and I could tell she was happy for me.

"Hi, this is Richard," he greeted me. "Kathy Bowlous gave me your number. Would you like to go to the movies Saturday? I have some friends we can double-date with." He didn't sound the slightest bit nervous. In fact, he was so relaxed his voice actually calmed me down.

"Sure, I'd like that," I responded. "What time?"

"The show starts at seven. How about six?"

"Okay. Do you know where I live?"

"Yup. All right, I'll see you then."

When I hung up, I fell backward onto my bed then immediately reached for the phone to call Leslie. "You *have* to get over here. Right now!" I screeched when she came on the line. "Richard just called, and I'm going to the movies with him Saturday, and I have *no* idea what to wear. God, you should see my room!"

Leslie's mom dropped her off for the night, and I went through my outfits and combinations all over again. With Dindy's help, we finally put together a suitable outfit. She provided a pair of slacks that she no longer wore but which I thought was neat. They were tight and had bright pink flowers running down the outside of the legs. And I had a bright pink sweater to go with it. *Oh yeah*, I thought, *I'll look terrific in this outfit!*

When Saturday night came, I had every strand of hair back behind my ears and in the right place. I wore gold hoop earrings, dark eyeliner, tons of mascara, and pale pink lipstick—frosted, of course. Everyone in my family was waiting to see what Richard looked like. Mom and Dad greeted him at the door, Murray and Dindy stood staring from the entrance of the living room, and I, who'd been waiting in my room, made a grand entrance coming down the stairs.

Richard said a polite "Hello, Mrs. Howell" then nodded to my father while shaking his hand. When Murray and Dindy came over, Richard smiled and nodded to them too. My first thought was relief that he'd managed the introductions, but then I began to feel that it was unfair, the way everyone was checking him out. To his credit, he handled it well. When the various greetings were completed, he took my hand, said a gracious good night to everyone, and whisked me out the door.

"Be home by twelve, Sarah . . . please," Mom called after us. As I was getting into Richard's Chevy, I realized how much my family had distracted me. I was so worried about how they'd see Richard because he was an Italian townie that I'd just wanted to escape. I hadn't even really looked at him. So I took a closer look as he held the car door for me. His hair was jet-black and perfectly positioned—just like mine, I suppose. It looked like he'd spent a lot of time getting it slicked back. Plus he had long sideburns. It wasn't a look I was used to.

"Hi," someone said from the backseat. I hadn't even noticed there was someone there. "I'm Louie Faillace."

"Hi," I replied. I tried not to look like I was checking everyone out, but it was hard. Louie, also Italian, was even darker than Richard and well built. He was leaning back, slouching was more like it, with his arm around a girl he introduced as Gail. Gail had shoulder-length, light brown hair, which was shorter on the inside. It looked as if they'd cut a hole in her hair for her face, the way they do with those little dogs. Her clothes were tight, far tighter than mine, and she was chewing and popping gum amazingly fast. It was bubble gum, and every once in a while, whether she was talking to you or not, a bubble would appear, grow to about five inches across, and burst. When the bubbles splattered, she rubbed the gum off her lips and face then chewed it off her finger. With all that going on, it was hard to take your eyes off her mouth. When I said hello, she made the popping noise, smiled, and waved a few fingers.

Richard looked at me and smiled. I was struck by the beauty of his hazel green eyes and the way they contrasted with his black hair. I also couldn't help but notice that he had broad shoulders; strong, chiseled features; and healthy, olive skin. With all this and his green pants and button-up sweater, he sure didn't look like the summer kids I was used to. The sweater wasn't even wool. Unlike most sweaters, the material in the body was stretchy, and the sleeves were suede. His pants were tight too, the opposite of the bulky khakis prep school boys wore.

The engine started with a roar. As usual when I was anxious, my left side jumped. I brought my right leg to the rescue and laid it over my left. No one really knew why crossing my legs relaxed my left leg; it was something I'd discovered. It has something to do with the nerves in my left leg being comforted by contact with my right leg so that they stop firing the muscles. I was glad I knew the trick that night because I was really nervous.

Louie leaned forward and whispered something to Richard, into his outside ear then sat back, laughed, and slapped Richard on the shoulder. Richard wasn't amused. He looked in the rearview mirror, said, "Shut up, Lou," then turned to me and said, "Don't mind him. He thinks everything's funny."

I smiled, looked down, and took a deep breath. The car took off with a burst of energy. Richard drove fast, shifting as often as possible so as to hear the sound of the engine.

"This is quite a car," I said.

"Yeah, I rebuilt it myself. Painted it and everything." It certainly wasn't like any car I'd been in, with its loud engine and raised rear end. The radio was on and loud, and the music seemed to be coming from everywhere. As I was looking around to figure out where the sound was coming from, I noticed that we weren't going in the direction of the movie theater.

"I thought we were going to the movies," I said.

"We are. The passion pit," Louie chuckled from the backseat. Gail laughed, and he pulled her to him and gave her a hard kiss on the mouth.

Suddenly, I wasn't so sure about the whole scene. But I didn't dare say anything. When we got to the drive-in, Richard paid then drove in and parked so that the speaker would have to go on the rear window next to Louie. Louie, who seemed to know the drill, rolled his window down and hung the speaker on it. When it wouldn't transmit, he slapped it, and it went on too loud, and he turned it down. Richard shook his head. "Do you want something to eat before the movie starts?" he asked.

"Maybe a soda," I replied. "Yeah, a soda would be great, thanks." Richard got out, held the speaker so Louie could get out, and the two of them headed off for the snack bar.

It was a warm night and clear. I rolled down my window to take in some fresh air. Behind me, Gail sat in silence. I was feeling uncomfortable because I didn't know what to say to her. I felt I ought to say something. The silence was killing me. But it didn't seem to bother Gail. I couldn't see her, but she seemed content, chewing and popping her gum. When I heard her rummaging around in her purse, then snapping a compact open, I turned and looked back at her. She was behind the compact, looking at herself as she poked her fingers into her hair to make it stick up more.

Okay, I thought, here goes nothing: "How long have you and Louie been going out together?"

She lowered her compact enough to make eye contact, stared at me for a few seconds as if considering how much to tell me, and said, "Oh, we're not dating. We're just friends." Snapping the compact shut, she added, "Louie and I are just helping Richard out. He thought it would be easier if we came along." She smiled. "Hey," she continued, "you live next to the Rathburns, right?"

"Yes, I do."

"Well, you must know Warren," she said.

"I know who he is," I replied. "He's kind of short and has two elder brothers."

"Yeah, that's the one. He is a friend of ours."

I began to relax. Richard and Louie were coming back with our drinks. A couple of horns honked as they got closer to the car. "Hey, Rich, baby," some guy called out, "What'cha got in the car tonight?" It seemed to embarrass Richard. He got in without answering, handed me my soda, and stared straight ahead. As I looked at his profile, I thought he was sweet. A voice inside me said, *Ah, Sarah, you're just taken by his looks.* Immediately, as if debating, another voice said, *Well, he is popular with his buddies.* He had a certain charisma, that's for sure.

We talked a little. He told me he worked at a garage in Watch Hill, pumping gas and driving the summer people's cars back and forth to their homes. He was trying to impress me, but it wasn't necessary. It was all I could do to keep from reaching out and touching his big, workman's hands. I was sipping my soda and thinking about them and how they might feel, when the screen lit up and the movie started. In the backseat, Louie slapped the speaker. My leg was jumping again, so I was relieved when the soundtrack started. Maybe Richard wouldn't notice, plus I knew the jumpiness would stop when I got into the movie.

A cup of popcorn with legs walked across the screen. He had a very smiley face. Then all the things you could and could not do at a drive-in flashed on the screen. When the direction not to honk your horn came on the screen, Louie reached over Richard's shoulder and honked the horn. Then, it seemed everyone in the drive-in honked his horn.

Richard looked at me and burst out laughing. Louie was already laughing. I looked back at Gail who was laughing and hitting Louie at the same time. I could feel Richard's eyes on me, and when I looked at him again, our eyes locked. He reached out and took my hand. Happy, I smiled. He changed the hand with which he was holding my hand, put his free arm around me, and drew me toward him. It was a little difficult getting past the stick shift, but I managed. As I snuggled up, I realized that right then, right there, all he cared about was the beautiful, dark-haired girl sitting next to him.

My leg kept jumping, probably because it was touching his, and he noticed it. Whenever it happened, he'd feel it, than look at my lap. I didn't like it, but I reasoned that he'd seen me walking around town with Leslie, so he must have been aware of my limp. Yet he'd asked me out and was holding me snug against him. Did he not care that there was something wrong with me? These insecure thoughts were racing around in my head as we watched the previews, but I got through them. I reasoned that he must want to be there with me, or he wouldn't be. I thought about how warm and safe I felt against him. The combination helped me relax. It occurred to me that maybe my experiences with the boys at Woodstock were coming in handy.

We watched in silence. Cozy against Richard's shoulder, I didn't move an inch. Finally, "Bambi" flashed across the screen. *Oh my god*, I thought, *the main feature is a children's movie!*

"Hey, Rich," Louie said, clearly frustrated. "What, you didn't look at the paper? Ah, man, I don't believe this." But he laughed good-naturedly.

Richard thought about it for a moment then said, "Well, I don't know about you guys, but I've seen this fifty times. How 'bout we go to the beach?" He looked at me. I felt his arm around me and his breath on my face, and I suddenly realized that not only was I physically attracted to this guy but it was starting to get to me.

"Sure," I said, smiling back at him, "I'd like that."

"Okay, let's go," he said enthusiastically as he pushed me up. I wiggled around the stick shift and across the seat so he could drive. The loss of his green eyes looking down into mine was almost physically painful.

"Yeah man, lets go. Wahoo!" Louie yelled as he put the speaker back on its rack. Then, playfully, he said, "Come here, you," grabbed Gail, and pushed her down on the seat.

Gail started wailing on his back. "Get off me. Get *off* me! Sarah, help me!" She was pretending to be hysterical, but I knew she was having fun. I turned and got up on my knees and started hitting Louie on the back.

We weren't hurting him, but Louie cried, "Okay, okay. I give up, I give up." He sat up, looked out the window, straightened his shirt, and ran his fingers through his long dark hair. He was pretending to sulk. He wouldn't look at me. I put on my expression of severest reprimand. When he could no longer resist peeking at it, he burst out laughing.

We headed for the beach. Louie asked me about my school and how long I'd lived in Rhode Island. He said that the boy who mowed my parent's lawn was Steven Tetlow, a friend of theirs. Louie seemed genuinely interested in me, and Gail was as nice as could be. I decided I was having a good time, better than I had with the Watch Hill kids. The Watch Hill boys were full of themselves, with their cocky attitudes and preppy clothes. They were either spoiled and self-centered, or pretending to be something they weren't, or both. It got to me. I'd survived some horrible experiences, from teasing to outright abuse. I could tell when people were trying to impress me, and I didn't like it a bit.

That was it, Richard, Louie, and Gail were completely natural with each other and me. And they all were obviously devoted friends. Richard had wanted to go out with me, a girl from Watch Hill, his friends supported him enough to come along, and they welcomed me. I appreciated it.

When we reached East Beach, the stars were out, and the waves were lapping on the shore. I was ready to get out and go for a walk, but Richard grabbed my arm and stopped me. He backed the car up, got a running start, and we were off through the deep sand to the harder base at water's edge. When we got there, he turned parallel to the water, and we roared along the shore.

"Oh my god," I yelled. "Won't we get stuck?"

"No, I do this all the time," he said, shifting down. I wondered how many times he'd gotten stuck learning how to do it right.

I was impressed with his driving skills. Louie and Gail were sliding around in the back, playing bumper cars with their bodies, and I was holding on for dear life. I don't know how many times we went up and down that stretch of beach, but time passed; and before I knew it, it was time to go. As we rode through town, all I could think about was going out with Richard again. Was he going to ask me? Was I was everything he hoped I'd be? When we got to my house, I was conflicted about going in. Part of me wanted to go and call Leslie—I'd promised to, no matter how late it was—but another part wanted to stay out on the porch with Richard. No, I had to go in. When I said I was going, Richard paused then stepped forward and took my hands. Back in the car, Gail and Louie were still laughing. Richard and I looked into each other's eyes without speaking. In slow motion, he leaned in and kissed me on the lips. It was short, but ever so sweet. After he kissed me, he gave my hands a squeeze. His hands were warm and strong.

"Thanks," I whispered. "I had a great time."

"Yeah, me too," he whispered back. And then he turned and walked away. I clutched my hands in front of me. I could have stood there and watched him drive off and then stared at the point where he'd disappeared, but I didn't want to look foolish. I didn't want him to think I was completely starstruck.

I passed my parent's bedroom on the way to the stairs. Their door was ajar, and Mom was reading. "Did you have a good time, dear?" she asked, peering over her glasses. I said I had and was on my way on to my room when she stopped me. "Wait. Come tell me. What did you do?"

I went into their bedroom, to Mom's side of the bed. She slapped the mattress, inviting me to sit, but I wouldn't. Daddy turned over so he could see me. "Let's see," I said. "We went to the movies and then to the beach. It was fun. But I'm tired now, so I'm going up, okay?"

Daddy understood. He winked at me and said, "I'm glad you had a good time, Sarah." I knew he meant it. Dad had always been in the background, cheering me on. Through all those years at House in the Pines, and getting Ringo, and changing schools. His love was without conditions. When he told me I looked pretty, the next sentence never started with a "but." Mother might tell me I looked pretty, but I needed to stand up straight, or my bangs were too long, or I was wearing the wrong necklace. My father had never been strong enough to fight my mother, but as the years went by, it bothered me less and less. It wasn't that I was giving up on him. It was more that I didn't need to look to him for help. I was getting better at handling my mother. Nanny and then Ringo had given me the unconditional acceptance; then, the people at Woodstock had convinced me that the stuff that had happened at House in the Pines wasn't my fault. The more I got that into my head, the stronger I felt.

I said all I wanted to say to my parents. The rest was for Leslie. When I got to my room, I dialed her number so fast, I screwed it up and had to start again. The phone seemed to ring forever, but she finally answered. "Shit, Leslie," I hissed. "Where the hell were you?"

"I had to come downstairs. So my parents won't hear me. Well, spit it out, how was it? Did he kiss you?"

"Yes, he did." I giggled shyly.

"Oh my god! He didn't! He kissed you? Oh, he's going to ask you out again for sure."

"I hope so. Because I really like him. Louie Faillace is his best friend. We double-dated with him, and a friend of theirs named Gail. She was nice. Both Louie and she were nice as could be. The movie we went to see was *Bambi.* Can you believe it?"

"Did he do that on purpose?"

"No, of course not, but he handled it well. We ended up driving out on the beach, down to Napa Tree Point."

"You mean he drove his car on the beach?" she asked incredulously.

"That's what I mean," I teased.

"Oh god, that must have been fun."

So that was my first date with Richard. Several weeks went by without hearing from him. One beautiful Friday afternoon, wondering what was up, I rode Ringo down past the garage where Richard worked. I bridled him but rode bareback. All right, I was showing off a little. But Ringo was good on roads, even those that were busy with summer traffic. Nothing scared Ringo, not even ten-wheelers. So as I got closer to the garage, I saw that Richard was out front pumping gas. Ringo was anxious to get to the beach, plus he wasn't keen on boys in general, so he didn't want to stop. I had to talk to him, walk him around in a circle a few times.

Richard was finishing up with a customer. "Thanks, Mr. Griffin. I'll be down to pick that car up," he said. Then, as Mr. Griffin drove away, Richard saw Ringo and me. "Oh," he said. "Hi, Sarah."

"Hi," I said, somewhat sheepishly. "I was on my way to the beach, and thought I'd stop and say hello."

Richard tried to pat Ringo on the neck. Ringo's ears went back, and I spoke to him sharply then said to Richard, "Sorry, he doesn't really like too many people."

"That's all right. I have to get back to work." I noticed that his black wavy hair was messy, and his garage uniform coated with grease. But as he walked off, I again noticed how broad his shoulders were. But why did he rush off? This was the guy that wanted to go out with me? Ringo continued to bug me about standing still. As I tried to restrain him, I realized that I was standing there alone; there was no need to even be there. That was it? The weekend was coming up, and he wasn't going to ask me out? I gave in to Ringo, and we continued on to the beach. "Okay, Ringo, what's going on here?" I said as we walked along the road. "I guess he doesn't like me, after all. I guess I blew it. I mean, what other explanation is there?" Ringo was listening—I could tell by the way he moved his ears back and forth, one and then the other—but he didn't have any advice.

I got to the beach and galloped along the shore in shallow water to my favorite spot. I was trying not to think about Richard. My favorite spot was the ruins of an old fort. It was the same place Carter and I had liked to go. It was a great place to get away from people, and that's what I wanted right then, to be alone. I rode to the top of one of the dunes and sat facing the ocean. The air was clean and warm, and a soft breeze was blowing through my hair, and out on the water the sun was scattering sparkles like diamonds. There were a few people on down the beach, but no one close. One man stood up with his camera and took a picture of me. He had a photographic lens, probably a bored bird-watcher. He waved at me, but I didn't wave back.

I thought about Carter. I'd heard that he'd hit a child with his car on Halloween night. I wondered how he was and considered writing him a note. "No," I said. "That wouldn't be a good idea, would it, boy?" Ringo flipped his head up and down and chewed on his bit. "Oh? You think it would be?" Ringo shook his head. "Oh? So now you're changing your mind?" I slapped him on the neck affectionately. "Well, you be careful, because I'm going to do whatever you tell me to." Ringo pawed the ground with his front leg. "All right. Let's get along home."

I couldn't resist going back past the garage. When I got there, Richard was under a car working and didn't notice us. The rest of the way home, I was looking forward to talking to Leslie about the whole thing. When I did, she had no idea what was going on.

The next morning, when I walked up to the barn to feed Ringo, I was surprised to see Richard's car. He and Louie were perched on the hood, waiting for me. I was walking straight toward them when I saw them, and it made me uncomfortable because they couldn't miss my limp. My embarrassment made my leg tense up, which made me even more awkward. I wanted to stop walking, but I couldn't just stand there. So I did the next best thing. Avoiding eye contact, I tried to act casual. "Hi, Richard. Louie. What are you guys doing here?"

They said hello and followed me into the barn. I was glad I had Ringo to take care of. I walked back and forth, getting hay and grain, and every once in a while I said, "Excuse me," when one of them got in the way.

Louie put his hand over the top of the stall to touch Ringo's head. "I wouldn't do that if I were you," I said with a smile on my face. "He'll bite you."

"Whoa, thanks for telling me. Wouldn't want that now, would we?" Louie said. Backing away from the stall, he nearly tripped over a bale of hay.

I caught Richard staring at me. I was wearing my hip-hugger, bell-bottom jeans and a short blue-and-white-checkered top that showed my stomach. I had a cute figure, and I wasn't afraid to show it. I always thought my looks made up for my disability. At least the disability wasn't the first thing people noticed. Richard's eyes were on my flat stomach. But he wasn't saying much, which made me wonder. Plus whereas Louie had on jeans, Richard was nicely dressed, with tan pants with a belt and a pale yellow button-down shirt.

I sat down on the bale of hay. Ringo was munching his grain. I was at a loss for words. Why had they come, and why was Richard so dressed up? I was afraid to ask. I thought I'd made a fool of myself at the garage. Richard and Louie crouched on their haunches in front of me.

"So, Sarah," Louie broke the silence. "What size sweater do you wear?"

"What?" I said, taken aback by the question. Why did he want to know? "Oh, I don't know. A medium, I guess. Why?"

"No reason, we're just shopping for a friend. Right, Rich?" Louie replied.

"Yeah, right. I gotta go, Lou," Richard said, standing up and heading for the door. Just like that. I followed them out and watched as they got into Richard's Chevy. He popped the clutch and spun out in the driveway, spitting gravel around; and then they were gone, and I was left standing there, totally confused. Was Richard going to buy me a sweater? I couldn't figure it out. All I knew was that it was Saturday, and Richard hadn't asked me out.

I led Ringo down to the pasture behind our garage and let him out. He ran around briefly then came back to the fence and pawed the air with his front foot. Knowing that was his way of telling me he wanted me to go in and play with him, I climbed the fence and dropped down into the pasture. The minute I looked up and made eye contact with him, he squealed and galloped off. He ran down the field and went behind a bush. "I'm going to find you," I said, trying to create a little tension for our game of hide-and-seek. It was absurd because the bush didn't nearly hide him, yet there I was, pretending to sneak up on him.

I was talking nonsense and laughing such that I didn't notice that Warren Rathbun had come up and was standing by the gate. When I "surprised" Ringo and he ran back up the field, and I started after him and saw Warren, I nodded a greeting.

"Hi," he said. "Sarah it is, right?"

I was startled and a little embarrassed that he'd seen me being foolish with Ringo. "Yes, I'm Sarah. And you're Warren Rathbun. Nice to meet you." I walked over to the gate, and we shook hands.

"Nice horse," he observed. "What's his name?"

"Ringo," I replied, always proud to say it.

"That wouldn't have anything to do with the Beatles, would it?"

"Well, yes, I'm a Beatles fan. I went to both of their concerts."

"Really? Cool."

"Hey," I changed the subject, "I've seen you at some of the beach parties, haven't I?"

"Yeah."

"You're a friend of Richard Skarrow's too, right?"

"Yeah, we hang out." And then, just like that, he said, "Well, I gotta go. See you," and walked away. And I hadn't had a chance to ask him anything about Richard. Something strange was going on, no question about it.

Late that afternoon, I decided to take Ringo down Browning Road past Richard's house. I was going to think about Richard for a little while; then, I was going to put him out of my mind. The Brecks of Breck's Shampoo were having a party that night, and I figured that would help, plus Leslie wanted me to go to her house for the night afterward.

I saddled up and started down the road. The closer I got to Richard's driveway, the more nervous I got. When I saw Richard's car coming down the hill, I tried to pull in behind a tree, but it was no use. Richard saw me, or at least I thought he did. There was a girl sitting next to him. She had blond, shoulder-length hair. My heart sank. "Shoot!" I exclaimed. "I don't believe this." I turned Ringo around and headed for the beach. We both needed a good run. When we'd gotten it, I walked Ringo home. "Well, so much for that guy, Ring," I said as I was bedding him down.

When I went through the kitchen, Maria was standing by the stove in her blue uniform and white apron, shaking a pan of vegetables she'd just drained. "Where are you going in such a hurry?" she asked.

"I'm going to a party with Leslie Ahern," I called back from the stairs. Halfway up, I realized that no one was home. I stopped. "Hey, Maria," I shouted, "where is everybody?"

"At the club. Your mother is swimming, and your father is playing golf. From there, they're going to a cocktail party. You have to eat dinner before you go, Sarah."

So the vegetables were for me. "I will, I will," I yelled as I continued up the stairs.

I changed, spending quite a bit of time in the bathroom, making sure my makeup and hair were just right. Satisfied, I went down to eat, passing Murray on the stairs.

"Going out with Ricardo tonight?" he said in a teasing tone.

"No, actually I'm not. There is a party at the Brecks. I'm going with Leslie."

"Oh, maybe I'll see you there," he said to my back. I liked the idea of Murray coming to the party though I didn't expect he'd spend much time with me.

In addition to his college friends, Murray had a group of local guys with whom he spent time. The first year we were in that rented house in Watch Hill, they got into trouble. Murray, Frank Copley, and Hank Somebody-or-other painted a local landmark, a statue of a group of Indians who'd lived in the area. The police came to the house to question Murray; then, he and his pals had to remove the paint. Mom rolled her eyes and said she was "fit to be tied."

That had been the summer before Murray's breakdown. A lot had changed since then, but he was still a bit of a troublemaker. He drank a lot of beer and had too much free time, pretty much like all the summer people in Watch Hill.

Murray dropped me off at Leslie's on his way to see his friends. Leslie's mother greeted me at the door of their Cape Cod house. She was a school teacher, and her husband ran a textile mill in nearby Norwich, Connecticut. They had five children, and while they didn't have as much money as many of the summer residents, they'd lived in Watch Hill for years and were well-known and liked.

Mrs. Ahern was of medium height. She wore her peroxide-blond hair in an efficient pageboy and looked right at you when she spoke. She was clear and assertive, but too funny to be strident. Mr. Ahern, invariably cheerful, was a dark, handsome man with beautiful, deep blue eyes. He was always talking about the book he was reading; I think he thought of himself as an intellectual. The Aherns were a devout Catholic family and great supporters of the Kennedys—the opposite of my parents who were WASP Republicans and thought the Kennedys were trash.

"Hi, Mrs. Ahern," I said as I started for the stairs.

"Hello, Sarah." Lifting her head, Mrs. Ahern called, "Leslie . . . Sarah's here." Leslie appeared at the top of the stairs and waved me up. Just then, Mr. Ahern walked in from the dining room. He was carrying a book and doing his whistling thing. He had this way of whistling with his lips shut. At least they looked shut. And his whistle sounded like a tiny trumpet. It was a riot. So he came into the front hall and stopped and looked at me and said, "Hello, young lady." It was hearty, he always gave you a hearty hello. Then he started whistling again and continued on into the living room.

I looked up at Leslie, and we both laughed. It was one of our favorite things, her dad's whistle. I went up, and we went into her room. It was small but cozy, with twin beds and a slanted ceiling. We sat lotus position on one of the beds, facing each other.

"So? What's going on with Richard?" Just like her mother.

"I don't really know. When I saw him a little while ago, he was with another girl. I think she's staying at his house."

"You mean he asked you out and he's seeing someone else?"

"Doesn't make sense, does it? Anyway, it's not like I was the one chasing him. He's the one who wanted my phone number."

"What a snake!"

"Yeah, well, I can't think about it any more. Let's just go have some fun, okay?" I got up and started pulling her arm.

The Brecks were only a few blocks from the Aherns, so we walked. As we got closer, the music became louder. Leslie said, "You know, Johnny Hemmingway thinks you're the most beautiful girl in Watch Hill."

"He does?" It was news to me. John Hemmingway, a neighbor of Leslie's, was older than we were, good-looking and wealthy. He later became a host on a TV show called *Travel*. I didn't know anything about him really, but I was flattered that he found me attractive.

"Yeah, you and Kate Burke." Kate was another friend of Leslie's. Her family owned a big department store in New York City. I was also flattered to be considered in the same category as Kate Burke.

The Breck's large front hall was jammed with Watch Hill kids. Leslie and I pushed through the crowd and out to the back porch. As we went, I glimpsed Murray across the living room. He was leaning on the shoulder of some girl I'd never seen before, and he was rocking back and forth like he was already bombed. His friends were with him, and they looked just as bad. I looked away before he saw me.

There didn't seem to be any parents around. When I observed it, someone said Mr. and Mrs. Breck were away. "That explains why there are so many people here," I yelled into Leslie's ear. We were out on the porch. I didn't know a lot of the kids who were there. Leslie saw Kate and took off; then, I saw Warren Rathbun. Wanting him to see me so he'd tell Richard I was at the Breck's party, I walked over and said hello. We talked for a while, but he was watching some girl; and when he saw an opening, he left in midsentence.

I found myself alone and bored. After a while, a boy came up behind me and started talking. His name was also Richard, but he was a far cry from Richard Richard. I'd seen him at beach parties. He liked to stare at me. He was creepy and made me nervous.

"Want to take a ride in my car?" he asked. That was the kind of a guy he was. He needed you to know he owned his own car. "I'll take you to my place."

"No, thanks, Richard." I walked away. When I thought it was safe, I glanced back. He was still watching me. I slipped into the living room, hoping to find my brother, but he'd already left. When I saw Leslie and Kate in the kitchen, I pushed through people to get to them, excusing myself as I went.

"Hi, Sarah," Kate said when I came up. "We were just talking about going to the beach club tomorrow. Want to come?" Kate was pretty, all right. She had dark hair that fell over her shoulders like a silk scarf, deep brown eyes, pale skin, straight white teeth, and a small, delicate nose. But she was also smart and sophisticated. Her family, more Irish Catholics, was close friends with the Aherns.

"Sure, I'd love to." My parents went to the club almost every day and always for Sunday dinner. Leslie and I agreed to meet Kate at the snack bar around noon.

The three of us stood around for a while; then, Kate moved away. For all the people there, it wasn't much of a party. Leslie and I hung on until midnight then walked back to her house. The salt air was fresh and cool, and the streets were so quiet we could hear the waves pounding in the distance. It all made me appreciate how lucky I was to be there. I had Ringo to ride on the beach during the day, no end of parties at night, and quiet, safe streets to walk home on.

"You're deep in thought, Sarah," Leslie observed.

"I was just thinking about how much I like it here."

"Yeah, it's really nice."

When we got back, we went straight to bed. The moon was streaming in through the window, lighting up the room. I hunkered down, pulled the covers up to my chin, and said, "I'm having a big eighteenth birthday party, Leslie."

"I know," Leslie said.

"How did you know?"

"Your mother told me." She sat up, took something out of the drawer of her bedside table, and shone a flashlight on my face. "Don't look so surprised. Of course you're having a party, eighteen is a biggie."

"Yeah, I suppose. It's going to be a Hawaiian theme, with lanterns and a pig roast. Do you think I should invite Richard?"

"No, I don't think you should invite Richard." No hesitation. "Come on, Sarah, you saw him with another girl."

"I know, I know, but it's not as if I own him or anything." I rolled over, exasperated by the vision of the blond in the car with him.

"You don't, but she may think she does."

The next morning I went home right after breakfast so I could feed and play with Ringo before going to the club. I'd been out of school since the middle of May, so I had a head start on my tan; but Kate and Leslie wanted to work on theirs.

It was nearly noon when I got back to the house. Mom and Dad were packing their beach bags when I walked into their bedroom.

"Sarah," Mom said, "I've been meaning to talk to you."

"About what?"

"Remember the Stevensons?"

"Yeah. Susie Stevenson. In England. We visited them when I was thirteen."

"'Yes, Mom,' will suffice, dear."

"Yes, Mom. What about her?"

"Well, we just got word that she's coming to stay with us."

"Really?" I sat down on the bed. I liked Susie. I even liked her accent. It reminded me of the Beatles. "How long will she stay?"

"Oh, maybe four to six weeks. I thought it would be fun for her to see some of the United States, so we're going to take a trip." Mom was always building up to something.

"You mean I'd go?"

"Yes. You, Susie, Mrs. Moore—if she wants to—and me."

"What about Dad?"

"Oh, he wouldn't enjoy this trip, Sarah. We're going to a dude ranch in Wyoming."

"Great! So, like, we can ride and camp out?" I jumped up from the bed. Dad came out of the bathroom. There was a spot of shaving cream on his cheek. I walked over, took the end of the towel he had over one shoulder, and wiped it off.

"Thanks, honey." He smiled and gently patted the back of my head.

"Don't you want to go, Dad?" I asked.

"No, honey. I think you and your mother should go."

I watched him button his shirt. I wanted him to come. He spent all week in New York, and I only saw him on weekends, and not much then, and I thought it would be fun if he came.

Mom was going on about how we'd fly to Chicago then take the train on to Wyoming so Susie could get a taste of the West. I had to admit it sounded great.

It wasn't until we were walking out to the car that I remembered Ringo. "What about Ringo? Who'll take care of him?"

"Mr. Phelps said he would." That was just like her, to make all the plans without consulting me and then spring them on me.

We got to the club, and Mom got out and started for the clubhouse. I called after her, "Mom, wait. Ringo hates Mr. Phelps. You *know* that."

She stopped, turned, looked at me, and said, "Don't worry, Sarah. Dr. Barrett will be around. He's promised that if Mr. Phelps has any problems with Ringo, he'll come to the rescue."

"But it's the other way around. It's Ringo who has the problem with Mr. Phelps."

"They'll manage, Sarah." And that was that.

It was a fine day for the beach. Leslie, Kate, and I bodysurfed until we were too exhausted to do anything but float. Afterward, we flopped onto our towels and lay there like sunning seals, sharing our fantasies about the lifeguard. I didn't think about Richard once the whole day.

When we got home, I was on my way out to the pasture to take Ringo back to the barn when the phone rang. Maria yelled out the door that it was Richard.

"Richard?" I asked in incredulously.

"That's right," Maria said, smiling. "Hurry, hurry. Come, come."

Maria graciously left the room when I picked up the phone. I could barely breath, but I tried to act calm and disinterested. "Hello."

"Hi, Sarah, this is Richard. I'm going to a party at Gail's house Tuesday night. Want to come?"

Hmmm, did I? I'll say. Actually, I wanted to say no, but there wasn't much chance of that.

Two nights later, as we were riding along to Gail's, he said, "I saw you riding past my house last weekend."

Darn, I thought, he did see me. "Yeah," I answered as calmly as possible, "I took Ringo down Browning Road. I do that sometimes. It's nice, quiet." I was rambling, so I stopped, crossed my legs, and looked down at my hands. They were sweating *and* trembling.

"I had a girl at my house. Her name is Dianne," he said.

It popped out: "Is that who the sweater was for?"

Richard looked shocked. "How did you know?"

"Well, it wasn't too hard to figure out, since you never ended up getting one for me. I figured it had to be for someone else." I was wondering why Richard was telling me about this girl, Dianne.

We pulled into Gail's driveway, and he turned the engine off. I was waiting for him to get out, but he just sat there. Finally, he looked at me and blurted out, "I broke it off with her."

"How long had you been going with her?" I had to ask, but I didn't want to know.

"About a year."

"Wow, that's a long time."

"Yeah, she was pretty upset. But when I saw you, even before I met you, I knew it was going to change things. Sorry about *Bambi*." He laughed.

"That's okay, I had a good time. And I liked Louie and Gail. It was fun."

When I looked over at him, I could see that he was relieved to have it off his chest. He reached for me, drew me to him, and was about to kiss me when Louie knocked on the window.

"You guys coming in or what?" Louie was obviously pleased to have caught us about to kiss.

"Yeah, yeah, keep your shirt on," Richard growled at his friend. We got out and went into the house.

Gail's parents were warm and friendly. Her sister, June, was there, as was Stephen Tetlow, the boy who mowed our lawn.

"So you're the one who's always lying around in a bikini?" he teased.

"Yup, that's me," I giggled, giving it right back.

That night, I also met Robert Gouvin and his girlfriend, Mary Lou. They'd been going together since the fifth grade and were planning to get married when they graduated. Robert was Richard's other best friend.

All the kids I met that night went to school together. They were the townies that Leslie was talking about who never mixed with the Watch Hill kids. They knew I was one of the summer kids, but they didn't care. Since I was with Richard, I was part of the group. I had a really good time. *Really* good. And then, before I knew it, I was home and saying good night to Richard.

"I'm going to be eighteen on July third," I whispered. "My parents are giving me a big party. Want to come?" I bit my lower lip and smiled.

"Yeah, sure." And then he kissed me, really kissed me. And then he took my face in his hands and looked into my eyes, and there was passion all over his face. I felt it too, and it wasn't like anything I'd felt before.

The night of my party finally arrived. My parents had gone to great lengths to make it colorful and fun. They hung lanterns around the yard, put up torches, and arranged to have a pig roasted on a spit. From our porch, we looked east, down across the Pawtucket River; and as the moon came up, its reflection sparkled on the water. Murray had discovered a local band he liked, so we arranged for it to play. The band members catered to me as if I was their kid sister.

But the best thing about the party was Richard. He was one of the first to arrive, and we walked around, hands entwined, greeting people. Leslie was there, as were a few of my Watch Hill pals; and my parents had a few friends over. At one point, when Richard and I heard a great explosion of laughter inside the house, I knew immediately that it was Mom telling a funny story. Mom's sense of humor and contagious laugh were among her best qualities, and I admired them.

Richard and I sat on the porch, watching the guests. As the evening wore on and it became cooler, Richard took off his jacket and put it over my shoulders. "Boy, this is some party!" he said.

"Yeah, Mom knows how to entertain."

Richard put his arm around my waist. "Do you want to go out for a while after it's over?"

"Sure."

Leslie walked by and winked. "Hey, Leslie," I responded, smiling. "See you tomorrow?"

"You bet."

Richard and I waited until almost everyone was gone. Mom had told me that tonight, on the occasion of my eighteenth birthday, I could stay out as late as I wanted. As we were getting ready to leave, she came out and asked if she and Dad could have a few words with me. Richard got up with me and would have accompanied me in, but Mom stopped him. She looked him in the eye, smiled, and said, "Richard won't mind waiting outside for a minute."

She led me into the living room. Dad was sitting on the couch. I didn't know what was going on.

"Sit down, dear," she said. Dad patted the sofa next to him, and I joined him. Sitting down next to me, Mom handed me a tiny gift-wrapped package and said, "This is your birthday present."

Inside the package was a black box, and inside the box was a gold ring. It had a sparkling dome with small diamonds in a circle and a ruby in the center. "Mom, it's beautiful! Really amazing! Where did you get it?"

"My mother gave me a ring when I turned eighteen. It had two rubies on it. Do you remember it?"

"Vaguely."

"Well, I took the rubies off that ring and had two rings made, one for Dindy and one for you."

"Oh, right. I've seen Dindy's."

"You have such beautiful hands, Sarah, I thought this setting would look stunning on you."

I took the ring out of the box and tried it on. It was dazzling, no question about it. I flashed it for Dad, and he smiled and gave me a kiss on the cheek.

"Take good care of it," Mom instructed. "It will be worth something one of these days."

"Thanks, Mom. Thanks, Dad." I kissed one then the other. "This is the perfect end to a perfect party."

I went out to show Richard my present. He was amazed. His female friends didn't get presents like that. After enjoying the ring for a few minutes, I took it up to my room and hid it away in my jewelry box.

Richard and I took off to find his friends over in Watch Hill. Louie was in the beach club parking lot. Richard drew his car up next to Louie's so the driver's windows were side-by-side, and they drank beer and kept watch for their friends while we talked. Occasionally they would start their cars, back up, and squeal around the parking lot making "donuts."

Richard and I dated regularly after that. It meant I saw less of Leslie, but that was all right. She was happy for me, plus she had lots of other Watch Hill friends.

I met Richard's mother and stepfather. Then, I met his aunt and her husband. Richard's mother, Mary, and her sister, Camille, owned a beauty parlor in nearby Westerly; and Richard would visit them when he needed money. When he'd show up, his mother and aunt would fuss over him. They'd insist that he kiss them then allow them to introduce him to the ladies under the dryers. A lot of their customers were summer people who knew me. They were surprised to see me there, especially since I didn't get my hair done. "Sarah," they'd exclaim, "what in the world are *you* doing here?"

"I'm with Richard," I'd reply.

The sign over the door read Skarrow's Beauty Shop. Richard's mother was married to her second husband, Bob Capalbo; but since everyone knew her as Skarrow, she'd kept her first husband's name for her shop.

Camille was a bright and cheery woman with sparkling blue eyes and dyed and permed hair with gold highlights. She had a snappy figure and lots of energy, and she loved Richard as if he was her son instead of her sister's.

Mary was taller and plainer than Camille. She wore her black hair rolled into a twist at the back of her head, had long, perfectly manicured fingernails, and was heavier through the hips. She, too, had lots of energy though her energy came across as quiet strength rather than get-up-and-go. Both women were open, friendly, and exceedingly polite. "So we finally get to meet the little girl," Camille said, shaking my hand. Richard seemed embarrassed.

One Sunday afternoon, Mrs. Skarrow invited me to dinner at the grandmother's house to meet the rest of the family. Richard's grandmother's name is Anna; his grandfather's, John. They were gracious and hospitable, the family patriarch and matriarch.

That's where I met Mary and Camille's elder sister, Lena. She was thin and frail. Richard later told me she suffered from seizures. He'd spent a lot of time with her when he was a child. It had been her job to take care of him while their mother was at the beauty shop, but he'd also had to take care of her. He told me how, when they'd be walking down the street with Lena holding his hand, she'd sometimes have an attack and fall right down on the sidewalk. He'd have to kneel down beside her and hold her head until the seizure passed, and she could get up and lead him on.

When he told me about Lena, I found it easy to tell him about my seizures. It just came out. He said Lena's seizures were grand mal, and that they came on during the day. I told him mine came only at night, and how I was taking Dilantin, and it seemed to stop them. He said Lena had started taking Dilantin, too, with equally positive results.

When I then went on and took the risk of telling him about my cerebral palsy, his only comment was, "So everyone has something they have to deal with." And when I then had the courage to ask if he'd noticed my limp, he said, "Yeah, but it doesn't bother me."

I spent the next few weeks either riding Ringo or with Richard. And sometimes I'd do the two together. I might take Ringo to the beach and run him down the shoreline while Richard drove his car beside us. Or Richard would bring his camera and photograph Ringo and me. I was the only girl Richard was dating, and I had no interest in anyone else, so we spent nearly all our time together.

In time, I also met Richard's father, Rudolph. He was a nice-looking Polish man who owned a junkyard near Louie's house. Richard told me how his dad had helped Louis and him build go-carts out of parts they found in the junkyard. His dad's hands were large and dexterous, good at fixing things, a trait he'd passed onto his son. Richard also told me that his father had once been a professional photographer with his own studio.

"What happened? Why isn't he still doing photography?" We were driving back from a visit to his dad's.

Richard looked over at me, considering how much to tell, and said, "I had a sister. She died before I was born, at eighteen months. My father never got over it. As a result, he started spending a lot of time alone. And the more time he spent alone, the harder it was to be nice to his clients. And you know, you have to be nice to people if you're going to get good pictures of them."

Richard took an old, cracked picture of his father out of his wallet and showed it to me. It was of a much-younger Rudolph, in a three-piece suit, smoking a pipe. His hair was neatly combed, and he had a big smile on his face. He was in his studio, with his tripods and lights and cameras in the background. The man in the picture didn't look anything like the man I'd just met. His clear eyes had become bloodshot, and his face bloated from too much drink. The house he now lived in wasn't much more than a shed.

Despite the tragedy in Rudolph's life, he clearly adored his son. He never said as much, or much at all for that matter, at least to me, but I could tell. His face lit up when he saw Richard. He was a gentle and sensitive man.

I enjoyed Richard's entire family. They obviously loved and admired him. He was their shining star in the night sky. And as I experienced the quality of attention they all gave each other, I realized how different they were from my family. The love I received from my parents wasn't nearly as freely expressed. Richard got lots of hugs from his aunts and mother, and his dad would often reach out and take his arm or put his hand on Richard's shoulder. They sure weren't like my family. My mother might pat me on the leg, or my father might wink, but I never got hugged. Richard could walk into the room with his family, and all eyes would turn to him, and they'd listen to every word he said. And when I spoke, they'd listen to every word I said. Without understanding why, I began looking forward to our visits.

Mom Makes Her Choice

August arrived, and along with it came Susie Stevenson and our trip to Wyoming. I was excited about going to a ranch although I didn't want to leave Richard. He didn't want me to leave either, but he convinced me that the time apart would pass quickly.

He was right. I was so engrossed by the magnificent scenery from the double-decker train we took from Chicago to Wyoming that I completely forgot about everything else. Plus the ranch was great. The rest of the trip is somewhat blurred, except for something that happened to my mother.

Mom met a man from New York City who was really interested in her. They went riding together almost every day. I didn't think much of it until Mom came to me one afternoon near the end of our trip. Susie and Mrs. Moore had gone on a walk, and I was sitting on the porch of our cabin, taking in the setting sun. Mom sat down in the rocker next to me. After swinging in silence for a few minutes, she said, "You really are a good rider, Sarah."

"Thanks, Mom." I was gratified that she appreciated my skill.

After another, shorter pause, she said, "Mr. Andrews wants me to meet him in New York."

"He does?"

"Yes. Your father hasn't touched me in months."

I was flabbergasted to have her say such a thing to me—speechless, and then embarrassed. Why was she telling me this?

"Do you think I should go?" she asked. And then, when I didn't answer, she added, "I don't think I can. I don't think I should."

I didn't know what to say. I knew my parents' relationship wasn't great. Mom was forever bossing Dad around, and he often mumbled under his breath at her. One night during their cocktail hour, I heard him call her an "asshole." It startled me because Dad almost never swore, certainly not in front of Mom, and I'd never heard him call anyone such a name. I hadn't really thought about their sex life. I mean, what daughter does? So

I was thinking of all this stuff when I suddenly blurted out, "I think you should go. Have some fun, Mom." I had no idea where it had come from, or why I'd said it.

"No . . . I can't, it's just not right." And then, as suddenly as she'd brought the subject up, she got up and went into the cabin.

I've always remembered that short interaction with my mother. It revealed so much about her and my parents' relationship. I don't know what it was like in the beginning, but by the time I was aware of such things, there was little show of affection. I don't know why, what might have embittered one or the other, or both of them. What child ever knows such things? All I know looking back is that for those few moments out on that porch, it seemed my mother stopped pushing and showed her true feelings. She allowed me a glimpse into her real self then immediately thought better of it and slammed the door. As far as I know, she never saw Mr. Andrews again.

Susie had a wonderful time visiting our Wild West, and I certainly enjoyed her company; but like me, she had a beau who couldn't wait for her to return home, so neither of us was sorry to see it end. We were young, things were changing fast, and we both wanted to get on to whatever might be coming next.

There wasn't much time left for Richard and me before I had to return to Woodstock. Nor was there much time left for our family in our house by the river. We had spent five years there, but it was coming to an end. My father was retiring, and my parents were in the process of buying another Watch Hill house. They planned to spend their winters in Florida, where they wanted to build their dream house on a piece of property they owned in Siesta Key, and their summers in their new Watch Hill residence. This meant that all but my summer vacations would henceforth be spent in Florida.

Of course I went out with Richard on my last night home. He was more upset than I'd ever seen him about my going away. I think he was afraid he'd lose me. He had tears in his eyes, and he promised to drive up to visit me every weekend. "No matter what," he kept repeating. We hugged each other tightly and kissed gently and soulfully. When we got back to my house and it was finally time to part, I gave him the phone number at my dorm. I went into the house crying and, quietly making my way up to my room, locked the door behind me.

Senior Year

Ringo had become a seasoned traveler, so I wasn't worried about his trip back to school. He remembered the barn, and even Emily and Bruce.

Betsy and I were no longer newbies. We'd been writing to each other all summer, but even so, it was great to see her again. In fact, it was great to see all the kids and to feel comfortable about returning to school.

We got the room we'd requested. It was on the second floor at the front of the house, looking out across the upper yard to the barn. Our first night back, we lay awake talking about our summers. I'd told her about Richard in my letters, but now I could give her the details. She listened with great interest.

The next morning we got up early and went directly to the barn to check on Ringo. Bruce and Emily were there, looking and behaving exactly as they had the previous spring. Bruce observed how healthy Ringo looked, and how he'd grown. I told him Ringo had had a great summer then patted Ringo on the neck as he thrust his head into his feed bucket.

"Betsy, come here," Emily called, as she came out of the tack room. "I want to show you something."

We followed her out to the outside stall. In the corner of the stall, standing quietly, was a beautiful chestnut mare.

"We just got her yesterday," Emily said. "Maybe she can be your project this year."

I smiled at Betsy, happy for her. "I'll help you, Bets."

"Okay," Betsy said, ambivalently.

Betsy wasn't very confident about her horsemanship, but the mare turned out to be a great horse for her, gentle and easy gaited. Plus she was so mild tempered that we could pasture her with Ringo. Betsy and I rode all over the place that year. Among other things, it helped fill the time between Richard's visits.

Debbie Carman returned for her senior year, as bossy as ever. I didn't enjoy her. The fact that she'd taken up with our French teacher made me feel she was kind of weird.

There seemed to be a number of students having relationships with teachers. I guess it was part of the school, like the panty raids that went on—a game the boys came up with. Every couple of months, the boys would come running into the girls' dorm in the middle of the night, throw blankets over our heads, and carry us off. David Bailey eventually grew tired of this and decided we all—girls as well as boys—should be punished. So he loaded a group of us into the farm truck, took us miles away from the school, and dumped us off with the instructions to make it back on our own. He made Betsy and me go even though we hadn't participated in the raids. There were a lot of boys. They took up the whole road, hooting, yelling, and whistling such that the people who drove by honked their horns in greeting.

Richard lived up to his pledge about driving up on weekends. David Bailey let him eat in the dining room. At night, we went to the motel where he stayed, and he brought me back to my dorm around ten. It made the year go by fast.

Christmas was the last time I stayed in our house in Rhode Island. That spring vacation, I went to Florida. It was awful being away from Ringo and Richard for the three weeks. It was also strange not to come home to the bedroom I'd grown used to. In Florida, I had a new bed in a new room in a house I'd never slept in before. Even after I was there for a while, I felt as if I was just visiting. Richard called every night, and even though Florida was nice, I couldn't wait to get back to school—where Ringo was waiting and Richard would soon visit.

Spring vacation finally ended, and I made it all the way back to school. That first weekend, I could barely control myself; I was so excited about seeing Richard again. I remember sitting in my room and listening for the familiar roar of his Chevy. Finally, I heard it in the distance, coming past the soccer field and up the hill. By the time he pulled into the drive and got out of his car, I was down the stairs, out the front door, and running down the steps toward him. He caught me in his arms, and I savored his strength and the familiar smell of his cologne as he pressed me against him. "I've missed you *so* much!" I hissed in his ear.

"Yeah," he growled. "That was *too* far away for *too* long." He looked down into my eyes and then at my face. "I don't *ever* want to go through that again."

Graduation was in May. My grades were poor, but in David's mind, the school had done everything it could for me. And it had done a lot, that was for sure. I'd grown stronger, to the point that I hardly ever thought about House in the Pines or the treatment I'd suffered there.

The only problem was that, unlike the other girls, I wouldn't be going on to college. My mother had long since decided that, since I'd gone through so much getting through high school, college wasn't an option. That was the way she put it—that *I'd* gone through so much, but I think what she was really saying was that *she'd* gone through so much. I don't know how David Bailey and my teachers felt; all I know is that there was never any mention of my taking SATs or visiting colleges.

My mother always told me that I was exceptionally pretty, and I guess her opinion had been confirmed during that last spring break. She and Dad had a cocktail party at which there was a photographer from *Sarasota Magazine*, and he asked Mom if I'd model for him. When she told me, I thought it was kind of cool that a professional photographer had noticed me. Why not? It could be fun.

The shoot was at a house on the beach. There was a swimming pool, and I wore a jazzy bikini. It was an awesome feeling, having everyone stare at me and the bulbs flashing and cameras snapping. Plus it was something I was naturally good at. It didn't involve walking, so no one saw my limp, and the photographer was careful not to show my scarred foot or wandering eye.

Mother picked up on my enthusiasm and, without my knowledge, began planning a future in modeling for me. First on her list was a final operation to fix my toes. Their constant tucking under was driving me crazy, and something had to be done. The surgery was done in June and was simple and painless compared to my earlier operations. It was the last time I would ever see Dr. Wilson.

After the surgery, I went back to Watch Hill, to our new summer home. It was a beautiful old farmhouse with large porches and a yard full of manicured hedges and bright flowers. The ocean was right across the street, so the pounding of the waves and the salt air were a fixture in my life. My bedroom was a big sunlit room on the back of the house.

I saw Richard every day while my foot recovered. He asked one of his friends who had a horse to board and exercise Ringo while I was laid up. I thought it was sweet of Richard to think of Ringo that way, especially since Ringo was so consistently nasty to Richard.

Sarasota, Florida, 1969. mother took this picture of me after one of her cocktail parties. She was pleased that I'd been gracious to her guests and thought I looked pretty. Whereas Mom saw me as nice and pretty but believed I was "not college material," I saw myself as nice, all right looking, and in some ways gifted. I didn't think it was my failing that my family didn't understand me, or that I was more comfortable around instinctual animals than supposedly rational people.

A One-way Ticket

I was settling into my world of Ringo and Richard. Ringo had been a major part of my life for three years; and Richard, for one. Together, they'd become the big constants in my life. Plus Richard and I were in love, and we knew it was real. We'd even begun talking about being together forever. So it seemed as if my life was starting to take shape. But then I began to notice something. My mother wasn't as nice to Richard as she'd been the first summer we'd been together. Or maybe she'd never been nice except in front of me. Whichever, I noticed that when I was in my room and Richard came to pick me up, she made him wait outside. At first she did it just when her Bridge friends were there because she didn't want to interrupt her game to introduce him, but she got into the habit of doing it whenever he came. She wouldn't come right out and say it, but I think it was her way of suggesting that he go away and never come back. I thought it was unbelievably rude.

Little did I know. One evening in late August, I was sitting in the living room in front of an early fire when she came in and sat down next to me. She was holding something in her hand, and when she handed it to me, I saw that it was an airline ticket. Her face was stern and determined.

"What's this?" I asked, opening the folder. It was a one-way ticket to England in my name. "Mom, what's going on? England? A one-way ticket? Where's the return ticket?" I rummaged through the other papers in the folder.

"There is no return ticket, Sarah," she said. "You'll stay with the Stevensons until we can find you a flat. It will be fun seeing Susie again. Then, once you get settled in your own place, you can start modeling school."

Stunned, I stared into the fire.

"You're too young to be in such a serious relationship," she went on. She was pressing her advantage of surprise. "Besides, there has never been any Italian blood in our family."

So that was it. Shocked, hurt, and beginning to feel anger, I replied, "What's that supposed to mean?" I wanted her to say it out loud. She knew what I was trying to do and wouldn't answer.

I stood up, and she stood up with me, so there was no advantage gained. Bringing her face in close to mine, she said, "Look, Sarah, modeling is your only hope. At least you have a pretty face. If you refuse to go, I'll . . . I'll tell my friends that you'll never amount to anything."

I could feel the flush in my cheeks. She didn't move, didn't even draw her head back. I knew she wasn't sorry for what she'd just said. It was so like Mom to go too far like that. Too furious to speak, I turned away. It occurred to me that her cold rejection was the exact opposite of the warm embrace of the fire. I didn't know what to say or do—except go to Ringo.

It was an unseasonably cool night, and very dark, and a fairly good walk to where Ringo was boarding. I shuffled along what I thought was the edge of the road, but I was blinded every time a car passed, with the result that I went back and forth from the grass to the pavement. The cars honked at me when I got too far out, but I was too distraught to care. In an effort to bolster my spirits, I tried to remember the good things the teachers at the country school had told me. When thinking them wasn't enough, I spoke them; and when speaking them wasn't enough, I yelled them. "I *am* a good person. I *am* worth something! My mother is *wrong!*"

Mom just wanted me away from Richard. Well, I wasn't going to let go of all the good feelings I'd found. I'd figure a way. I would! When I got to Ringo's barn, I went directly to his stall, buried my face in his neck, and let the tears flow. I stayed with Ringo until I calmed down then continued on to Richard's.

Richard met me at the foot of his driveway. "I called your house," he said with obvious concern. "Your mother didn't know where you were. She sounded *very* weird." He took my hand. "Where have you been?" The streetlight shone down on us; there was a soft but chilling breeze. I shivered, and Richard put his arm around me. He could tell I'd been crying. "What's wrong?" he asked.

"I was with Ringo."

"Oh no. When you go to see that horse at strange hours, I know something's wrong. What is it?" He took my hands and rubbed them as he started drawing me up the driveway.

My arms stretched out, but I couldn't move my feet. "I'm going away, Richard. My mother is sending me to England, to modeling school," I said it all very quietly, as if it was a death sentence.

Richard thought about it for a moment then asked, "When will you be back?"

"That's just it. I don't know. She's going to rent a flat for me in London."

"A what?"

"An apartment."

Richard turned away and slammed his fist into the palm of his other hand. It was the first time I'd seen him that upset. Ordinarily, he was a gentle soul, somewhat like Ringo. And like Ringo, he accepted me for who I was. They were my only true friends, Ringo and Richard, and now I was leaving them both. I stood in the driveway looking at Richard's back. "Richard," I said. He didn't move. I took a step toward him and put my hand on his shoulder. When he turned and I saw the anguish in his eyes, I took him in my arms and squeezed with all my might.

"Will you watch out for Ringo?" I whispered.

"You're not going, are you?" he replied.

"For now, yes, but I'll come back." I felt resolve replacing my sadness. I had spent too many years away from home doing everything my mother wanted me to do. I'd finally found someone I really cared about, and I'd been thinking that I was going to have this great year with him; and in a matter of minutes, my mother had ruined it, swept it all away. But I'd survived four years at House in the Pines, and two more at Woodstock—where I'd discovered my strengths—and in the process, I'd become a *very* determined person. I'd go along with my mother for the time being, but I'd get my way in the end.

I spent my last night home with Richard. I couldn't bear to see, much less say good-bye to Ringo. The last thing I did as Richard was leaving was go in the house and get the rest of the Oreo cookies for him to give Ringo after I'd gone.

At Last, Sweet Defiance

I spent the flight to England with my head buried in a one of Richard's sweaters, feeling alone and desperately unhappy. As we came down out of the sunny blue and through the clouds to rainy London, I put makeup on to hide my puffy eyes.

It was nice seeing Susie again. We spent afternoons in the backyard of her home, catching up, and recalling our trip out West. Susie's parents did all they could to make me feel at home; and I made an effort, but it was hard.

The Stevensons showed me London, which was only a half-hour drive from their home. And they took me across to Ireland, which was beautiful. I got to go riding in the Irish countryside.

But Susie knew there was something wrong. I spent a lot of my time alone in my room, reading and rereading the day's letter from Richard, or staring out the window.

One day, to my surprise, I got a letter from Louie. It was about Richard, and it was very disturbing. As I was reading it over a second time, Susie came into my room. Seeing her sympathetic expression brought tears to my eyes. I got up and stood with my back to her so she wouldn't see them. "Sarah," she said with clear concern, "what's wrong?"

I was too upset to speak, so I simply handed her the letter.

"Do you want me to read it?" she asked, ever the well-mannered Englishwoman.

I nodded. She took the letter, sat on the edge of my bed, and carefully unfolded it. The room was hot, and the combination of the warmth and silence, oppressive, so I unlatched and opened the window. Mrs. Stevenson had created a truly magnificent garden behind their cottage, and I let my eyes wander around it while waiting for Susie to finish reading.

"Oh, Sarah," Susie said as she completed the letter. She went back to read one part again then got up and came over to stand next to me. Placing her hand on my shoulder, she read the letter aloud:

Dear Sarah,

I wanted you to know that Richard has not been doing well. The other night he took a gun and shot the hell out of a car he just bought. He stood in front of the car and shot the headlights out first, then the windshield. Glass was flying all over the driveway. It was an old car that he was going to fix up and use at the beach. Warren and Stephen Tetlow were there with me and we just stood there, watching him. After he emptied his gun into the car, Warren and I grabbed him and got him on the ground. It wasn't easy, but we did it. When are you coming home? I've never seen Richard so crazy about a girl before. We sat on the grass with him after he shot the car, and he talked about you and why your mother sent you away. He said he's going to join the army and go to Vietnam. Anyway, I thought you should know.

Take care,
Louie

Susie put her arm around me. "Poor thing. So this is what's been making you so distracted."

"My mother made me come!" I cried. "She hates Richard because he's Italian."

"What!" Susie exclaimed. She was clearly appalled. She grabbed my wrist. "Come with me. We are going to tell my parents." She pulled me after her, out the door and down the hall to the living room where her parents were sitting. She made me tell her parents the story, and then she read them the letter. It was a relief not to have to hide my feelings anymore. Also, I was exposing the manipulative, controlling side of my mother to her friends. Boy, did that feel good. The Stevensons seemed taken aback, but I didn't care. I didn't care if I completely undermined my mother's whole social status.

Mrs. Stevenson didn't believe my mother would embarrass me with her friends. "I know your mother can be strong willed, Sarah," she said, "but I don't believe she'd do such a thing."

"Oh, she'd do it, all right," I replied.

"Nor do I believe she'd fault Richard simply because he's Italian. That doesn't sound like your mother to me."

Susie came to my rescue. "I believe her, Mother," she injected. "I spent the summer with them, don't forget. I don't think Mrs. Howell ever approved of Richard."

Mrs. Stevenson thought about it. Mr. Stevenson asked if my mother had really said she'd tell her friends I wouldn't amount to anything. When I told him that had been exactly what she'd said, he stood up, came over to me, patted me supportively on my upper arms, shook his head, and heaved a great sigh of resolve. In a measured, rational tone of voice, he told me that I'd attained my majority, reached the age where my parents no longer had legal control over me; and that being the case, I could do anything I wanted, including return home.

Mrs. Stevenson helped me get an airplane ticket, and I called my parents that night. When my mother got on the phone, I told her I was coming and gave her my flight number. There was long silence on the other end of the line, followed by some sharp words. The conversation ended without her agreeing to meet me at the airport.

Then, I called Richard. It felt so good to hear his voice. I couldn't wait to see him. He was amazed that I was going against my mother's wishes. He said he thought I was brave.

"I'm not brave," I said. "I'm just sick of her telling me what to do. I love you, Richard, and I'm coming home." I felt new power coursing through me when I said it.

"I love you too, Sarah," Richard replied. "Always. Call me from the airport if your parents don't show up."

"No, you call them and ask if they're going to meet me. If they're not planning to, you come."

When I got off the plane, my parents were there to meet me. My mother was cold and didn't say much. My father, though clearly nervous, at least tried to make polite conversation. I didn't care. For the first time, I really didn't care. My mother had bullied me for the last time, and I was standing up to her, and it felt good. In fact, it felt better than good; it felt *right*. I'd found a life with Richard and Ringo, Ringo and Richard, and no one was going to stand in my way.

My mother was surprised by my new independence and resolve, but to her credit, she accepted it for what it was. She realized that I'd won, and she was going to have to back down. So we negotiated an agreement. Richard and I could get engaged, but the engagement would have to last a full year. I knew what she was thinking. She was postponing the wedding in the hope that, given a year, she could figure out a way to undermine our relationship. She said she and Dad would pay for me to live in an apartment in Watch Hill. Ringo would continue to stay at Richard's friend's house. I knew it was her last-ditch effort to get rid of Richard, and that she'd meddle as much as she felt she could get away with to break us up. But that was all right because for the first time in my life, I thought I could handle her. I looked her straight in the eye and told her that if she said one word about Richard or stuck her nose in our relationship, our deal was off; I'd marry him on the spot and never speak to her again. Ah, it was heaven. I was finally free and in control of my own life. As things turned out, Mother was never able to tell me what to do again. She tried a few times, but it didn't work.

Richard and I were married at my parents' house in Watch Hill on a sunny June day in 1970. I was a month shy of twenty-one. Ringo was at the wedding, as was his vet, Dr. Barrett, who kept trying to persuade Ringo to sip his champagne. My sister, Dindy, was the matron of honor. She'd married several years before, a Vietnam helicopter pilot who'd become a flight engineer for TWA. And my two best female friends in all the world, Leslie from Watch Hill and Betsy from Woodstock, were my bridesmaids. My mother and Maria polished everything they could lay their hands on, and the house looked beautiful. Dear Maria served as an unofficial maid of honor, following me around and making sure my needs were met. At the end, a little teary, she said she couldn't believe her little Sarah was actually getting married.

I still go back to see that old house by the beach where I was married. It was a great family house. When I drive by it and see the overhanging roof and screened porch, inviting you in, I remember whiling away summer afternoons on our white wicker furniture, listening to the gulls and ocean. The house gave the impression of perfect family life, which was of course what my mother wanted to convey to her friends at the club. What they didn't know was that the boy in that family had slit his wrists. What the house didn't show was that the older daughter, while still barely more than a girl, had been the one to find the bloody boy and call the ambulance, then receive and take the EMTs up to the boy's bedroom, all because the perfect, pretty mother couldn't bear the truth. What the house didn't show was that the younger daughter, the sweet little girl who could ride like the wind, had been pushed aside by the perfect family, then told she'd never amount to anything. All three children had been hurt in some combination of oppression and neglect. We'd all been denied love in the perfect, loving family. But unlike Murray and Dindy, I'd had Nanny to accept me as a child, Ringo to appreciate me as an adolescent, and Richard to love me as a woman.

My relationship with Ringo made me aware of the bonding that all creatures must have when they're infants. When Ringo and I bonded, we created a door that either of us could pass through, a door that led into a space of complete acceptance and trust by the other one. Nanny had done the same thing, provided me with the same door to the same space, but I'd been too young to be aware of it. And the thing about such acceptance and trust is that once you receive them from another, you know how to provide them for yourself. Because when someone else trusts your instincts, intuitions, and feelings, you learn from their example. I think it's the same with all creatures, at least mammals. Baby mammals bond with their mothers to learn the things they need to know in order to survive, and one of those things is a sense of self. My substitute mother, Nanny, believed in me and, by doing so, gave me faith in myself. And then, after Nanny, Ringo came, and he trusted me; and I followed his example as I had Nanny's and developed even more confidence.

I think that's how we learn the truth, by trusting ourselves enough to open up to it, bit by bit. That was the real gift Nanny and Ringo had given me: the example of their faith in me that led to my faith in myself, that enabled me to open to the truth.

Dindy and Murray never went through that bonding and affirming process as children. Well, a little perhaps with the family pets, but not to the extent I had it with Nanny and Ringo. Instead of being shown trust, Murray and Dindy were shown distrust. And so they didn't develop faith in themselves. They developed confidence in certain areas, but not real faith. And because they didn't have real faith in themselves, they didn't dare open to the truth. Mother taught them to deny, deny, deny, and as a result, they denied their instincts, their true feelings. Because they denied them, they were desperate, and because they were desperate, they were dangerous.

*Rhode Island, June, 1970. I was 21 and about to marry Richard.
My great grandmother, Dad's grandmother, was married in this
dress, at about the time of the Civil War*

Rhode Island, June 13, 1970. Head table at our wedding reception. From left to right: Betsy, my roommate from Woodstock; Murray; Dindy; Richard and me; Richard's best man, Robert Goudin; my friend, Leslie Ahern; and Warren Rathbun

Rhode Island, 1970. Mom asked me where Ringo's saddle and bridle were while I was getting dressed for the wedding, but it didn't occur to me why she wanted to know. Richard's friend, Peter Lamphere, dressed Ringo and brought him to the reception. I was delighted; Richard was, as always, a good sport. Dr. Barrett tried to get Ringo to drink a champagne toast. Ringo put up with us.

The Hunter Pace Event

Richard and I spent the first year of our marriage in a small rented house by the water in Watch Hill. There were two other couples on our street, and we became friends, ate at one another's houses, and shared various adventures. Ringo was just down the road, so I had Ringo and the ocean during the day, and Richard and our friends at night. I'd never been happier.

Things got even better our second year. When our lease in the first house expired, we were able to buy a house in Ashaway, about fifteen minutes inland. It was a cute little eighty-year-old house with two acres and a barn so I could have Ringo in the backyard. When we got settled and I started riding, I learned that my old friend, Leslie, who had gone off to college, had a younger sister who also rode. Her name was Loran. I guess she'd been so young I hadn't noticed her when I'd been hanging out with Leslie. At any rate, when I looked her up, I liked her immediately. Plus it was nice being back in contact with the Ahern family.

Loran worked for a man by the name of Cottrell. A retired state senator, Mr. Cottrell had a magnificent one-hundred-acre farm and three fine horses. Loran's job was to feed and exercise the horses. It was a great job, and whenever I had the time, I'd walk Ringo over to Mr. Cottrell's farm, and Loran and I would ride together.

Mr. Cottrell and his neighbors, also horse fanciers, held weekly foxhunts during the fall and spring when the weather was suitably cool. Loran participated in them and, after seeing how well I rode, suggested that I might like to, as well. I was thrilled, despite the fact that neither Ringo nor I had any experience jumping. Loran made her suggestion in Mr. Cottrell's study, where we occasionally visited him after our rides. Mr. Cottrell was a slightly built man with a fair complexion, always immaculately dressed—he reminded me of Fred Astaire. He was almost always sipping an old-fashioned, complete with fresh fruit, out of an engraved crystal glass.

"Don't you worry," he said when I told them I'd never hunted. "Loran will teach you everything you need to know."

Loran wanted to start teaching me immediately, but I delayed for a few days while we walked the course, and she explained everything. The truth was, I was frightened. But she was patient. When I was ready, we started with the lowest post-and-rail fence. Ringo was more willing than I, which was good since he was the one who'd be doing the jumping. It was also good because his confidence was infectious. When the day came to start in on the higher jumps, I invited Richard to watch. He stood to one side, and as I came around the corner and went past him, I could see that he was as anxious as I was. At the last minute, I grabbed Ringo's mane, he jumped—well clear of the fence—and I managed to stay on his back. Ha! So there! Another challenge met! Richard clapped and I laughed and Ringo pranced around proudly. After a few more tries, I was able to do it without grabbing his mane. I could even keep my eyes open. By the end of the afternoon, we were looking pretty sharp. One of the things I liked most about it was that Ringo and I were working together, learning a new partnership skill. Talk about trust and bonding. Loran was overjoyed, I was tentatively enthusiastic, and Richard, well, I guess Richard was simply relieved.

Within a few weeks, when Ringo and I had become confident on the highest rail jumps, Loran started us on the more solid stone walls and hedges. I remember it as if it was yesterday. Ringo and I were cantering around an open field when Loran, on foot, pointed to a low, thick hedge and nodded for me to jump it. Her long, blond ponytail was jerking this way and that from under her hard hat, and her blue eyes were clear and sure. "Go ahead," she directed. "It's a piece of cake."

I was turning Ringo in small circles beside her. He knew something was up and was ready to go. "Yeah, right," I sneered, skeptically.

"No, really," she persisted. "Just keep him moving forward and set up in your low-point position." When, still uncommitted, I continued circling, she added, "Hang onto his mane if you want to. That way, you won't pull on his mouth if you lose your balance." I started studying the hedge. "Go on," she pressed. "Then I'll get Rosie, and we'll go on a trail ride."

I trotted Ringo along the hedge then went back and circled in front of it to make sure he got a good close look. Then I trotted him back twenty to thirty feet, turned him in another circle to the point where I wanted to approach the jump, leaned forward, and gave him a little nudge with my heels. He jumped into a canter and started for the hedge.

I thought we were doing fine as we closed on the jump, but I guess I was wrong. For some reason known only to himself, Ringo slammed on the brakes at the very last minute. He stuck his front hooves into the ground, dropped his hind end, and pretty much sat on his haunches. But I was long gone by the second part. When he set his feet, I went between his ears and over his head as if he'd aimed and fired me. He did it so skillfully that I went all the way over the hedge, doing a flip as I went, and landed on my butt facing in the same direction I'd been riding.

Fortunately, I landed on sod and wasn't hurt. After checking myself out, when I looked back, Ringo was leaning over the hedge looking at me quizzically. His expression was slightly incredulous, as if he was wondering why I'd want to jump off him like that.

The whole thing, the combination of the dance-like precision with which he'd thrown me, my indignity, and his bemused expression made me burst out laughing. I was laughing so hard that when I got up and started dusting myself off, I had to pause, lean back, and let her rip some more.

"Hmm," said Loran. "Perhaps we should try that one again."

Ringo nickered, and I was reminded that horses laugh too. But there was never any question that I'd get back up and try again. I guess Ringo had gotten to know the hedge—if at my expense—because we went over easily the second time. It was a great feeling, the more so because we'd failed the first time.

"Good job!" Loran congratulated us. She walked up and gave Ringo a pat on the neck. "Now, let me saddle Rosie, and we'll give you your reward." She'd done a good job, and I appreciated it. Watching her walk toward the barn, I thought that while she wasn't as cute as Leslie, she had a warm smile and devilish sense of humor. Plus she understood horses and was a good rider and teacher. While we weren't exactly better friends than Leslie and I had been, our friendship had a lot more to it.

The hunts were fun, if sometimes scary. A couple of the stone walls were as wide as they were high, but I put my faith in my horse, and he didn't let me down. Once was enough, I guess. After each hunt, Loran and I went in to report to Mr. Cottrell. We joined him in his living room, where he was always comfortably ensconced in his easy chair with his old-fashioned, and he'd ask questions and listen attentively. The room was filled with prints of hunting scenes. Loran told me that Mr. Cottrell had sustained some kind of back injury that kept him from riding. So I guess he lived through Loran's riding experiences—and mine, too—for the short time I was around.

One afternoon, after telling Mr. Cottrell about the day's adventures, he turned to me and said, "Sary . . ." That's what he called me, Sary. And then he paused until he was sure I was paying attention. "How about going into the hunter pace event with Loran?"

I knew about the hunter pace event, but it hadn't occurred to me to enter. Loran glanced at me with an encouraging expression. She knew Ringo could do it. The course wended through the countryside for three miles and contained sixteen jumps, some natural and some set up in fields. The ride, a timed event, was done with a partner. You rode in tandem until the last jump, a stack of hay bales that you jumped side by side. "I really haven't given it much thought, Mr. Cottrell," I replied evasively.

Loran was planning to ride her favorite mount, a Connemara that Mr. Cottrell had brought over from Ireland. Rosie was just a little white mare, but she was well built, if a bit stocky, and very competitive. I'd seen her and knew: If you asked her to, she'd go through or over anything in front of her. And Loran and Rosie were a good team, often at the head of the hunt, helping with the dogs.

Ringo was also strong and spirited, so keeping the two horses from competing with each other would be a challenge. That was part of the test, how well you controlled your mount while staying together and getting through the course as quickly as possible.

To make a long story short, Loran and I agreed to ride together, and we signed up. It would be more challenging than any competition Ringo and I had entered, but I felt we'd hold our own. Just the same, when the day finally came, we were both tingling with excitement. My eyes were wide, sucking up the sights, and Ringo pranced as if he was doing a firewalk.

We checked our tack and walked the horses while waiting to be called to the starting line. Neither Loran nor I said much. We'd discussed the event and course ad nauseam, plus we were focusing our attention on connecting with our horses. When the call finally came, we mounted up, grasped each other's raised hand in encouragement, and walked to the gate. Sensing the coming challenge, Ringo and Rosie had worked their bits to the point where they were frothing at the mouth.

We stood even with the timekeepers as they synchronized their watches. When they were ready, they looked up at us, and we nodded to let them know we were ready as well. I could feel the tenseness in Ringo. He stood at his full height, and his muscles danced with anticipation. Like Pegasus, he was winged and ready to fly. And fly he nearly did when the signal was given. He leapt forward from a standing stop, and suddenly we were roaring down the course.

Rosie and Loran were more experienced than Ringo and I, so as planned, they took the lead. Unlike Ringo, I was happy to be led. We cantered through the woods, going as fast as seemed reasonable, dodging trees and having our legs whipped by the brush. Then we were jumping over stone walls. Between jumps, and especially when crossing open fields, I was having an increasingly difficult time holding Ringo back. When we'd started out, it was as if he simply resented being second, but as we moved into the course and he gained confidence, hit his stride, and got his second wind, he became more assertive. "Easy, boy. Settle down," I kept reminding him. "Whoa. Hold back. Whoa!"

And then, suddenly, without my being aware that we'd gone the whole three miles, we cleared the last jump in the woods and came out into the final field. We were abreast of Loran and Rosie, galloping uphill to the remaining two jumps, when Ringo yielded to his excitement. Tucking his hind end so he could dig with his driving feet, he sprinted for the line. Great spirit that he was, while he wanted to serve, he wanted to win even more. As we went by Loran, I glanced over at her and shook my head.

Laughing, she yelled. "Just *go!*"

And go we did. The steeper the hill became, the deeper Ringo dug and the faster we went. But Rosie stayed with us. Loran must have known she would. To her credit, spunky devil that she was, she wasn't about to be beaten either.

With the first jump coming up, I gave Ringo a squeeze with my legs, and suddenly, before I was quite ready for it, we were airborne. It was different from the other jumps. He went over the hay bails like an arrow instead of a jumping animal; we hardly seemed to leave the ground. As we came down, Rosie pulled even with Ringo, and together Loran and I reined them back from their sprint. I was amazed at their strength and endurance. Loran and I glanced at each other with massive grins on our faces. We'd ridden the course as we'd wanted to, as it ought to be ridden, and we knew it. Now all business, we sat upright in our saddles, heels down and hands high, galloped to the last jump stride for stride, took it in close formation and crossed the line together.

I was excited, though shaking with fatigue. You name it, I was feeling it. I jumped off Ringo and gave him a big hug. He rubbed the side of his face up and down against my ribs, drew back, and shook frothy spittle all over me; I was proud. Loran came over, and we slapped hands and yelled yes together. Then Richard was there too, giving me a huge hug and Ringo a pat on the neck. When all was said and done, we placed second, less than a minute behind the winners.

We told Mr. Cottrell the whole story from beginning to end, interrupting each other with details. Our enthusiasm clearly delighted him. For the rest of the day, having related the details, I couldn't resist rerunning the race again and again in my mind.

"If I knew what it would be like, the way I know now," I told Richard, "we could have been a minute faster, for sure."

Later that night before turning in, I went out to the barn to check on Ringo. His low nicker greeted me, and I brushed him thoroughly and lovingly as he munched on his hay. The rhythm of his chewing reminded me of those cold nights at the country school. I stopped brushing and leaned against him as I recalled climbing out of the dorm window and sneaking up to the safety of the barn. His chewing sound was still a comfort to me. Woodstock seemed so long ago. Was I really that tortured little girl? The answer was yes, but I'd survived it and broken free—free from my childhood, then from my mother. Ringo had shown me the way. And he still was. By his example of his trust in me, he was showing me how to trust myself and others.

Richard and Ringo were my family now. Richard supported me in whatever I wanted to do with Ringo. He knew Ringo, and I would never part, and he accepted it without complaint. It was a tribute to how much he loved me because he was always outside my relationship with Ringo. Ringo felt threatened by Richard to the point where he'd tried to bite him and chase him off for years. Richard couldn't even go into Ringo's stall alone. Ringo's ears would go straight back, and he'd swing his head as if it was a club with teeth, and sometimes he'd actually charge right at Richard. I tried to get him to accept Richard, but I never succeeded. When he got older, he ignored Richard, but he never accepted him. It didn't matter that I was a different species, nor that he was gelded; to Ringo, I was his mare, and all other males were to be driven off.

There were other competitions that summer. Ringo and I were in a number of horse shows, and we almost always ended up in the ribbons. He had developed into a beautiful, mature Morgan. His breeding was from the old type, working Morgan, bigger boned and strong; and he'd grown to sixteen hands and almost twelve hundred pounds. Plus I'd become a steadily more confident rider. The hunting and horse shows taught me a lot about myself. With Ringo's help, I gained the respect that I needed from my fellow horsemen. No one mentioned that I was disabled because when it came to horseback riding, I was anything but disabled.

Richard and I liked Ashaway, but the entire state of Rhode Island was losing its countryside. Everywhere you looked, new houses were springing up, and most of them looked like shingled weeds. As I looked back over my life, I felt that I'd gotten my start in Vermont; and the more I thought about it, the more I liked the idea of moving back there. Richard had grown up in Rhode Island and followed his uncle and stepfather into Electric Boat in Groton, Connecticut—where they built submarines—but he was game. He said he thought it would be good to have the experience of living somewhere else. Plus he knew and liked Vermont from his visits to Woodstock. So we talked about it and decided to put our house on the market. It sold in four days.

It wasn't easy saying good-bye to Loran. I don't think she understood why I might want to leave the life we shared. The night we parted, she gave me a braid she'd woven out of Ringo and Rosie's tail hair. When she presented it to me and I'd thanked her, she said simply, "I will miss you, Sarah."

"You'll have to come visit," I replied. "And I'll be back. This isn't the end of our friendship." That was in 1973, thirty years ago; we still talk and see each other several times a year.

Our first home in Vermont was in Woodbury, up in the Northeast Kingdom. We found a beautiful old barn on twenty-seven acres and converted it into a house. It was summer when we moved up, and we had to work hard to get the place closed in by winter. Plus we had the problem of where to put Ringo. Since it had housed cattle, Richard suggested we put him in the basement. So he ripped out some of the old stanchions and broke up enough of the concrete floor to build Ringo a twelve-by-twelve stall with dirt underfoot. He gave the stall strong walls and a heavy door because Ringo liked to kick while eating, a habit he'd acquired as a starving foul who'd had to fight for his food. When Richard completed his part, I filled the stall with sweet cedar shavings. Ringo seemed to like his new accommodations. I think he especially liked being able to hear my voice overhead.

The barn was much bigger than the three of us needed, but that was all right. It had been built into the side of the hill and had two huge front doors opening out onto the valley. We kept the doors in order to maintain the structure's integrity. When we fenced Ringo's pasture, he'd come out of his stall and stand in the doorway, ears up, looking out across the valley then gallop off down the hill. If there was frost in the air, he might kick his heels out to the side as he went.

During that summer of closing in and fencing the pasture, we made new friends. We were pioneers together, plus some of them had also moved up from Southern New England—"flatlanders," the locals called us—so we had things in common. It was a new adventure, and we were young, healthy, and full of ideas—bad as well as good.

It was while in Woodbury that I got into competitive trail riding. We had a neighbor, a summer resident named Gail, who got me interested. Gail leased a horse that had been trained for competitive trail riding, so she was familiar with the event. I thought that with his get-up-and-go, Ringo would be perfect for it, so I began training with Gail. We started with a twenty-five-mile ride, which meant we took long excursions out along dirt roads and logging trails. It was fun exploring the beautiful backcountry of Vermont. I don't know of anything to compare with its flora and fauna, especially its birds and trees. When we started those long rides, I felt as if I'd been away a long, long time, but had finally come home.

We did well from the beginning. In our very first ride, Gail, whose horse was smaller than Ringo, came in fourth in the lightweight division, and Ringo and I took first in the mid-weight division.

*Ashaway, Rhode Island, 1972. Ringo in his very own pasture
at our first home.*

*Rhode Island horse show, 1973. when I look at this picture, I see a
confident and competent team. I was in charge of planning and strategy
and Ringo was responsible for getting it done. To me, my cerebral palsy
contributed and enabled far more than it detracted and curtailed.*

Rhode Island horse show, 1973. My friend, Lauren Ahern, taught Ringo and me to jump so she and I could hunt, then ride in the Hunter Pace Event together. Thereafter, we rode together whenever possible, entering shows as a team. Here, we are proudly displaying our second prize ribbons.

Woodbury, Vermont, 1974. we had goats at our first home in Vermont. Here, Ringo looks on while I try to get everyone into a group shot. When it rained, Abby, the brown goat I'm holding, would go over and stand under Ringo.

Woodbury, Vermonth, 1975. Please permit me to introduce you to my friend, Ringo . . . . Seeing how his ears were up in all these pictures reminds me of how alert and aware he was

Two Steps Back

Unfortunately, jobs were scarce in Vermont. We managed to close the barn in and were warm that first winter, but the following summer, when Richard still hadn't found work, we were forced to move back to Rhode Island. Our last night in our Woodbury house was very sad. Richard lay on the bed, too numb to speak. I lay next to him and massaged his neck and shoulders. "Do you think we'll be able to come back?" I asked.

"I don't know," he mumbled into his arm. "We'll just have to rent this place and see what happens."

"I feel bad that we have Ringo," I said.

"Don't worry, we are not getting rid of him. That's not even an option. The house has that field. I'll talk to the owners, see if they'll let us fence it in. And I can put up a shed, or at least a lean-to." Richard's plans always included Ringo—which is more than Ringo could say for Richard. "I have to call the tenants to let them know what time we are leaving," he said, rolling over and getting up.

As we drove down our road and out through the little village of Woodbury, some of our friends saw us and waved. Behind us in his trailer, Ringo whinnied his own good-bye.

Vermont, 1977. Richard, friend, husband, father,
a good man and gentle soul.

The Farm

My parents offered us their summerhouse in Watch Hill, but I didn't think it would be fair. Their original plan had been to sell the house and give Murray, Dindy, and me the money. Murray and Dindy thought we should take the proceeds, buy a farm, and live on the property together; but I wasn't sure I wanted the family to give up the Watch Hill house. I also had mixed feelings about the three of us living on the same land. On the other hand, it didn't seem right that I impose my preference on the two of them.

One afternoon, we got together in the living room at Watch Hill to discuss the situation. Murray did most of the talking. "Look, Sarah," he said to me, "if we don't sell this house, we're all going to be responsible for its upkeep. And we simply can't afford it."

"Yes, I know," I said, "but they gave us the house or the money, and I'm choosing the house. We can use it during the summer. It will be fun." It was then that I got clear that I didn't want to live on the same property with them.

But Dindy was in agreement with Murray, so I was outvoted. Richard and I moved into a rental, and the family house was put on the market. We also sold our house in Vermont. Reluctantly, we joined Murray and Dindy in their search for a farm. It was looking as if we wouldn't get to live in Vermont after all.

The family house sold quickly. After looking at a few farms in Connecticut and Rhode Island, Murray and Dindy started looking in Vermont. I was encouraged by this, especially when a beautiful property in Chelsea came to our attention. It was on top of a mountain, with beautiful fields around an old farmhouse and a log cabin about one hundred yards behind the house. Dindy and her new husband could live in the farmhouse, Murray could live in the log cabin, and Richard and I could build our own place. Murray had gotten a horse, and we'd ridden together a few times; so I thought, well, if we all live together, perhaps Murray and I will finally get to know each other.

So we put the money into the farm, and Richard and I started planning our house. We discussed it at great length until we'd settled on a style and layout. In the meantime, we built a house for Mom and Dad to live in during the summers then moved into that house in the fall when they returned to Florida. At last we were back in Vermont, ready to settle down for good.

But there was a problem. We'd put Ringo into the ancient barn on the property when we'd moved in, but it was damp and drafty, not to mention a long walk from where we planned to build. So Richard and I decided that when we built our house, we'd put up a second barn next to it. This seemed reasonable, but one night when the four of us were having dinner at Dindy's, Murray challenged our plans. "I don't want to look up the road and see a house with a separate barn," he complained. "The barn we've got is fine."

"What do you mean, Murray?" I replied. I was shocked by his attitude. I put down my knife and fork and placed my hands in my lap. It was really too much, his interference. And Dindy was no better. I would take care of her animals when she went away, but she always complained when I asked her to take care of Ringo. And she snarled every time I set foot in her house. I think part of it was that her second husband, Duncan, couldn't stand me. He called me a jerk and stupid, or worse, and he ignored me when I spoke to him. It didn't matter that Richard got up before dawn on the coldest winter days to plow the long drive for everyone. I don't remember that Duncan ever thanked Richard for any of the things he did in all the time we were there together. And now they were telling us what kind of house we had to build? No way. Suddenly, sitting there at the dining room table, I'd had enough of all of them.

"Okay," I said, looking straight at Murray. "We want out." Richard, was speechless.

"What do you mean, you want out?" Murray responded.

"I want my share of the money. Richard and I are leaving. Which part don't you understand?"

Murray sat back in his chair and sighed. "But I don't want you to leave, Sarah," he tried to explain. "I didn't mean for you to leave."

"But Murray, don't you see, this isn't going to work. You can't tell me what kind of home to have. When we all moved in here, you took the cabin, and Dindy took the farmhouse. That was all right because we were going to build our own place. But now you want to tell us what we can and can't build? I don't think so. I'm sorry but I've *had* it!"

Murray looked surprised and saddened. Dindy sat there, eyes averted, saying nothing. It was obvious that she didn't care about Richard and me. She and Duncan probably wanted us to go. I was surprised by my brother's sudden concern, but on the other hand, if he was really concerned, why was he being so obtuse?

West Brookfield

Murray and Dindy found the money for my share of the farm, and Richard and I bought our own place, a beautiful 150-year-old cape on ten acres of land in West Brookfield. It was about ten miles north of Randolph and a half hour from what was coming to be known as "the family farm" in Chelsea.

Our new home was on a dirt road that ran along a high ridge and looked down across a number of farms in a beautiful, "Curious George" valley. I always expected to see the man in the yellow hat emerge from one of the houses in the distance. It was quiet up there, and there was a lot of old growth. Our property had some monstrous old apple trees.

The house had a lot of character. Built on a slate foundation, it had a large, elegant front door and a brick entranceway. Inside were high ceilings, charming wainscoting, and the original wide floorboards. The floorboards were covered with dents and scratches, a thousand stories to tell. One problem was that the house had sat empty and unheated for fifteen years, with the result that the plaster was soft and the wallpaper peeling. Plus like all those old houses, there was no insulation. We had a lot of work to do before we could move in, but we were full of energy now that we had our own place.

There was no barn, so along with winterizing the house, we built a small stable for Ringo. We had a barn raising. Richard and I provided the food and drink, our friends and neighbors came, and together we got the skeleton and frame up in a day. Richard had done a good job on the design. When it was completed, the structure looked like a small house. It faced out onto a lush pasture and our pond. The entrance was sheltered so that we could leave the door open, and Ringo could walk in and out.

I was happy to have a good barn because Ringo was developing heaves, a lung disorder usually caused by allergies. He always had a slight rattle in his throat. I think I was the only one aware of it because I knew him so well. But it had gotten louder in Vermont. I'd found a good vet by the name of Will Barry. He explained that because of the long, harsh winters in Vermont, horses were exposed to a lot of dry hay, and that in Ringo's case, the dust was irritating his lungs. His prescription was to take Ringo off hay, altogether, and put him on a diet of oats, corn, pellets, beet pulp, and molasses—with extra beet pulp for good measure. "We want to keep him going," he explained. "He has quite a few years left." That was 1976. Ringo was sixteen, but his age didn't seem to bother him. In fact, Dr. Barry was amazed by Ringo's condition. "This horse is built," he liked to say.

Just the same, the diagnosis and prescription concerned me. It's hard, not giving a horse hay during the long Vermont winters. There are long days spent standing on dank, frozen ground, and munching on hay gives a horse something to do. A bored horse is more likely to grind his teeth or chew the beams in his stall. With this in mind, I felt I had to give Ringo a little hay from time to time. I soaked it in water to wash out the dust, and then spread small clumps around his pasture. That way, he had to take the time to find it as well as eat it. And sometimes it would freeze, so he'd have the delicacy of iced sweet hay. I did this faithfully all winter, plus I kept his door open so he'd have a lot of fresh air. He seemed to appreciate it, and his coughing didn't get any worse.

We got the house fixed up so that it was a cozy home, and Ringo stayed healthy; and a few years later, Richard and I had a baby girl. We named her Tayo, after a friend of my mother's. It's a Japanese name meaning everlasting life. It seemed appropriate, given that I'd had two miscarriages before getting pregnant with her. She had jet-black hair and beautiful olive skin. Even as a baby, Tayo loved sitting bareback on Ringo. As I had with Peanuts, she enjoyed the warmth and softness of his body and coat.

West Brookfield, Vermont, 1984. When Tayo was 3, Richard took a series of mother-daughter shots. This is my favorite. After two miscarriages, I felt Tayo was truly an angel from heaven.

West Brookfield, Vermont, 1987. I'm walking, Tayo, 7-8, on Ringo, with our Blue Merle collie leading the way.

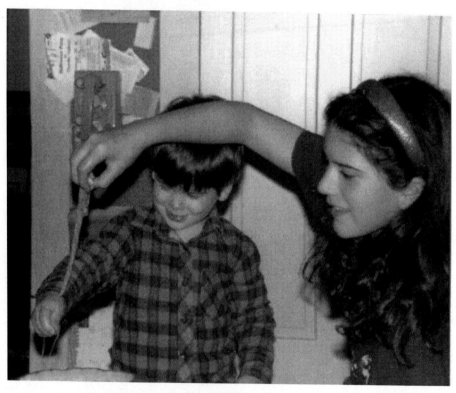

West Brookfield, Vermont, 1991. Tayo, 11 and Richie, 3, de-sliming a pumpkin for Halloween

The Last Trail Ride

Ringo and I controlled his heaves, and I continued to ride. I even joined a local riding club so we could make new friends. One day in the summer of 1983, the club posted an announcement for a competitive trail ride. Ringo was twenty-three by then, and I knew our competitive riding days were coming to an end, but he was in such great shape that I thought we could do it one last time. On the rides we took with club members, he always insisted on taking the lead. Plus we'd been together for so many years that when I was on his back, we didn't just act as one, we *were* one. I gave him my full attention, and he gave me every ounce of strength he had to give. So I knew what he could and couldn't do. I knew he could still manage even as I knew that it would be the last time we competed together.

To prepare for the ride, I put Ringo on an extra high-protein grain and slowly increased the length and difficulty of our rides. The more we went out, the clearer his lungs became. Dr. Barry explained that when the mucus built up, it seeped down into the air pockets in the lungs, restricting their effectiveness and eventually damaging them. He said heaves are similar to emphysema and that exercise diminishes the buildup of mucus. It was reassuring, having Dr. Barry on our team.

On the day of the competition, Cliff Murray came to trailer Ringo to the place where it was to be held. Richard and I had been forced to sell our trailer when we left Woodbury, and we hadn't replaced it. Cliff was a member of our riding club and much admired for his generosity toward young people. They were always welcome on his farm, and he was happy to trailer their horses for them. He had a big, old GMC flatbed truck with side panels and a hinged ramp. He bred and raised Appaloosas, which are spotted horses, so he painted spots on the outside of the ramp so that when it was closed, the back of his truck looked like the rear end of one of his horses. "They may not know me when I'm coming," he liked to say, "but they will when I leave." We liked Cliff so much we never did get another trailer. He transported Ringo for sixteen years.

Climbing down out of his cab that morning, his happy voice eased my tension. I can see old Cliff so clearly, even after all these years. He was a short man with gray hair combed straight back and dark-rimmed glasses, and he always had a smile on his face. Tayo watched as he dropped the big loading door. "Hello there, young lady," he greeted her. He always greeted her the same way, and for some reason, though she was too shy to respond, it always made her smile. Ringo let out a whinny of greeting from the barn.

"Hi, Cliff," I said, happy to see him.

"Well, look at you," he replied, giving me the once-over. "All dressed up and ready to go. Well, go get Knucklehead, and we'll be about it." Knucklehead was his pet name for Ringo.

Richard walked behind us as I brought out Ringo. He was always there for me and always encouraging. "I'm not worried," he said when I'd led Ringo up the ramp. "I know you'll do well." He was a lot like Ringo—steady, sweet, and always encouraging. In fact, I sometimes wondered if I'd fallen in love with Richard because he was so much like Ringo. I thought it, but I didn't say it to Richard.

Cliff tied Ringo's lead line to a ring in the front of the truck then climbed down and raised the ramp. Ringo didn't threaten Cliff. When he saw Cliff, he seemed to understand that he was going somewhere, and he liked going places and having adventures. And Cliff wasn't put off by Ringo's possessiveness toward me. That's what the name Knucklehead was all about, Cliff's affection for that male energy. "I'll be at the ride all day," he said. "So feel free to use the trailer if you need it." He winked, smiled, and gave me the thumbs-up sign.

I gave Richard a kiss and a hug and picked up little Tayo. She put her arms around my neck and gave me a five-year-old's squeeze, followed by a wet kiss on the cheek.

Ringo was stomping to get going. "Come on, girl," Cliff ordered as he climbed up into the cab. "This horse wants to meet the competition."

I had to weigh in with my equipment. The horses and riders are judged by different weight classes. Horses with more weight are going to perform differently than horses that are carrying less weight. As I stepped onto the scales, I saw Richard drive up next to Cliff's trailer. I hadn't expected him to be there, and wondered why he'd come.

"Age and breed of your horse, please," the lady behind the desk said.

"Twenty-three, and he's a Morgan," I replied.

"Did you say twenty-three?" She was clearly taken aback.

"That's right, twenty-three, going on five," I laughed.

She didn't think it was funny. I think she was worried about Ringo. I got off the scale and walked back to the trailer where Richard was standing with Cliff. Richard was carrying Tayo on his shoulders. "You forgot your drinks," he said. "Since we're here, why don't Tayo and I stay with Ringo while you get organized."

"Great." I had one more table to go to and sign some papers, so I crossed the street and stood in-line. It was starting to get busy. I was anxious to get the signing part over with so I could get Ringo ready. Standing there, I watched Ringo and Richard. It was plain that their relationship was never going to change. Richard reached out and gave Ringo a pat every once in a while, but his pats were invariably met by laid-back ears and an evil eye. Finally Richard tired of being rebuffed and just let Ringo be. Amused by the whole thing, Cliff smiled and shook his head. At times I'm sure it got to Richard, the way Ringo treated him; but he knew Ringo and I were forever, and that was that. So in his kind, forgiving way, Richard backed off and never tried to force himself on Ringo.

Ringo was nicer to Tayo. He seemed to know that she belonged to me, and he was always careful when she was around or sitting on his back. When she got older and became a good rider, he'd tolerate her in his stall as long as I was there, even allowing her to bridle him for me. He was more forbearing with her than with Richard, but still, there was no mistaking it, he was a one-woman horse.

Finally, it came time to mount up and report to the starting gate. As I got in line, I started worrying about getting lost, but a nice lady rode up and asked if she could ride with me. She said she didn't want to take the course alone. I told her I'd be happy to have her along, we could get lost together.

The stopwatches were set, and off we went. Ringo's ears faced straight ahead, and I could tell he was ready to catch up with the horses in front of us. As always, we were one and having the time of our lives.

The countryside was beautiful. While we covered a number of rolling hills, Ringo showed no signs of fatigue. I let him trot; he didn't seem to want to stop. It wasn't easy to get him to walk downhill, but I insisted. The pounding and stress of trotting downhill take a toll on a horse's front legs, especially on a long ride, and I didn't want him to come up lame.

Anne, the lady I was riding with, was fun and interesting. She'd done a lot of competitive riding. She said she liked Arabians because of their long stride and athletic ability. Her mare, a dapple-gray, trotted along with her tail up.

We were soon at our first checkpoint. We approached the vet in charge, David Lamb, at a fast trot. David smiled and shook his head as I got off then checked Ringo's heartbeat while his assistants checked the rest of him. One of the assistants pulled the skin on his neck to test for dehydration. If the skin snapped back into place, it meant the horse was okay; but if it remained sticking out, it meant the horse wasn't taking in enough water. Despite the fact that he'd refused to drink at any of the water stops, Ringo was fine. While I didn't know it that day, David Lamb was to become an important person in our lives.

Anne and her horse were also all right, so we mounted up and set off again. Ringo was into his trot before my right foot hit the stirrup.

The lunch stop was welcome. Both Anne and I needed to stretch and walk around, so we took turns holding the horses. Then we ate our lunch and were off again. As David Lamb watched Ringo go by, he said to an assistant, "That horse is amazing."

It started to rain on the last half of the ride. My sweatshirt was soaked; I bet it weighed five pounds. Plus my ankles were stiff, and my legs were numb from posting. So I was relieved when we finally saw the finish line. Ringo's ears were straightforward, studying the small group of people who were clapping and cheering. The rain had stopped, the sun had come back out, and steam was rising out of the dirt road as Ringo and I, and Anne and her beautiful white Arabian, crossed the finish line.

At last we could dismount. Cliff came to the rescue. "You okay, girl?" he asked as he reached for me. Fortunately he had his arm around my waist as my feet hit the ground for my right foot and ankle were completely numb.

"I think so, thanks," I replied, when I'd taken stock. He released me, and I stood hanging onto the saddle. I rolled my ankles around until the feeling came back. Ringo stuck out his leg, lowered his head, and rubbed his frothy cheek on his knee. When Cliff took his saddle off, he shook his entire body from head to tail.

It was all I could do to get my sweatshirt off. When I was ready, I walked Ringo around in circles. It was important to keep him moving lest his ankles swell and get stiff. I couldn't wash him down or even give him a drink until the vet had checked him one last time. I was hoping they'd hurry as he had drunk at only one of the water stops, and I was a little concerned about him. Finally David Lamb came over. He smiled at me and pinched the skin on Ringo's neck. To my surprise it snapped into place, meaning that he was still not dehydrated. David ran his hand over the girth area and said something to his assistant, which she wrote down. Then he ran his hands down Ringo's legs. Ringo was resting on three legs with his head down, enjoying the massage. David smiled again and walked away without saying anything.

Anne was cleaning her horse off when we got to Cliff's truck. Cliff was ready with a bucket of cool, clear water, and Ringo dove into it. I let him drink half of it but then pulled him back. Cliff got the bucket with my sponges and scrapers in it. The sweet smell of Absorbine filled my nostrils as I wiped down Ringo's legs then dumped the remainder of the water over his back. His belly muscles twitched as the water ran down around his rib cage then dropped onto the ground. I think it tickled him. Satisfied that he was comfortable, I left him tied to Cliff's truck and went to sit down.

David Lamb and his assistants were ready to give out the awards. I found it hard to sit still because the muscles in my legs were cramping up, causing me considerable pain. Unable to stand it, I got up and walked. When someone turned up the microphone and it squealed, I jumped. I was more exhausted than I dared admit. The head judge started out with the lightweight division. The winners were announced, and everyone clapped. I wasn't expecting to get a prize. It was enough that we made it through the ride. I tried sitting down again, couldn't stand it, got up, and continued pacing. I heard the judge speak Ringo's and my names, but it didn't register.

Cliff tapped me on the shoulder. "That's you!"

"Oh my god," I gasped. "You're right!" I walked over to where the judge was standing next to the table with all the ribbons. I was still somewhat out of it when she handed me a ribbon and shook my hand. It was a blue ribbon for first place in the mid-weight division. I was stunned for a second; but when I started smiling, my grin went ear to ear, and there was no stopping it. On my way back to my seat, staring at my ribbon, I felt pats on my back. Then, the minute I sat down, our names were called again, and I had to go back up for another prize. The second one, also a blue, was for the highest number of points. The other riders and onlookers were getting to know us, I guess, because when they heard I'd won again, they cheered and clapped enthusiastically.

David Lamb took the microphone. "At the age of twenty-three, this horse has ninety-nine points, almost a perfect score." He gave me the ribbon and then a hug. The combination was too much for me, and I started sniffling. David handed me the vet's notes for the day. The first one read, "Unbelievable! This horse is still rocking and rolling twenty miles into the ride."

It was a day I'll never forget. Cliff couldn't get over it. He couldn't stop patting Ringo on the neck. Nobody could get over it, least of all those who knew Ringo. As for me, I couldn't wait to get home and show Richard my ribbons.

Exhausted but high, I waved the ribbons out the window as we pulled into the yard. Richard came out of the house pumping his fists in the air. When Cliff stopped the truck, Ringo stomped his feet, glad to be home and impatient to get down. Cliff unloaded him, and Richard held him while I took his wraps off; then, we put him in his pasture so he could roll and relax in the sweet grass.

Richard was proud and excited for me. When we'd waved good-bye to kind Cliff, we walked into the house arm in arm. Later, when I went out to feed Ringo, I took a handful of fresh carrots to mix in his feed. As he ate—with unusual gusto—I admired him. *You, my twenty-three-year-old friend*, I thought, *have been my savior; our souls are joined.*

Last Rides

That was our final competitive trail ride. I had a close friend in West Brookfield, and another in Brookfield, and we took pleasure rides together. We'd been riding together for so many years that our horses had become friends.

One of the last trail rides I went on was in South Woodstock, Vermont, at the Green Mountain Horse Association. It was called the Twilight Ride. The GMHA was next-door to my old school, the Woodstock Country School; but the school had closed by then, and David Bailey had died of emphysema. It was hard to see the buildings I had known so well as school buildings being used for other things. The main building, Upwey, was now a stable, and the library, a tack shop. It had been a stable before it became a school, so maybe that was the way it was supposed to be. But still, it was hard to accept. The school, which had lasted thirty-five years, had helped so many young people find their way.

It was a bit like returning to a childhood home. Being there transported me back to the sadness and pain of my first few days at the school. I think Ringo remembered his old stomping grounds as well. He seemed to recognize the trails.

Ringo was twenty-eight at the time. There were 150 riders, and we were there with my friends, Barrie and Elaine. One of the other riders was Christopher Reeves, the actor who would subsequently fall off his horse and break his neck. He was parked in back of us. He was there with his girlfriend, Dana, who later became his wife. They were a striking couple, tall, lean, and fit.

Barrie, Elaine, and I paused in lush green meadows as the sun dipped beneath the hills in the distance. When we finished, there were long tables, covered with white linen tablecloths and decorated with bright orange carrots. Beyond the tables, the horses stood tied on a picket line. Of every size, shape, and hue, they rubbed their faces on their legs then shook in relief when their riders took their saddles off.

"Look, there's a spot," Barrie said, guiding her bay Morgan, BJ, toward a space on the line. Elaine followed on her Morgan, Sun. He was slightly smaller than BJ and a light brown. I was next on Ringo who was the biggest and darkest of the three.

With the horses tethered and unsaddled, we made our way to the table. Barrie and I grabbed some of the carrots and went back to give them to the horses, but Elaine was too hungry. Ringo and BJ were rubbing each other's necks while Sun stood resting on three legs. Elaine had gone directly to the lunch table and then found a pleasant spot under a big maple next to an exercise paddock. I got a box lunch and followed, flopping down on the soft grass next to her. It felt delicious to stretch my legs.

I was about to bite into my turkey sandwich when Barrie said, "What is that woman doing?" Following her eyes, I saw an elderly lady talking to Ringo.

"I'm not sure," I said. "But whatever it is, it's probably not such a good idea." I was afraid Ringo might butt or nip the poor, unsuspecting woman. I put my sandwich back in its box and got up.

"Better hurry," said Elaine.

I was halfway there when the woman called out to no one in particular, "Whose horse is this?"

I raised my hand as if back in school and replied, "He's mine. Is something wrong?"

"Oh, no, my dear. He's a magnificent animal."

I moved around the woman, getting between her and Ringo then took him by the halter so he wouldn't get any ideas. The woman was charming. She had short gray hair and was wearing a fancy riding shirt with a stunning gray collar and tan britches that ballooned out at the hips. The britches contrasted stylishly with her black leather boots. She reached around me and ran her hand down Ringo's back. "How old is he, dear?"

"He's twenty-eight."

"Is he really? My goodness. Morgan?"

"Yes."

"He looks like the Morgans that came from the Ferguson Farm down in Rhode Island."

"He's out of the same bloodline," I said, amazed that she had such a good eye.

"Ah, yes, Broadwall Parade," she said.

"That's the one."

"Wonderful horses," she said. "My name is Nora." She stuck out her hand. She had a good grip for a slight woman.

We talked for a few minutes then went our separate ways. But I never forgot that woman and the way she recognized Ringo's lineage. In doing so, there at my old school and toward the end of Ringo's life, she seemed to tie the whole story into a neat package.

Barrie, Elaine, and I had many wonderful rides after that. Ours was an unconditional friendship, based on the love we felt for our horses.

The last group ride I took Ringo on was in West Brookfield, just below our house. Barrie and Elaine were there. Ringo was clearly struggling up the hills by then. At the end of the ride, as I headed home, I paused to look back at the people and horses and trailers on the church grounds. It was the Mid-State Riding Club, women for the most part, many of whom I'd ridden with for over ten years. I could see Julie, a native Vermonter with short-cropped hair, walking competently around her coal black mare, Slipper. Julie knew just about all there was to know about horses, particularly Morgans, because she'd grown up on a farm that raised them. She was the one we all looked to when there was trouble on the trail.

Laurie was beside Julie with her wonderful bay quarter horse, Liberty. I could hear Laurie's high-pitched voice drifting up the hill. Also a native Vermonter, her spirit and love for life shone like a beacon wherever she went.

Then I saw Barrie and Elaine. They stopped and waved when they saw us. It was understood that I wouldn't be bringing Ringo on any more group rides. I waved back and turned Ringo to continue up the hill. He took a few steps, swung his head around, and gave an over-the-shoulder whinny. It was as if he knew he wouldn't be back and was telling his friends he'd catch them later.

Back in the churchyard, Barrie cupped her hands over her mouth and called, "Good-bye, Sarah. Good-bye, Ringo." When the others heard her call and looked and saw us, many of them waved as well. Some stuck their heads out of their trailers; others put down their buckets or paused in their grooming. And when Barrie called a second time, "Good-bye," a few of them also called good-bye.

From that point on, we went out alone or with only one other person. I did it that way so Ringo would stay within his limits and not get upset that he couldn't keep up. His lungs had gotten progressively worse from the heaves, and he was on the largest dosage of medication Dr. Lamb would prescribe.

That last group ride was a turning point, the beginning of the end of all those years Ringo and I had been together. His sturdy legs had carried me thousands miles—five times around the earth—I once figured. My daughter, Tayo, by then twelve, had learned to ride on Ringo. He knew her. Toward the end, he allowed her to mount him and walk him down our road. I would watch them from the house. Tayo's hair flowed out from under her hard hat and down over her shoulders, a black rapids in the sun; her dark eyes sparkled, and there was a constant smile on her face. Ringo's step was slow and cautious. He took extra time and care because he knew he was still responsible for a part of me. He was the same with our son, Richie, then four. On Sunday mornings, I sometimes put Richie up on Ringo and led them around the yard. Despite his advanced age, Ringo never as much as stumbled.

Over the next two years, as Ringo and I shared quiet rides, I began thinking about living without him. Barrie and I talked about it. In her quiet way, she pointed out that our beloved animals never live as long as we do and that we have to steel ourselves to losing them. That was the harsh reality. At some point, I was going to have to go on without him. But no matter how often I thought about it, I could never hold the thought for long. It was too much; besides, I couldn't know how it would be. So much of my identity was tied up with Ringo, how could I separate it out?

When Ringo turned thirty, Richard and I gave him a catered birthday party. I wanted to celebrate our life together. Ringo's pals—BJ, Barrie's Morgan, and Sun, Elaine's gelding—were trailered over for the occasion. We planned to take a birthday ride in the morning, a short loop around West Brookfield, then have a picnic on the lawn. As always, Richard was helpful and supportive. He knew how much the occasion meant to me.

When Barrie arrived, she unloaded BJ and brushed him until he shone like a new penny. I gave BJ my extra stall since Barrie lived an hour away. Next to them, I brushed Ringo as he munched on his hay. It was early June, and he was still losing his winter coat. As I worked my way back over him, I realized that I knew every curve, muscle, tendon, and joint intimately. Every scar had its story and history of mending. Lost in thought, I was unaware that Barrie had finished brushing BJ and was standing next to me.

"Are you okay?" she asked.

I stopped brushing. Her voice had startled me. "I suppose." Ringo turned his head and snorted, as if to tell me to get back at it. The sensation of his warm breadth on my hand reminded me of how he'd blown on my cold face during those first nights at Woodstock.

I looked up at Barrie, smiled slightly, and said, "I know every inch of this horse. I know what he's thinking, and what he's going to do next."

Barrie put her hands on my shoulders. "You have had an unbelievable relationship with an unbelievable horse. I've never seen anything like it."

I smiled again even as my eyes filled with tears.

"Come on," Barrie said, "let's enjoy this beautiful June day."

Elaine was already up. I saddled up, and we set off on Ringo's birthday ride. It was a magnificent day, and I wished it could last forever.

West Brookfield, Vermont, Ringo's Thirtieth Birthday Party, 1992.
Five friends honoring a sixth who likes the friendship but not the honor.

West Brookfield, Vermont, 1988. Ringo, in his late twenties—gentle
eyes and the wisdom of age. Though I can tell by his mouth that he
was communicating with me, I no longer recall his message.

Crossing the Threshold

On the morning of November 16, 1993, it was cold, damp, and windy as I set out for the barn. A fine, light, icy snow was blowing about; and the flakes were gritty against my face. When I got to the barn, Ringo was standing quietly in the corner. For the first time I could recall, perhaps the first time ever, he didn't whinny a greeting or turn his head. When I looked over the edge of the stall and he saw me, he took two steps toward me. As he did, his knees cracked, a sure sign that he'd been standing in one position for a long time. It wasn't like him, and it concerned me. I scooped his measure of grain out of the feed bin, but when I emptied it into his trough, he wasn't interested. He stood there, staring at nothing and making no sound. When I realized that even his breathing was quiet, with none of the percolator noises his nostrils usually made, I knew something was seriously wrong. "I'll get help," I said, and I set off to the house to call David Lamb.

It was all new, and I was shocked. When I picked up the phone, I fumbled it; and when I jumped back, I noticed my hands were shaking. I took a deep breath and managed to dial David's number. Fortunately, he answered the phone.

"David, this is Sarah. Ringo's off his feed, and I'm worried. He's not acting right at all. You know how he is with food."

"Hey, hey, take it easy," David reassured me. "It could be nothing. I want you to walk him for forty-five minutes and call me back. I'll be on the road, but my secretary can reach me. Okay?"

I heard the words. Walk him. Outside? Forty-five minutes? I felt like I was falling into a nightmare.

"Sarah?" David asked.

"I'm here. All right. I'm going right now." I hung up and returned to the barn.

I stumbled on the raised door frame going in and was regaining my balance when I heard Ringo go down. I had to get him back up. When I entered his stall, he was lying on his right shoulder. His eyes were dull.

I slipped the halter over his nose then gently up over his ears. Attaching the lead rope, I urged him to get up. "Come on, Ring, we have to walk." I put a little tension on the rope. With one huge lunge, he got his front feet under him then his hind legs, and was up. Not wanting him to change his mind, I immediately turned him and started for the door.

Outside, we headed up the drive to the road. Ringo could move only slowly, and he seemed terribly stiff. When I encouraged him and he looked at me as if to say, "I just can't do it," I could see the pain in his eyes. Walking wasn't going to help.

I took him back to the barn, returned to the house, and called David again. His secretary reached him on his radio, and he called me back. When I told him what had happened, he said he'd come right away. When I got back to the barn, Ringo was standing in the corner of his stall, in shadow as if the light might be painful. I cried out in anguish when I saw him, then paced back and forth while fighting down tears. "Come on, Sarah," I berated myself. "This is no time for tears." I walked into the stall and rubbed his neck, and he brought his head around slightly and sniffed my hands.

After what seemed forever, I heard David's truck pull in, then his footsteps on the gravel drive.

"Sarah?" he called quietly as he entered the barn.

"I'm in here with Ringo."

He came into the stall, walked up to Ringo, and rubbed his forehead. When Ringo lifted his head to sniff David's face, David sniffed right back at him, nose to nose. It was a greeting I'd suggested to Dave, a way for him to get past Ringo's innate mistrust.

"Okay, old boy, let's see what's up, shall we?" David said as he ducked out of the stall, knelt, and opened his bag. Taking out a pair of long rubber gloves, he pulled them on and up his arm, worming his fingers down into the glove fingers. Watching his strong physique, reddish brown beard, and intelligent eyes, I was reminded of what a good vet he'd been for us and how much Ringo and I trusted him. He was soft-spoken and gentle, and he always seemed to know what to do next. When he got the gloves on, he took his Australian bush hat off, revealing a slightly balding head, and reentered Ringo's stall. Moving behind Ringo, he lifted his tail and—without the slightest hesitation, but with supreme gentleness—sank his arm up to the elbow in Ringo's rectum. Ringo's head went up in alarm, and I tightened my grip on his halter. "Whoa, Ringo, it's okay," I comforted him.

David shut his eyes and felt around for perhaps thirty seconds then withdrew his arm. Leaving the stall, he removed his gloves. My heart was racing. Turning to me with concern in his eyes, he sighed and said, "Ringo's lower intestine has a huge impaction. It's a six-to-eight-inch lump or wad of undigested food. I could feel it, but it's too hard to break up."

"What can we do?" I heard the words without being aware that I'd spoken them. I knew such blockages could be serious, even fatal. I felt myself slipping into shock.

"I'm going to give him some mineral oil to see if that won't break it up and flush him out." He said he'd be right back and went out to his truck. I was encouraged.

When he'd shot a measure of mineral oil down Ringo's throat, he instructed me to walk Ringo and keep on walking him. The idea was that the oil and exercise together might do the trick. And that's what I did. I spent the entire day walking Ringo. Darkness came early as it does in November, especially when it's damp and foggy, but still I walked him. I turned the outside spotlight on, and it lit the area with a silver-gray glare. When Richard came home, he walked alongside me. Ringo labored along, head down, staring at the ground.

Eventually Richard went in to feed the children, and I was again alone with my old friend. The night grew quiet, and the fog lifted, allowing the spotlight to cast our shadows out across the muddy ground. Richard brought me snacks and tea. At midnight, when we took a break, I began to feel that while we were together, just the two of us, Ringo and I were also in the process of separating.

Out at the edge of the field, an owl was hooting. I was cold and tired. I stood with my arms around Ringo's neck, my face in his mane the way I'd done as a frightened girl. Who was going to protect me from all those bad people? Would they come back if Ringo was no longer there? I sniffled a little, then made myself stop.

Ringo's intestine remained blocked. In the morning, David's assistant, Lisa Stanley, came and gave him another dose of mineral oil. A tall, sturdy young woman with short brown hair, Lisa seemed both confident and competent. She spoke reassuringly about the second dosage breaking up the impaction, and though exhausted and on the verge of more tears, I was again encouraged. Lisa said she'd wait with me to see what happened.

An hour passed, then two. We walked Ringo again, but still no bowel movement. After three hours, Lisa headed for her car.

"Where are you going?" I asked.

"Sarah, I'm going to call David. The mineral oil isn't working. We need to go to the next step."

"Which is what?" No one had mentioned a next step. Behind me, Ringo moved, clearly uncomfortable. He didn't want me to leave him.

"It's okay, Sarah, you stay with him. He needs you. I'm going to talk to David first, but I'm sure he'll agree on the next step." Lisa held up her hand, paused, and started to leave.

"Which is?" I repeated.

She came back and put her hand on my shoulder. "This is hard, I know," she started.

"No!" I said sharply. "You *don't* know. What *is* the next step?"

"It's the last resort. We have to force large quantities of fluids into Ringo to try to blast out that blockage. It takes time."

She watched to see my reaction. I lowered my head. "How do we do it?" I whispered. Ringo was pressing his nose against my back, trying to distract himself from the pain.

"I have some bags of fluid in the car. We'll put an IV in Ringo's neck, hook him up, and wait. We should hang the bags from the rafters and let gravity do the rest."

I got up on a chair and drove a spike into a rafter, and we hung the bags from it, one at a time. As each bag emptied, Lisa would grab another and go into the kitchen to warm the fluid in the microwave. It took six hours to get to the last bag. Lisa had given Ringo painkillers that were so strong they caused him to sway, but he wouldn't go down. She said it would be all right if he were to lie down, but he was determined to stay on his feet. He would *not* go down. The few times I moved away from him to get something or simply rest against the wall, he followed me, wanting to stay close.

I finally reached the point of exhaustion where I didn't think I could continue standing. I'd been up for more than thirty hours, most of which I'd been walking. Not wanting to leave Ringo, I lay down next to him in the straw. To my surprise—and Lisa's amazement—he very carefully lay down next to me.

It was clear from his breathing that he was in terrible pain. With me behind him, I put my arm across his neck, and we kind of spooned. *All right*, I thought, *it's my turn to comfort you.* He let out a long muffled groan. I could feel his soft, warm back against my stomach and thighs.

Lisa joined us in the stall and sat with her back to the wall. She said she'd never seen anything like it and didn't expect to again. "He's under extremely heavy sedation, so much so that by all rights, he should have gone down hours ago, yet he stayed up until you lay down then managed to get down next to you without rolling on you."

Time passed. Lying there, I told Lisa the story of my life and the role Ringo had played in it. Finally, cramping, I sat up and put my arms around my knees. The last of the fluid was dripping out of the last bag. Mesmerized, I watched it move down the tube. Ringo stirred. Lifting his head then shaking it slightly as if to clear it, he got up. His belly was massive above me. Alarmed, I got up with him. "What's going on?" I asked Lisa.

Lisa said she'd be right back and went out to her truck. I stared out the open door, waiting for her to return. From the lighted barn, it looked pitch-black outside, and it seemed eerily quiet. Ringo seemed relieved, strangely better.

Lisa came back with a large hypodermic needle, felt for the right spot, and plunged it into Ringo's abdomen. Holding the needle in with her left hand, she drew the plunger out with her right. As she did, the syringe filled with a dark, reddish brown fluid.

"His intestine has burst," she announced. "It's draining into his abdominal cavity." Her expression was horrified but resigned. "There's nothing we can do, I'm afraid."

I understood, but I couldn't believe it. My heart wouldn't let my brain accept it.

"Listen to me, Sarah. I want you to tell me where you want to put him down. And then we have to take him there and do it. We have about twenty minutes before he gets into real pain and dies on his own right here."

"I have to tell Richard," I said. It was the first thing to come to mind. I ran out and made for the house. Behind me, Ringo whinnied. Wiping my eyes furiously, I stumbled on.

Richard had known it was coming. He put his arm around me as we walked back across the driveway. When we got into the barn and he saw Ringo, he stopped, and tears came into his eyes, too.

I went back into the stall and put my forehead against Ringo's. It was time. "I'm so sorry, Ring," I whispered. "I can't help you anymore. I hope you can forgive me. I won't forget you, Ring, I promise." Even in a whisper, my voice was desperate.

Lisa's hand was on my shoulder. "Come on," she said. "We need to get him there."

It took all my willpower to let go, and even then I couldn't draw my hand back from his mane. Lisa took my hand, and Richard came in to help. Ringo's coarse hair was entwined around my fingers. It seemed magically knotted so as to hold me. "You lead him, I'll walk beside," I said to Lisa. I thrust my fingers still deeper into his mane, made a fist, and held it as we walked out of the barn. Out in the misty, mysterious night, it was as if some powerful being was hovering low overhead, watching the end of a great life and love.

We went to Ringo's favorite tree, an old oak that stood tall and proud at the edge of his pasture. Its branches disappeared in the dark mist above us. When we got to it, Ringo stopped. He was standing before me for the last time. It was too dark to see into his eyes, but I held his face and sent him my best love as Lisa went about her business. She slid the needle into his neck, and within seconds, his legs collapsed. His head slipped out of my hands, and I was left standing above him.

"Don't worry," Lisa said. "He was dead before he hit the ground."

I looked down at him. The life energy had left his face, the warmth gone out of his eyes. As gently as I could, I lowered myself down until I was stretched over him. I wanted to soak up the last of his essence.

Behind me, the lights from the house cast us in long shadows. Sobbing, I pressed myself against his still-warm being. He was going somewhere and leaving me alone, and I felt empty and scared. I wanted more than anything to go with him. I felt that if I didn't, I'd be up for grabs, for anyone to hurt me.

I opened my eyes to find that Richard and Lisa had gone in. When I tried to get off Ringo, I'd grown so stiff I fell on the ground. It was a horrible nightmare. I was devastated, weak, and lost.

Richard came back out, knelt down next to me, and rubbed my arm. "Lisa has to go," he said gently. "Come on, take my hand, and I'll help you up."

I took his hand as if it was a handle. My numb legs were wobbly, but we made it into the house.

Lisa was in the kitchen. She'd been crying too. We hugged then drew back, continuing to hold each other's forearms. "I will never forget your relationship with that beautiful horse," she said. "It's been a privilege to be here through this." She squeezed my arms and hugged me again. Then, turning to Richard, she asked, "You can take care of the burial?"

"Yes."

The backhoe man said the road was too icy for him to come up and bury Ringo that night. I didn't want to hear that. I was afraid coyotes or a pack of dogs would find his body; so I stayed up, the second night in a row, and watched over him from the kitchen window.

Tayo said a tearful goodnight. "I wanted to be able to ride together someday, Mom, when I get my pony." Upstairs, she slammed her bedroom door, shutting out the world.

Richard had little to say. He was sad too and concerned about me, but he knew there was no convincing me to go to bed. When he finally went up, his feet were slow and heavy on the stairs.

I stood by the window. The spotlight on the back of the house was on Ringo, but it was difficult to see out the window because of the glare from the kitchen lights. I turned the lights off and pressed my forehead against the cool pane. The house was silent. Occasionally, I drew back to check the time. The combination of the cool glass and regular clock checks helped me stay awake.

Around three, the silence was suddenly broken by the sweet, clear melody of "Happy Birthday." Where was it coming from? On top of the refrigerator? Something in the basket? I walked over, reached up into the basket, and picked up the small box containing Ringo's thirtieth birthday candle. The candle contained a tiny music box that had somehow been activated. But nothing had touched the basket, box, or candle. The box hadn't been opened. How could this happen? I took the candle out and went to turn the switch to off, but it was already off. I turned the switch on and off, on and off, but the music continued playing. How could that be?

I walked back to the window with the candle in my hand and looked out at Ringo. The light, whimsical music had lifted me out of my grief. Looking at the candle then out at Ringo then back at the candle, I suddenly felt his presence. He was telling me something.

"Are you trying to tell me you're okay, Ring?" Opening the window, I leaned out and asked again, "Are you okay, Ringo?" I held the candle out the window next to my head.

"You are, aren't you?" I asked in a choked voice. "Well, I got your message." And the minute I said that, the music stopped. My head was still out the window and my arm in the air, but the music was no more. It was as if Ringo, the maestro, understood that I'd gotten his message, and he no longer needed to conduct. I looked at the candle then drew back inside.

"I understand, Ringo," I whispered. "You don't want me to worry about you. Fair enough." I brought the candle to my lips, kissed it, and put it back in its box.

As the light came up, harsh reality returned. My friend was gone; and his body lay still, out in the cold, damp field. I walked out to be with him one last time. There was no longer any remnant of life or warmth about him. With my fingertips, starting at his nose, I traced his soft face and ears. There were no more tears as I ran my fingers through his mane and down across his back. His coat was still soft, and when I bent close, he still smelled like Ringo. Those familiar sensations—his smells, softness, strength, and warmth, the sensations that had affirmed and kept me safe—were all about to be gone. In a matter of minutes, I was going to have to begin moving on without them.

Behind me, I heard the backhoe coming up the road. As it got closer, I collapsed onto my friend once more. The backhoe operator stopped, and Richard came out of the house. Looking up at Richard, I said, "How do I say good-bye? You have to show me because I don't know."

We searched each other's faces for an answer, but there was none. I buried my face in Ringo's mane. "I feel so helpless," Richard wheezed.

"I want to go with him," I cried in desperation. "I want to be buried with him and lie next to him forever. He's going somewhere without me, and I won't be able to find him." Richard helped me up. I was chilled and numb. The backhoe operator, an older man, was a friend of Richard's. He walked up, knelt down, and gave Ringo a pat on the nose. No one said anything.

I watched the backhoe do its work. When the shovel teeth clanged and scraped on the rocks, they also clanged and scraped on my bones. The hole got deeper and wider. I felt as if it was being dug in my heart at the same time it was being dug in the ground.

As the backhoe went under Ringo's body and began lifting and pushing him toward the hole, his neck twisted back in an unnatural way. I gasped and cried out, "Wait! Please wait. Don't push him like that." I reached out to Richard because I knew he wanted things to go smoothly. "Please, Richard, don't put him in like that. Lie him on his side."

"He's doing the best he can," Richard said, stifling his frustration. He waved at the backhoe operator, who pulled back a few feet and idled his engine. Richard walked over and talked to him then stepped away. The engine started up again, the backhoe came forward, and the scoop went under Ringo's rear end, trying to lift him part by part.

One of the teeth on the front of the bucket caught and punctured Ringo's haunch. I grabbed Richard, but I knew there was nothing to be done. "He's too big, honey," he said. "We can't position him without chewing him up. It's best if we just push him in."

"All right!" I snapped, even as I was—once again—comforted by Richard's common sense. We stood there, Richard watching Ringo and I staring at the ground as Ringo was nudged toward the hole. And then, suddenly, he fell in and was being covered with gravel, and our thirty-year friendship was laid to rest.

Mending

I was totally lost. Wine and Excedrin were the only things that enabled me to sleep. Days ran into nights, and the nights into more days and nights and days. The mornings would come and with them the harsh reality of Ringo's death. The smallest household chores seemed overwhelming. I had to continue being a mother to Tayo and Richie. Life goes on whether you want it to or not.

The children saw my grief. One afternoon, as I was sitting on the front steps, watching the wind bend the branches on the maple tree in our yard, Richie came to me. He stood in front of me, held out his little-boy hand, and said, "Here, Mommy, I got this for you."

I looked into his round five-year-old face. He was proud of himself. "You did?" I smiled to show him I was pleased. Then I looked at his hand. He was holding a piece of paper towel, wrapped around something. I took it from him, laid it gently in my lap, and unwrapped his gift. When I saw what it was, I lost my breath and put my fingers to my lips. Before me lay a blacksmith's shaving of Ringo's hoof. I looked into Richie's face. "How did you get this, Richie?"

"In the barn. In his stall. I found it in his stall. I even got the piece of paper by myself. I know I'm not supposed to climb on the counter."

I put my hand to his mouth, stopping him. "That doesn't matter now, Richie. This is the most thoughtful thing anyone has ever done for me." I scooped him up in my arms, and we squeezed as hard as we could. "I will cherish this little piece of Ringo," I told him. "I don't have a piece of him. I didn't even cut off a piece of his mane or tail."

We looked at each other and laughed; then, he ran off. I thought how amazing it was that he had gone out to the barn alone and found that piece of hoof. The barn was scary to him, with its dark corners and musty smells. But he had overcome all that to support his mom. How do children know these things?

My life became more difficult. Tayo was sad because she thought that with Ringo gone, we wouldn't get to ride together. It had been a dream she and I had shared, exploring together. I tried to reassure her, but I felt I was operating with only half of myself, the other half having been buried with Ringo. It was an unnerving sense. Who was that other half that I had so willingly ceded to Ringo?

I thought about this question for weeks. Eventually, it became more than I could manage. One night, while standing at the sink washing dishes, I started crying and couldn't stop. Richard heard me and came into the kitchen. It was late, and Tayo and Richie were long since in bed. Richard came up behind me, and I turned and fell against him. "I'm sorry," I said, "but I can't do this anymore."

"You can't do what?" He held me away from him so he cold look into my face.

I wiped my face with my sleeve and turned back to the sink. After gathering my thoughts, I turned back to him. "I'm nobody, don't you get it?" I was surprised by the anger in my voice. "I don't know who I am without Ringo. I put my entire being into him. Without him, I don't exist! I'm a shell!" When Richard came forward to comfort me, I pushed him away and slapped my hand on the counter. "Get me out of here! I can't *stay* in this house another minute!"

Richard grabbed me. "Let me help. Can't I help you?"

"No, not now."

"Then tell me who." His voice was beseeching. In his eyes, I could see the anguish of impotence.

"The Coogans. I want to go see Dave and Dove." I don't know why I said the Coogans. I hadn't been thinking about them.

"All right. I'll call them right now. Do you want to go to their house?"

"Yes," I said it firmly so there wouldn't be any misunderstanding. I was determined to go see our friends.

Richard walked over to the phone and dialed their number. I let my knees give way and slid down the front of the counter to the floor. Drawing my knees up to my chest, I held them in my arms and rested my chin on them. Sobbing quietly, I started to rock myself. After all those years of having Ringo, I again wanted Nanny.

As if from a great distance, I barely heard Richard's voice. He hung up, came over, and sat down next to me. "We can go over to their house, Sarah, okay?" I nodded. "Good. I'll tell Tayo we're going."

He got up to go upstairs, but Tayo was already standing in the doorway. When I saw her, my first thought was that I'd made more noise than I'd realized. "What's wrong, Daddy?" she asked.

Startled to see her there, Richard moved between us and made an exaggerated effort to appear calm. "Your mother and I are going over to Dave and Dove's for a while," he explained. "Mommy needs to talk to our friends. Will you and Richie be okay for an hour or so?"

"Mommy?" Tayo asked, trying to see around Richard.

"I'm all right, Tayo." I stood up. "I just need to get away for a little while. It's all right, really, it is."

Tayo wasn't convinced. She looked into my eyes for more assurance then started upstairs. Halfway up, she turned to look back.

"The Coogans' number is right here on the pad next to the phone in case you need to call us," Richard reassured her.

"Okay, Daddy," she said, continuing on up.

Richard led me out to the car. When we got to the Coogans', Dove came out of the house, followed by Dave. I got out and went directly into Dove's arms.

"Let's go in the house," Dave said, his voice deep and soothing. He was a tall, thin, dark-haired man, younger than Richard and me. Dove, slightly older than Dave, was about five feet five inches with short wavy blond hair that circled her face like a halo. Inside, in the front hall, Dave said, "Let's go downstairs. There's a comfortable chair there for Sarah." He stepped in front of Dove to open the basement door.

I hadn't been in their basement before. It was finished and cozy, with a woodstove at one end. Dave motioned me to the chair, and I sat down and pulled my knees up to my chest. It was comfortable, all right, as well as deep and safe. I stared at the floor.

Dove pulled up a chair and sat to my left, Dave was across me, and Richard sat slightly back from us on my right. No one said anything at first. After a while, Dove reached out and lay her hand on my forearm. Her touch was light and gentle. The Coogans had sensitive hearts and were in touch with their innermost selves; they knew words weren't always necessary. I was hoping they could help me find the half of me that had died with Ringo.

"Afraid?" Dove whispered.

"Yes." I started sobbing again, but didn't bother wiping my eyes.

"Lost?" Dove whispered.

"Yes." How did she know?

"Close your eyes, Sarah, and tell me what you see." She said it confidently, and I trusted her completely. I closed my eyes.

"Take a deep breath."

I did so, and it caught in my throat and came out as a short whimper.

"Who are you now, Sarah?" Dove asked.

I cleared my throat. I was afraid to speak, but I knew I had to. "I'm a little girl," I began. "I feel like the girl I was before Ringo. I hear the teasing at House in the Pines. I hear Ms. Johndroe's footsteps coming to get me. But Ringo isn't here to protect me from them, to keep them away."

"Oh, yes, he is," Dove said, firmly.

Her comment got my attention, and I looked up. Glancing at Richard, I saw his concern and fear.

Dove went on. "His physical body is gone, Sarah, but his spirit is still here. Our spirits are the important part of us. Our bodies are just the containers that carry our spirits around. Ringo's spirit hasn't left you. It's in your heart."

Dave got up from his chair, came close, took my hand, opened it as if it was a flower, and pressed my palm to my heart. "He's right here, and he'll never leave this place," he explained. "Your essence and his spirit are in here together, they're just in slightly different forms. Ringo has given up his physical self, but that's all. His spiritual self lives on. It's in you. It *is* you, now, and you're it. You're him."

Dove reached in and toughed the back of my hand with her fingertips. "You are the same in mind and spirit, Sarah," Dave went on. "None of you is missing, it's simply changed form. If you look inside yourself, you'll always be able to find the part of you that was Ringo. Always." He stepped back and settled in his seat.

Dave's explanation calmed me. It felt true. And because of it, I felt Ringo had come back. "That's the reason for the birthday candle," I said.

"The what?" Dove asked.

"The night Ringo died, his birthday candle from his thirtieth birthday party wouldn't stop playing. It was the oddest thing. I was convinced that he was trying to tell me he was going to be all right. I even called out the window to him that I'd gotten his message."

"He was trying to say that he would never leave you," Dove replied. Then, after a brief pause, "There's no doubt in my mind that you had a deep spiritual connection with that horse. You had it because you were open to it. That's your gift, that openness, Sarah. You're like that with people too. You inspire them with your presence. It's what your life has added up to. Your life experiences—from your birth to today—have made you who you are, open to the endless possibilities that life offers. It's a great gift. And now, as you go on, you need to recognize it and open your heart to it." She gave me an encouraging smile.

And that was it. My intuition had led me to Dove and Dave; and now, though I wasn't completely clear, it told me I'd gotten what I came for. When I smiled back at Dove, there was relief in Richard's face. I stood up and faced Dove, and she got up and gave me a hug. From behind me, Dave put his hands on my shoulders and squeezed. "Thank you," I said, glancing back. He smiled and nodded once.

Epilogue

The next night, I got my pen and paper and started writing about my thirty-year relationship with Ringo. It was the beginning of the real healing, of me taking responsibility for my own healing. It was also the beginning of my keeping my promise to Ringo. While he was sick and dying, I'd promised him I would share our story to help others who need healing and inspiration.

My story became a seventy-five-page memoir. Since Ringo had helped me cross so many thresholds in my life and had crossed so many in his own, I entitled it *Crossing the Threshold*. After a friend typed it up for me, a local copy shop made fifty copies, and I began circulating them to friends. As I did, David and Dove's words about my gift came back to me, and I began to gain confidence in myself and the value of my story. I had found what I thought was the missing me, and I wanted to share the story that it might help others find the absent parts of themselves.

During this time of discovery, we sold our house in West Brookfield to move closer to Randolph. It was hard to leave the site of Ringo's grave, but by then I knew that he'd stay with me no matter where I was. I had had a gravestone made for him with the inscription, "Ringo, my best friend, 1962-1993." I brought the marker to our new house and planted a weeping willow over it and a flower garden around it.

The summer after Ringo's death, the oak under which he'd been buried died. Richard wondered if the backhoe hadn't perhaps injured its root system, but I chose to believe Ringo wanted the tree with him in heaven.

When we got settled in our new house, I approached the Randolph teen center and suggested to its director that my story might have value for his teenagers. After reading the story, he agreed, and a few evenings were set aside for me to read it to them. I had a small audience, but those who came seemed to enjoy it.

In the audience was a local playwright. When I finished my reading, she came over and introduced herself. She was tall and elegant and had an open, loving smile. "Hello, Sarah," she said, looking me straight in the eye. "My name is Maura Campbell." She stuck out her hand. "I love your story. Would you consider making it into a play?" She explained that the director, Kevin, had given her the story and invited her to my reading and that she thought it had dramatic potential.

Would I consider it? I'll say, especially if it might help teenagers. Maura and I had a number of meetings at my house, during which she dug for the kind of details that would dramatize the story. I liked her and we seemed to work well together. As the play took shape, Kevin agreed to act as promoter and handle the business end of things. The production would be sponsored by Project Youth, which was what the teen center was called, and would be performed on the stage at the high school. It was a dream come true, the fulfillment of my commitment to Ringo.

One beautiful fall day, Maura arrived with a troubled expression on her pretty face. After weeks of sharing my deepest secrets and having her share many of hers, I felt unusually close to her. "What's up?" I asked.

We walked into the living room, by then filled with my mother's antiques. The sliding glass doors gave us a panoramic view of the mountains. Maura plopped down on the couch. "All right," she said, "if Ringo could talk, what would he say?"

"If Ringo could talk," I repeated, considering it. "Hmm."

"Yes," Maura said. "This is my problem. I'm having a hard time getting your relationship with Ringo across to the audience. And of course, it's crucial to the story. So here's my thought. The simpler things are on stage, the more your story will stand out. So my idea is that the characters should be dressed alike—in black—and Ringo, even though he's a horse, should be on stage as a human figure and have lines, in the present. It's the only way I can think of to get your relationship across."

"Maura," I responded, "you are a genius. But of course you know that." We laughed, and I sat down next to her. "I know *exactly* what Ringo would—and, in fact, *did*—say. Come on, let's get to work. You give me the setting, the different incidents in the play, and I'll tell you what he said."

Maura and I trusted each other completely. We dove in and spent the afternoon writing out Ringo's words. It not only worked, it was surprisingly powerful. We thought it would be the making of the play.

And it was, and the play was a success. There were fourteen roles, fourteen kids ranging from ten to twenty-one. Tayo was in it as her grandmother. Ashley Warlick, a senior at Randolph High, played young Sarah. A tough but sensitive street kid named James Goodson played Richard. And Stacy Cumings played the adult Sarah. In all likelihood, Ashley, James, and Stacy would never have met if it hadn't been for the play. James played Richard with charm and dignity; and it was interesting to watch him, an outsider, and Ashley, a popular high school girl, in the roles of Richard and me. The entire cast learned from the material and exercise and grew from the experience. Stacey, who also played the narrator, had had a difficult childhood; so she was sympathetic with mine, and it came across in her performance.

Perhaps the best thing about the play was that it was based on actual lives and events. And I was there, in the first row, for every rehearsal. And so, through me, was Ringo. It made it more real, and thus more compelling for the kids. There was even a boy with cerebral palsy in the company.

As opening night got closer, the excitement grew. It was to be put on in the theater at the Randolph Union High School. The *Times Argus*, a statewide paper, wrote an article about the play that came out the day it opened. It was a three-page spread, complete with pictures and interviews. The article got the attention of our local paper, which, not to be outdone, sent a reporter to the opening night. He gave the play a rave review.

It was amazing to see the reaction of the audience. Many of them cried a number of times during the play; and they all stood, cheered, and stomped their feet at the end.

Richard said it was touching how successful the play was. When it closed, we threw a cast-and-friends party at a local restaurant. Richard and I lived off the good feelings generated for weeks. For months afterwards, I had the odd experience of having strangers greet me on the street.

But I wasn't through. I'd promised Ringo I'd get my manuscript published to give our story broader distribution, and I was determined to do so. To this end, I found an agent in Burlington, Vermont, and she put me in touch with a ghostwriter. I worked with the ghostwriter for several months, during which time I paid him our entire savings, but nothing came of it. The more he wrote, the more his voice replaced mine. The experience convinced me that my story could only be told by me.

But I couldn't write! I had cerebral palsy. The left side of my brain, the language, reasoning side, didn't work right. Shoot, I'd barely gotten through an alternative high school. Sure, I'd scribbled a sixty-page anecdote that Maura had then made into a play, but I didn't think I could stretch it into a full-blown memoir.

I did it though. "With a little help from my friends," as the Beatles song goes. Especially Ringo. I got guidance and support from within as well as without. It's strange how things work out. I was able to write this memoir because I started opening to myself and my life. I began listening to myself, really listening. As I did, I started sharing more of my story with others. I have a friend who thinks I have a gift. He says that when I tell people my story I inspire and motivate them. I'm not sure about that, but I like talking with people, especially young people; so when my friend suggested I start giving talks, I agreed to give it a try. He made up a flier, and I sent it around. Before long, I started receiving invitations to speak. I talked with young adults at the Association for Cerebral Palsy. I've been doing that for three years now. Plus I spoke to a class of graduating seniors and their families at a local Kiwanis Club dinner. My most recent talk was for the Self-Determination Project for the mentally challenged.

As I've given these talks, I've come to see that my story does give people hope, not only the disabled, but people in all walks of life and at all ages. This realization has given me the courage to write the story down.

My life since Ringo's death has been one of self-discovery and growth. At first, I was afraid, but I've come to welcome the process. I'm now fifty-five. It's been nearly ten years since Ringo died. During that ten years, my brother, Murray, died of cancer. After Murray died, our father and mother passed away. With Mother gone, Dindy and I have grown closer, discovered and come to appreciate each other. We've talked about how and why Mom kept us separated, our individual struggles, and how we held back from each other. We're trying to make up for lost time.

In a sense, I have become Ringo. I began life severely impaired. Because my mother lacked faith in herself, and therefore couldn't trust me, I started out doubting myself. But like a puppy, I sensed my needs and trusted my instincts. When Ringo came into my life, I grabbed onto him with all my might and he thenceforth provided me with the model of his unceasing faith. Completely open to life, he exhibited absolute confidence. And because he was confident, he placed his trust in me. It wasn't his choice, it was his inherent nature. His joy in my being and presence reflected his essence, not mine. He modeled acceptance and faith day in and day out for thirty years. When he died I was forced to acknowledge and take responsibility for all his example had taught me. I began exhibiting his faith and openness. I see it in my relationships with Richard, our children, our family and friends. I see it in my relationships with animals. It seems to me such openness, such unbiased attention is the essence of love. It was the way Ringo loved me. To the extent I love, I learned it from him. He didn't teach me how to *do* it, he taught me how to *be* it. He be-ed it for me, and I'm now trying to be it for others.

In Ringo's memory, I founded a therapeutic riding program called Ringo's Gift. The summer of 2002 was our first season and it was a great success. To celebrate, we had an end-of-year party in our backyard. It was a beautiful day. The volunteers who worked on the program came, and awards were given out. That evening, when the sun had gone down and a few of us were relaxing around a campfire, listening to Kathy, our riding instructor, play her guitar, one of the volunteers suddenly shouted, "Look!" and pointed up at the sky. In the northern heavens, there were red and green lights flashing and dancing. "It's Ringo!" the volunteer exclaimed. "He's celebrating our success."

Though I'd lived the better part of my life in New England, I'd ever seen the northern lights. *How strange*, I thought. Watching them flair and churn, I imagined Ringo galloping across the sky, kicking his heels out behind him. "Hey, Ring," I whispered, in greeting. Then, laughing, I raised my fist and shouted, "Ringo forever!"

Randolph, Vermont, our first Christmas on Fish Hill Road, 1995.
Richie, Richard, Sarah and Tayo, the human side of our
much extended family.